Praise for *Becoming Justice Blackmun*

"Highly readable and interesting . . . Greenhouse has mined [Blackmun's private papers] brilliantly to create a moving narrative."
—*Los Angeles Times Book Review*

"[A] fascinating volume . . . *Becoming Justice Blackmun* is as welcome as it is interesting . . . informative and moving." —*The Washington Times*

"[Greenhouse] is a riveting writer. She vividly depicts Blackmun's trajectory. . . . Her report from the subterranean regions of Harry Blackmun's papers and mind is absorbing." —*Slate*

"Should inform anyone with an interest in the law and how the court operates . . . Blackmun, a precise writer and exacting editor, would approve." —*USA Today*

"A model biography of a Supreme Court justice . . . Greenhouse delivers a crystal-clear, and sometimes painful, portrait of the way personality shapes history." —*The Courier-Journal* (Louisville)

"[A] highly readable story . . . Greenhouse's book illustrates . . . the value of a truly independent judiciary." —*The Nation*

"Absorbing . . . Greenhouse paints a rare and wonderfully human portrait of one of the Court's most extraordinary justices." —*Ms.* magazine

"This book's singular literary character justifies Ms. Greenhouse for consideration for a Pulitzer Prize." —*New York Law Journal*

"Greenhouse sets a high standard in offering an intimate look both at the man and at the development of his judicial thought."
—*Publishers Weekly,* starred review

Becoming Justice Blackmun

LINDA
GREENHOUSE

Times Books
Henry Holt and Company
New York

BECOMING

JUSTICE

BLACKMUN

Harry Blackmun's

Supreme Court Journey

Times Books
Henry Holt and Company, LLC
Publishers since 1866
175 Fifth Avenue
New York, New York 10010
www.henryholt.com

Henry Holt® is a registered trademark of Henry Holt and Company, LLC.

Distributed in Canada by H. B. Fenn and Company Ltd.

Library of Congress Cataloging-in-Publication Data
Greenhouse, Linda.
  Becoming Justice Blackmun : Harry Blackmun's Supreme Court journey /
Linda Greenhouse.—1st ed.
    p.   cm.
  Includes index.
  ISBN-13: 978-0-8050-8057-5
  ISBN-10: 0-8050-8057-0
  1. Blackmun, Harry A. (Harry Andrew), 1908–   2. Judges—United States—
Biography.   3. United States. Supreme Court—Biography.   4. Constitutional history—
United States.   I. Title.
  KF8745.B555G74 2005
  347.73'2634—dc22   2004063772

Henry Holt books are available for special promotions and premiums.
For details contact: Director, Special Markets.

First published in hardcover in 2005 by Times Books
First Paperback Edition 2006

Designed by Fritz Metsch

Printed in the United States of America
1   3   5   7   9   10   8   6   4   2

FOR

GENE AND HANNAH

CONTENTS

PROLOGUE

JUSTICE HARRY A. BLACKMUN gave the country a great gift. At his death, in 1999, five years after retiring from the Supreme Court, he left his vast collection of personal and official papers to the Library of Congress. Five years after that, on March 4, 2004, under the terms of his will, the library opened the collection to the public: more than half a million items, contained in 1,585 boxes that take up more than six hundred feet on the shelves of the library's Manuscript Division. This book is the story that Blackmun's papers tell of his life, and of the Court on which he served for twenty-four years.

It is neither a conventional biography nor a comprehensive survey of a judicial career. I did not interview family members or former law clerks. I did not try to reconcile his accounts of cases with those contained in the papers of other justices. I made only minimal use of secondary sources, and most of those were my own articles for the *New York Times,* written during the sixteen years—1978 to 1994—that my assignment to cover the Supreme Court overlapped his tenure. Instead, my goal was to extract from this immense collection—from childhood diaries, personal correspondence, internal Court memos, and drafts of opinions, as well as the transcript of a thirty-eight-hour oral history—a coherent narrative of a consequential life that spanned the decades of the twentieth century and left its mark not only on the law but on American society.

The project began in January 2004, when the Blackmun family gave me access to the collection for two months before the public opening so that I could write an article or series of articles for the *Times*. The family's aim was to enable the kind of methodical journalistic consideration of the material that would not be possible on a frenzied opening day, when the prospect of examining the original files of *Roe v. Wade* could be expected to attract large crowds—not only journalists—to the Manuscript Division reading room. The result was a series of articles that appeared over three days in early March 2004. This book is an outgrowth of that project.

In an essay for the *Times* that accompanied the series, I compared the sensation of entering the reading room to plunging down a rabbit hole into a separate world, so different from the surface where I had spent twenty-five years as an observer of the Supreme Court's public activities. When I returned to the library to begin working on the book, yet another image came to mind. I was standing in front of a huge open-face mine on which seams of precious metals were visible, running in various directions. I was the miner. I could not, as a practical matter, follow every seam, but I could choose the most promising and see where they led.

In addition to writing the majority opinion in *Roe v. Wade*, the 1973 decision that established a constitutional right to abortion, Blackmun participated in 3,874 Supreme Court rulings. He wrote significant opinions on such varied subjects as the federal income tax, Indian law, antitrust, and the courtroom use of scientific evidence. Many scholars will use the Harry A. Blackmun Collection to illuminate those areas of law. Still others will use the collection to study various aspects of the Court's processes. The *Buffalo Law Review*, for example, has published an article by Nancy Staudt, a law professor at Washington University in St. Louis, who used the collection to examine the Court's selection of federal tax issues to consider. Under a grant from the National Science Foundation, another Washington University professor, Lee Epstein, is compiling a digital archive of law clerks' memoranda advising the justices on which cases to accept. On only one or two days during my summer in the library was I the only researcher exploring the Blackmun papers. In fact, the library staff told me that of the eleven thousand collections housed in the Manuscript Division, the Blackmun collection was the most intensively used from the moment it opened.

So as I worked the mine, I faced many choices of direction and emphasis. I was selective, searching for those subjects that would shed the most light on a career that was also a remarkable personal journey. The seams I chose to follow most closely were abortion, the death penalty, and sex discrimination, as well as Harry Blackmun's complex and fascinating relationship with his boyhood friend Warren E. Burger, who would serve as the fifteenth chief justice of the United States, from 1969 to 1986. Burger's papers, housed at the College of William and Mary in Williamsburg, Virginia, will remain closed until 2026. For the next generation, anyone seeking to understand Burger's life and career will of necessity turn to the Blackmun collection. Its trove of correspondence between the two men stretches over more than sixty years of a relationship that would seem unlikely if depicted in a novel. Anyone interested in the Supreme Court during the last quarter of the twentieth century will turn to the Blackmun collection as well, for many generations to come, thanks to Harry Blackmun's gift.

Becoming Justice Blackmun

MINNESOTA BEGINNINGS

THE LITTLE LEATHER-BOUND book with the odd word "Day-logue" embossed on the cover contained a page for each day of the year, with places on each page for five entries. It was a five-year diary, in a format that invited pithy observations rather than rambling introspection. It cost $1.50. Perhaps Harry Blackmun requested it for his birthday. Maybe it was a Christmas present. In any event, on December 30, 1919, just weeks past his eleventh birthday, he opened it and began to write.

The act was hardly remarkable. Many children start diaries, keeping them long enough to record their teenage angst and dreams. Soon enough, the dreams having been fulfilled or forgotten, most of those journals lie abandoned in desk drawers or attic trunks. Harry Blackmun kept writing.

From a routine beginning—"Bright and fair. Snow melting."—he went on to chronicle his life and the world around him in astonishing detail. Soon outgrowing the space allotted for each day's entry, he would write a few lines in the book and complete the entry on the family typewriter. He filled hundreds of pages as the chapters of an examined life unfolded: high school, college, law school, a federal court clerkship, law practice. At first, he used his father's letterhead, CORWIN M. BLACKMUN, WHOLESALE FRUITS AND VEGETABLES. Later he typed on law firm stationery. The writing was vivid, rarely elegant, but never perfunctory. His anxieties and satisfactions, athletic feats and romantic adventures, the strains of a Depression-era household in which a son's prospects bloomed as the father's withered—all of it is there.

"I *am* beginning to acquire a name for myself," he wrote in late 1936, a twenty-eight-year-old lawyer on the road to partnership. "It comes slowly, but it comes." The diary peters out soon after that, the victim, perhaps, of too many late nights in the office, too many clients with tax problems to solve and estates to settle. Harry Blackmun's interior monologue had lasted for seventeen years. In other ways, it never really ended.

It is tempting to assume that only someone who knew, or suspected, or hoped that he was bound for glory would persist in such a project. But that almost certainly does not explain Harry Blackmun. The diary seems to have sprung, rather, from an impulse to order a world that was marked by sadness, where illness and death were tangibly present, where disorder of a profound sort lurked just beyond the horizon. It was a deep impulse that reappeared throughout his long life, in lists he kept of concerts attended, movies seen, books read, and in the handwritten "chronology of significant events" he maintained throughout his twenty-four-year tenure on the Supreme Court, in which he recorded everything from the birth of a grandchild to the collapse of the Soviet Union. At the end, the impulse may have accounted for his decision to send it all—not only the opinions, memos, and other official records but the high school autograph book, the law school notes, the honeymoon hotel receipts, and the diary itself—to the Library of Congress. The team of curators who would spend more than a year organizing and producing a 300-page index to the Blackmun papers achieved the ultimate ordering of Harry Blackmun's world.

Harry Andrew Blackmun was born on November 12, 1908, at his maternal grandparents' home in Nashville, Illinois, in the same room where his mother had been born, twenty-four years earlier. His parents had met at Central Wesleyan College, a small Methodist school in Warrenton, Missouri, and had been married for ten months when

Harry was born. The couple lived in St. Paul, Minnesota, but Harry's father, Corwin Manning Blackmun, needed to be on the road for his wholesale produce business that fall, so his mother, Theo Huegely Reuter Blackmun, arranged to stay with her parents toward the end of her pregnancy.

There was deep sadness in the Reuter home. Theo's brother, Harry, the pride of the family, had died of pneumonia the previous year. A brilliant young pianist, Harry Reuter had been studying in Berlin with Madame Teresa Carreño, a famous performer, composer, and conductor, and he and his teacher were about to leave for a concert tour to Australia and New Zealand when the fatal illness struck. Madame Carreño would later come to Nashville to express her regard for a young man whose potential and loss his family could barely comprehend. Theo Blackmun never fully recovered. She named her baby for the adored brother, and made certain that Harry took piano lessons as a young boy. While it soon became clear that he was not destined to be a performer, he embraced his musical legacy, singing in glee clubs as a young man and attending concerts regularly throughout his life.

Misfortune soon struck the Blackmun family again. A second child, a son named Corwin Manning Blackmun, Jr., was born three years later and lived for only two days. It is painfully apparent that as a young wife and mother—her third child, Betty, was born in 1917— Theo Blackmun suffered from depression. In his early diary entries, Harry noted in passing that his mother would sometimes remain in bed for days or weeks at a stretch, although there did not seem to be a diagnosis of physical illness. But time evidently eased the wounds it could not completely heal. Theo Blackmun lived to age ninety-three, the last thirty years as a widow, and saw her son take the oath as a Supreme Court justice. Her letters to Harry in later life were filled with optimism and pride in his accomplishments, and the occasional dispensation of parental wisdom.

Blackmun himself was dogged by intermittent melancholy that was seemingly unrelated to external events. In the fall of his last year in high school, he noted in his diary that he had been elected president of the senior class, certainly a mark of success and of the esteem of his peers. He was also president of the student council, winner of a citywide award for oratory, manager of the city championship swim team, and an A student, near the top of his class. Yet on November 21, 1924, less than two months after his election, he wrote: "What is the matter with me. I seem to have absolutely no courage, either physically or mentally. I must overcome it." A few years later, in the midst of a generally cheerful account of studying and moviegoing with his college friends, Harry's mood shifted abruptly: "I have been thinking lately that if I should kick off one of these days, that there would not be much loss to the world, for my existence has surely been unfruitful and rather non-accomplishing."

His early diary also contains a litany of somatic complaints—backache, eyestrain, colds. But his one encounter with a real medical emergency, an attack of appendicitis at age fourteen, became a source of lifelong fascination. "My Illness—Appendicitis" was the title he gave a five-page handwritten essay, dated March 21, 1923. "About 3 a.m. on March 8 I awoke with a dreadful pain in my stomach and right side," it began. Eleven years later, it was his sister's turn, and Harry obtained permission to witness the operation. "Little old tike, it was not easy to watch her writhing and grunting as they do at first under ethylene," he wrote in his diary. But his interest in the proceedings soon overcame his squeamishness. "Her appendix was not particularly large, about the size of a lead pencil, three inches long, but very pink and inflamed. What a lot of trouble such a little thing can make." He judged the seventeen-year-old Betty an exemplary patient. "I certainly learned that she has guts and a pile of courage. What a whale of a good sister she is."

For the rest of his life, Blackmun would mark the anniversary of his own surgery; March 8 attained a lasting significance. "Eight years ago tonite I hit the old operating table at Saint John's hospital," he wrote as a law student in 1931. Three years later: "Eleven years ago tonight I had me side cut open in a curious experiment." And on March 8, 1988, upon learning that his Supreme Court colleague Sandra Day O'Connor had just undergone an appendectomy, he sent get-well wishes with this note: "We are almost on the same 'wavelength.' Sixty-five years ago

Harry Blackmun at about age six with his maternal grandparents, Theodore and Mary Huegely Reuter, in front of the family home in St. Paul, Minnesota

today I had my first surgery. It was an appendectomy with a six inch scar. I suspect my mother thought that when they took me away in an ambulance, I would never return. It was ether in those days, and I did not like it one bit."

Blackmun grew up in Dayton's Bluff, a working-class neighborhood of St. Paul whose best days were behind it. By the 1910s and 1920s, it was home to many Irish immigrants. The Blackmun family, however, had no Irish ancestry. Blackmun was of German descent on his mother's side—her father was brought to the United States at the age of three from the Prussian province of Hessen-Nassau—and Corwin Blackmun's English and French Huguenot ancestors were among the early settlers of New England. Both of Harry's grandfathers had served in the Union army during the Civil War, a source of deep interest to the boy, although to his regret they resisted his questions about their combat experiences.

The neighborhood elementary school was Van Buren School, and it was in kindergarten there that Harry Blackmun met Warren Burger, who was fourteen months older but in the same grade. The two boys lived six blocks apart and were also Sunday school classmates. "We didn't have much, but the Burgers had less than we did," Blackmun would later recall. Poor as the Burger household was, it was welcoming, and soon the boys were in and out of each other's homes. Along with two other neighborhood boys, John Francis Briggs and Robert Damkroger, Harry and Warren made a foursome whose friendship and activities centered on sports. Of the four, Burger was the best athlete. As the boys grew older, they turned from softball to golf and tennis. During one particularly vigorous set of tennis with Burger, Blackmun noted, "We both had to remove our shirts and get down to our gym shirts in spite of the presence of the girls." Harry and Warren attended different public high schools, but they maintained their friendship through sports and occasional camping and fishing trips. They worked together at summer jobs as camp counselors. When girls entered the picture, they frequently double-dated for movies. Harry brought a date to Warren's senior prom.

Harry attended Mechanic Arts High School, and photographs show a serious young man with neatly parted hair and round glasses. "Theodore Roosevelt is my hero," he wrote in an essay on the assigned topic "My Ideals as a High School Boy." When the local newspaper, the St. Paul *Pioneer Press and Dispatch,* sponsored a high school oratory contest on the subject of the Constitution, Harry won the citywide award with a speech that ended: "May our great 'Ship of State' sail on, manned by those who dare to live and die for freedom's cause!" One of the contest's judges was an actual judge, John B. Sanborn of the Ramsey County District Court. In an enthusiastic report on Harry's victory, the newspaper singled out his opening lines: "The Constitution lives! Down through the years it has come, often assailed, the hope and fortress of a new nation." They provided, the report said, "the keynote of an oration which stood out above a succession of orations, any one of which would have done credit to a Daniel Webster."

In the spring of 1925, Blackmun graduated fourth in his class of

450 and expected to attend the University of Minnesota with nearly every other college-bound member of the class. No out-of-state college was economically feasible. His father's efforts to establish himself as an independent produce broker were foundering, and the family's financial prospects were highly uncertain. But two English teachers at the high school thought so highly of Harry's talents that they put him forward for a scholarship to Harvard, awarded to one student each year by a committee of four lawyers from the Harvard Club of Minnesota. It was late July by the time he learned that he had won. He was far from home at the time, working at a summer job he had obtained through a family friend, managing a store on a ranch outside Buffalo, Wyoming. "My dream of the past year is realized," he wrote in his diary when the letter from the Harvard Club reached him. "I am so shaky I can hardly write." The scholarship was a $250 gift and a $100 loan, to be paid back within three years after graduation, renewable if he kept his grades up, enough to cover tuition but not living expenses. It reflected "all-round competency and character as well as scholarship," the newspaper announcement said.

Just sixteen years old, Harry left home on a sixteen-berth sleeping car bound for Chicago, the farthest east he had ever been, where he changed for a train to Boston. This was to be a long separation, because there would be no money for a trip home for Christmas—not that first year, and not for any subsequent Christmas vacation, through four years of college and three of law school. Because his enrollment was so late, he learned on his arrival at Harvard that no freshman rooms were available. He was on his own. Joining forces with two brothers from Los Angeles who were in the same predicament, he walked the streets of Cambridge looking for an affordable apartment. It was an adventure that left him undaunted. "A woman finally asked us where we were going to stay for the night," he wrote in his diary. "We did not know and told her so and she then offered us to stay in her house with an old man which she called Hosea. She furnished us the blankets and we felt better. We got our beds fixed a little and then this old man who is 84 talked about three arms off of us. The house was built in 1640 and was sure an old dump. At eleven we hit the hay. We slept about two hours that night and froze the rest. At least it was free." The next day Harry learned that the last room in a five-man freshman suite had become available, and he took it.

The atmosphere at Harvard was almost completely unfamiliar. The university was dominated by graduates of the New England prep schools, and midwesterners who had gone to public school were a distinct minority. For students who lacked money or connections, much of the social life was inaccessible. But perhaps because Harry did not miss what he had never had, his spirits were high. He joined the glee club and took a job with the freshman crew, driving and maintaining a coach's motor launch, which paid a relatively generous $15 a week. Later he earned money as a math tutor. In December he wrote to thank his Harvard Club benefactors: "I really do not know how I shall ever be able to thank you and the Club for what it has done for me. I realize this help more and more as the days pass. I only trust that things will turn out for the best and that I will not utterly disgrace myself. Do not think, however, that I am pessimistic. 'All's well that ends well,' and I surely hope that this year shall end well!"

Summer brought a return home to St. Paul and jobs installing windows and delivering milk. It also brought a renewal of Blackmun's friendship with Warren Burger, who was working during the day and taking prelaw courses at night at the University of Minnesota. The two met often for tennis, and when it was time for Harry to return to Cambridge, Warren came to see him off at the train station. It was a bittersweet departure for Harry. The night before, knowing the full dimension of the separation that lay ahead, both Harry and his mother cried. "It is different this year from last in that I now know what a real and a personal home is to me," he wrote in the diary. "It is great, that is all. Last year, everything came in such a rush that I knew not where I was and when anything happened. It was Wyoming, Minnesota, moving, goodbye, and hello Boston. But this year—well, parting with the best home folks available and with one's greatest pals in the world, was one darn hard job."

Gradually, college life fell into a familiar, pleasant routine. The academic challenges were not overwhelming. There was time for glee club trips, including a first visit to Washington, D.C., blind dates, and a spring vacation trip with friends to New York City. A lover of live performances of all kinds, Harry was dazzled by a first encounter with Broadway. He got a ticket for *Show Boat* in the new Ziegfeld Theater. "The theatre itself is wonderful, perfumed air, and such accessories. The show was good, tho a bit dragged out, and sparked with some good songs, in 'Old Man River,' 'Can't Help Lovin That Man,' and 'Why Do I Love You.' The last is a peach."

In his senior year, with graduation approaching, he briefly considered and then rejected the idea of medical school, because he would have needed additional undergraduate courses to meet the admission requirements. Law school seemed a simpler, more plausible route to the status and security of a professional career. His father had always regretted not having gone to law school, and over the years had acquired a small collection of law books that occupied a prized place on his bookshelf. "In those days, people always said well, if you don't know what you want to do, study law because it won't hurt you any, it'll be good in whatever you go into," Harry later recalled. His friend Warren Burger had made the same calculation and had already earned a year's credits toward a law degree. Blackmun's undergraduate record was sufficiently impressive that admission to Harvard Law School was all but guaranteed, and it was the only place he applied.

But Blackmun was worried, as he so often was, about finances. To avoid accumulating more debt, he considered taking a year off to teach. Through Blackmun's mother, word of this plan reached Burger, who sent Harry a long, avuncular, advice-filled letter urging him to "stay by the guns for the last lap." Theirs had been an ongoing correspondence, as Blackmun's diary made clear. ("I read a regular book of a letter from Warren and was put quite in the right mood for the exam," one sophomore-year entry noted. A few days after his eighteenth birthday, he wrote, "Warren sent me one peach of a box of candy today.") But the "stay by the guns" letter, dated May 18, 1929, was the first one from Burger that Blackmun saved. "I have seen so many instances here where high ambitions and good intentions have been tempted from the path of struggling student days to bigger and better financial remuneration,"

Blackmun as a new college graduate,   Warren E. Burger as a young man
Harvard Class of 1929

Burger wrote. "Most of them left school for a year or two and most of them will never crack a law book again. I do not mean to infer that any such thing would come to pass in your case, but rather to point out what that never-broken law of averages has done to others." Burger himself had contemplated leaving law school "during the stormy and dark nights of last fall and winter," and he added that "I shall never cease to be thankful for that something, whatever it was, that kept me from finally quitting."

There followed a long paragraph that, in tone if not in particulars, would be repeated by one or the other of the two childhood friends throughout the decades-long correspondence that would take them well into middle age. Clearly Blackmun had unburdened himself to Burger, who now responded with encouragement and effusive praise:

> June holds much for you, but not a bit more than you deserve
> and I hope that the reward will prove, as I'm sure it will, ample

compensation for your four years of hard work and harder study to carry the old fight to them. You have given much for what you have gained, much that people do not ordinarily associate with going away to college, giving up family, home, friends, and no end of comfort for the damnable struggle to stay near the top and keep working to make those old ends meet. I can appreciate those things to some extent and I know that these four years have been anything but a bed of roses for you. Each one of us must plug in his own appointed way and much that is deserving of praise goes unsung but believe me, old man, I have no end of admiration for you, for your courage and for your determination and fighting spirit that has carried you to the top. I have always respected those qualities in you but as the years roll by and take us nearer each day to our far set goals, I have become more aware of them, and along with those few things of which we can always be sure, and in which we never lose faith, I am sure and know that the day is not far when you will come to a place as high in life as you are now in the esteem of your friends.

Harry may well have saved this letter to buck himself up, because Harvard Law School was discouragingly difficult for him. The diversions of college life, modest though they had been, were absent, replaced by cutthroat competition. Exams were terrifying—"Three boys passed out in our section," he noted in an account of an "absolutely terrible" exam in Evidence—and his grades were disappointing. He failed to earn a place on the law review. Paid jobs ate into precious study time. After a 67 average for his first year—which placed him about midway in the class—he hoped for better but dropped to a 66 in his second year. It was a "sorrowful time," he wrote after his transcript arrived in St. Paul during the summer of 1931. "It is the real first time I have overestimated myself, and I do not know when anything has quite so completely taken the wind out of my sail. The scholarship, the hoped-for Eastern position, and all, even a job here seem to have glimmered down the way. Oh, well, life is full of disappointments and I should be getting used to

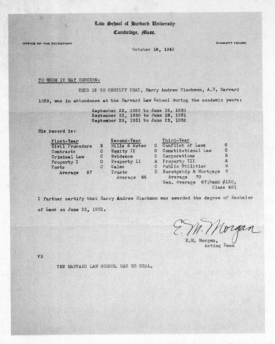

Blackmun's Harvard Law School transcript. His class rank was 120 out of 451.

them." A professor he consulted explained that the law school's grading scale was a harsh one, with few A's or B's awarded, and that "considering everything, I did mighty well to get my sixty-six." He followed this account with his own rueful comment: "Maybe."

One bright spot was his membership on the student team that won the Ames Competition, a high-profile moot court contest built around briefing and arguing appellate cases. The pressure eased when Blackmun realized that he had saved enough money, from his various jobs, to give them up and get through his third year with a manageable amount of borrowing. His final class rank was 120 out of 451, respectably near the top quarter of the class but a comedown for a student who three years earlier had been one of only twenty-four Harvard seniors chosen for Phi Beta Kappa and had graduated summa cum laude in mathematics. His memories of law school would remain raw for decades. For his seventieth birthday, in 1978, his oldest daughter, Nancy, sent him a copy of *One L,* a best-selling book about the rigors of the first year at Harvard Law School. The author, a young Harvard Law School graduate named Scott Turow, had autographed the copy at Nancy's request, and Blackmun wrote him a note of thanks.

"You certainly captured and poignantly described life at the Law School, with its worry and concern, its tension, its competitiveness, and its deep-seated discomfort," Blackmun told Turow. "Surely there is a way to teach law, strict and demanding though it may be, with some glimpse of its humaneness and its basic good—the art of getting along together—as well as its demands for perfection. You so properly point out that there is room for flexibility and different answers, and that not all is black or white. If I ever learned anything on the bench, it is that."

Blackmun graduated from Harvard Law School in 1932 and returned home to St. Paul without a job. He studied for the Minnesota bar examination over one weekend and passed it. He applied for a clerkship with a newly appointed federal court of appeals judge, John B. Sanborn, who kept his chambers in St. Paul. This was the same Judge Sanborn who, as a state court judge eight years earlier, had awarded first prize to Harry Blackmun's high school oration on the Constitution. But now, in the midst of the Great Depression, everything was uncertain, including whether emergency restrictions on the judiciary's budget would even permit Judge Sanborn to hire a law clerk. But on August 1 the clerkship came through, at $2,200 a year instead of the usual $2,400, although Blackmun did not mind the reduced salary. "How much that looks to me now! It may mean a way out of things," he wrote.

Judge Sanborn was one of seven judges on the United States Court of Appeals for the Eighth Circuit, then as now one of the most diverse of the federal appeals courts. The seven states of the Eighth Circuit ranged from the Dakotas and Minnesota, in the north, to Arkansas, then officially segregated and anchored to the Deep South. Its official seat was in St. Louis, to which the judges traveled on a regular basis from the courthouses in their home states where they kept their chambers.

Blackmun's early assignments included preparing memos in compli-cated copyright and tax cases. He was tense, suffering from eye prob-lems and headaches, and the judge seemed cold and distant toward him. After a month he wrote in his diary: "The judge said two words to me today—good morning. Dad says there will be two Monday—get out!" But in time, the relationship would emerge as one of the most significant and rewarding in Blackmun's life. Sanborn became his teacher, mentor, role model, and, perhaps because he had no children of his own, surro-gate father. He and his wife gave Blackmun free use of their weekend house on the St. Croix River and treated him as a member of the family.

The clerkship, which lasted eighteen months, saw the young lawyer through the worst of the Depression. Law firm positions now seemed possible. But Blackmun was still living with his parents, who were suf-fering under the burden of hard times. Corwin Blackmun's wholesale fruit business had failed, and he held a series of jobs, with local banks and insurance companies, that had respectable titles—"representative," "district manager"—but carried little security. Blackmun was critical of his father not only in several diary entries but also in the oral his-tory he recorded in his retirement. "He was pretty stubborn and never would compromise on things, and he often alienated people," Black-mun would recall. That in his own old age he would offer such an un-charitable judgment, nearly fifty years after his father's death, indicates the depth of his resentment at his father's failure as a reliable provider for the family.

"This morning first thing Dad asked me for $300.00. I knew it was coming eventually," Blackmun wrote in his diary on September 27, 1933. "I will hand it over, but it wrecks my own plans, puts me into a jam on my insurance and in my paying off my own notes, and ab-solutely upsets any plans that I may ever have had of getting married. I am tied down now to support the family. Betty I want to go thru school, but—. Never can I remember a time when Dad was ever a step ahead of the world; he was always worrying and stewing about when he should get the instant batch of bills paid off."

Two years later he recorded the news that his father would lose his most recent job: "He says they attribute it to general economy, but

The wedding of Warren Burger and Elvera Stromberg, November 8, 1933. Black-mun, far left, was the best man. The bridesmaid is Ella Caroline Anderson.

I believe again he has been saying too much. He has a terrifically inflexible code of ethics, which is all very fine and wholesome in its place, but it does not protect jobs when one is desperately in need of them. That such things exist does not speak well for our system of existence, but they do exist. What will be done I do not know."

While Blackmun was struggling to support his parents and his sister, Warren Burger was already in law practice in St. Paul and preparing to marry Elvera Stromberg. With the two friends living in the same city, there were no more letters, but Blackmun's diary noted frequent lunches, with accompanying long conversations. He was best man at Burger's wedding, which took place in the bride's parents' house. "As usual, when someone close to me is married, it 'got' me a little," he wrote. "It is a solemn and aweful ceremony, for large are the promises made. And how worthwhile it seems to have kept one's self clean and pure and to have some one who loves you as dearly as you do her. There are a few things in life worth while, after all." For himself, though, Blackmun's interest in marriage was at that time largely theoretical. He was dating, occasionally brought young women home, and frequently mentioned them in the diary. But he did not appear close to proposing marriage to any of them.

Despite the tensions at home, Blackmun turned down an attractive opportunity to leave Minnesota. A law school acquaintance, Charles E. Wyzanski, Jr., a brilliant young lawyer and protégé of Felix Frankfurter, then a professor at Harvard, had recently completed his own clerkship and was serving in the Roosevelt administration as solicitor of labor, the top legal position in the Labor Department. One year into Blackmun's clerkship, Wyzanski wrote and offered him a job. Anticipating another six months of clerking before finding a position with a local law firm, Blackmun turned him down. More than a year later, in April 1935, Wyzanski wrote again. The work would be interesting, Wyzanski insisted—not simply routine administration but regular contact with the International Labor Organization, in Geneva. "Once you get down to Washington there are many opportunities to get into big and interesting fields of law and politics," he said.

This time, Blackmun was "exceedingly" tempted, he told Wyzanski. "What to do what to do," he mused in his diary. But in the end, he said no. He was, frankly and self-consciously, risk-averse. He was in his second year as an associate at Junell, Driscoll, Fletcher, Dorsey & Barker, the best law firm in Minneapolis–St. Paul. Wyzanski was offering him hundreds of dollars more a year than the $200 a month he was earning at the firm, but after a year or two in Washington, where would he be? "As a sporting proposition your offer would be immediately accepted; but I hesitate to lose what little progress I have made here," he wrote Wyzanski on May 2, 1935.

For Blackmun the episode signified a road not taken. When Wyzanski died, in 1986, after serving forty-five years as a federal district judge in Boston, Blackmun told his widow, Gisela, that the death "brought back a question that has always been in my mind since 1934." Blackmun said in his condolence note that he had declined Wyzanski's invitation to Washington "with great reluctance," adding, "I often wondered what would have happened had I accepted. It was a compliment and a most difficult decision."

At the Junell, Driscoll firm, Blackmun worked in the tax department. One of his first assignments was a Supreme Court brief that had to be turned out in less than a week, including a weekend of nonstop labor. The client had been assessed federal tax on the income from a trust he had set up to generate alimony payments for his former wife. His legal argument was that because the ex-wife received the income, the tax liability should be hers as well. The Eighth Circuit had rejected the reasoning. Blackmun accompanied two senior partners to Washington for the appeal, which the Supreme Court heard on October 14, 1935. It was his first visit to the Court, which had just moved into its own building on Capitol Hill, after having met in the Capitol building since early in the country's history. The justices unanimously agreed with the appeals court and less than a month later issued an opinion in *Douglas v. Willcuts,* upholding the client's tax liability.

Blackmun found himself frazzled by the pace of the work. After one appellate argument, conducted on short notice, he wrote in his diary: "I discovered at five this PM that I had been wearing unmatched sox all day! Not such a good day, thus." But there were diversions from work: frequent dinners with the Burgers, skiing, tennis, squash, bridge, and the Minneapolis Symphony, to which he had a subscription, filled his free time. He bought his first car, a Ford coupe with a rumble seat, for which he spent $702.14, naming it Mignon. During this period, his professional prospects blossomed as well. He became a junior partner in 1939 and a general partner in 1943.

Also during this time, Blackmun fulfilled his ambition to get married and establish a home and family of his own. On the tennis court in August 1937 he had met a young woman named Dorothy Clark. It was an unusually hot summer Sunday, and Blackmun and one of his regular tennis partners were wilting in the heat after three sets. They noticed two women playing at the far end of the row of courts and decided to invite them to play a set of doubles as a less strenuous alternative to the singles game. Dottie Clark was a secretary for a local businessman. "I thought her legs were rather pretty," Blackmun said later. Swimming followed tennis that afternoon. The two dated for more than three years before Blackmun arrived at her bedside while she was suffering from a minor illness and proposed marriage. They were married on June 21, 1941, and moved into a new apartment complex within walking distance of the law firm. The next years saw the birth of their three daughters: Nancy in 1943, Sally in 1947, and Susan in 1949.

One of Blackmun's clients at the law firm was the Mayo Clinic, headquartered ninety miles southeast of Minneapolis, in Rochester, Minnesota. He was, in fact, spending most of his time on matters related to Mayo, providing both tax advice for the clinic and estate planning and other personal legal services for the doctors who worked there. In 1949 the clinic's management asked him to become its first resident counsel, a position in which he would function not only as a lawyer but as a member of the senior management of the multimillion-dollar nonprofit corporation. After several weeks of indecision, including a house-hunting trip with Dottie and an investigation of what the schools in Rochester would offer the three girls, he accepted. The community was inviting, and he enjoyed the doctors' company. The Blackmuns, who were just finishing the construction of a custom-built home in Minneapolis, sold that property and bought a lot in a new development in Rochester called Sunny Slopes, on which they could build a house to the same plans.

Harry Blackmun's nine years at Mayo, he would say later, were the happiest of his professional life. He was deeply involved in the enterprise, leading the reorganization of a management structure that dated to the clinic's founding by the two original Mayo brothers, in 1919. He gave advice on everything from malpractice to public relations. He was a regular guest at the surgeons' biweekly dinners and the monthly meetings of the clinical staff, listening to the doctors present their research papers and analyze one another's mistakes. He watched medical procedures and laboratory experiments. "I felt the more I could learn about how medicine was practiced there, the better off I would be in advising the physicians," he said later. He also took an active interest in community affairs; in 1955 he was elected president of the Rotary Club of Rochester.

As Blackmun moved from private law practice to senior management of a public-interest institution, Warren Burger was going through a transition of his own. Burger, who had been active in Minnesota Republican politics since the 1930s, was now playing on the national stage. He attended the 1952 Republican National Convention in Chicago as a delegate supporting Minnesota's former governor Harold E. Stassen. But in a crucial credentials fight between General Dwight D. Eisenhower and Senator Robert A. Taft, Burger helped swing the Minnesota delegation for Eisenhower. After the election, Burger's reward was an offer from Herbert Brownell, the attorney general–designate, to join the Eisenhower administration as an assistant attorney general in charge of the Civil Division of the Department of Justice. There he would lead a staff of 180 lawyers and take charge of some of the federal government's most important litigation.

Burger accepted, arriving in Washington in January 1953, in advance of Eisenhower's inauguration. The correspondence between the two old friends, suspended for two decades, resumed almost immediately. Burger, a partner in a successful St. Paul law firm, took a leave and a pay cut to join the new administration. "The decision was not easy but was inevitable," he wrote to Blackmun on January 8. "In both of us there is something deep which makes service a thing which neither of us can avoid. You have elected one form which gave you more positive expression than the practice. Temporarily now I elect another." Burger never returned to Minnesota to live.

APPEALS

WITH THE TWO friends now separated by one thousand miles, letters flew between them. Warren Burger, who had never lived outside Minnesota, was the starstruck voyager, his reports home filled with wonder. "You find yourself carried on into streams never before experienced and yet somehow avoiding the rocks," he wrote after arguing a case before the Supreme Court. While his training and experience helped him meet the challenge, he said, "at other times there can be no explanation except that an Angel has one by the hand."

"Every minute of it was actually spine tingling," Burger wrote after attending President Eisenhower's inauguration. And he sounded awestruck by an encounter with J. Edgar Hoover at a White House dinner, describing for Blackmun the "force of character that stands out in the shape of his face and head. He looks for all the world like one of these Holland Dutch fellows that Rembrandt immortalized even down to a slight suggestion of coloring in his face but with it all a tremendous strength and power in his whole makeup and bearing and in the piercing blue eyes that are so marked in his countenance."

Back in Rochester, Blackmun was a one-man cheering section for his friend, urging Burger to keep the reports coming. "They mean a great deal to me for I share through you and your letters the wonderful experiences you are having in Washington, and the great contributions you are making."

Almost immediately, Burger looked for a way for Blackmun to join him in Washington. Without clearing the overture with Blackmun, he approached Attorney General Brownell in March 1953 to see if there might be an administration job for his friend. When Blackmun said that, in any event, he was not ready to leave Mayo, Burger drafted a letter for him to send to Brownell by which he could introduce himself and express interest in being considered for a future, unspecified position. Blackmun retyped the letter and sent it to Brownell as his own.

In 1954, as he marked his first anniversary in government, Burger told Blackmun he would "unequivocally" make the same choice again. "Working in public service convinces one that the world, one's own world, can be almost exactly what you care to make it and wherever you want to make it. It has also underscored the unimportance of making money. Not that I was ever very much concerned—but here is a town with literally thousands of people who really lead dedicated lives—some in small slots—and many in large ones, but in doing what they really want to do they lead full happy and satisfying lives."

In its tone of self-satisfied idealism, this letter marked a high point of contentment for Burger, as money worries and a growing restlessness soon became a theme. Just seven months later, in August 1954, Burger wrote: "I have the feeling that my stay here is drawing to its closing stages. I can't stand it financially & in another 6–8 months most of the targets I had set will have been substantially reached." But having breathed the rarefied air of the nation's capital, Burger viewed a return to law practice in St. Paul as unappealing. He was tempted, he said, by the prospect of a federal appeals court seat.

Blackmun encouraged Burger in that plan. A judicial appointment "would be a tremendous thing both for it and for you," he wrote. But he did not want Burger to foreclose the possibility of returning to Minnesota or to law practice. "I am tempted also to think, as we used to once in a while, of the firm of Burger and Blackmun and wonder just where that would take us. In other words, I guess I need a good long visit with you."

The next year Warren Burger got his wish as President Eisenhower nominated him to a seat on the United States Court of Appeals for the District of Columbia Circuit. Then, as now, this was a significant nomination. The D.C. Circuit's docket of important cases from the federal agencies made it the most prestigious of the eleven federal appeals courts (today there are thirteen), and it was, and is, regarded as next to the Supreme Court in the judicial hierarchy. The nomination thrilled Blackmun. He wrote to Burger's mother, saying, "This is just another of the many honors that he so richly deserves, and all of us who have known him for these many years are very proud of him as indeed you must be." He also sent letters to Minnesota's two United States senators. The senior senator, Edward J. Thye, was a Republican and thus presented no obstacle to Burger's confirmation. But Senator Hubert H. Humphrey, a prominent liberal Democrat, required more targeted advocacy. "I realize that Mr. Burger is not a member of your party," Blackmun wrote to Humphrey. "On the other hand, I think he has been at all times associated with the so-called 'Liberal Wing' of the Republican party." Blackmun said he was writing out of "my deep conviction that he will be a splendid addition to the District's Appellate Court." In reply, Humphrey offered a prediction without an endorsement. "I am confident that Mr. Burger will be confirmed," he said.

A minor controversy—over three disgruntled Justice Department employees whom Burger had dismissed—delayed the confirmation vote until March 28, 1956, but the outcome was a happy one. Blackmun came to Washington for the swearing-in. "I can't tell you how much it meant to me to have you on hand last Friday—again as my Best Man in a sense," Burger wrote by hand on a D.C. Circuit memo pad. "It was a tremendous thing as far as I was concerned," Blackmun replied. "You have a great future and experience lying before you." To Blackmun's inquiry about a gift suitable for the occasion, Burger suggested: "What about some vanishing ink for my first dozen opinions?"

Warren Burger and Harry Blackmun at Burger's swearing-in to the U.S. Court of
Appeals for the District of Columbia Circuit, April 13, 1956

This was not false modesty. Burger, in fact, harbored doubts about
whether he was "qualified for this damned job," as he expressed it to
Blackmun after several months. "It takes some doing to do it right and
I am not sure yet I have what it takes." He wondered why he had ever
wanted to go on the court, and whether he should stay. "Sometimes I
feel like a guy who woke up and found he was married to Marilyn
Monroe. Everybody thought that was wonderful and envied him. But
he wasn't sure on account of he had never thought he wanted to be
married to la Monroe."

Burger was Eisenhower's third and, as it turned out, last nominee to
the nine-member appeals court. When Burger arrived, the chief judge
was Henry W. Edgerton, a leading liberal named to the court by
Franklin D. Roosevelt in 1937. David L. Bazelon, soon to become chief
judge, was another liberal, one of five Truman appointees, who would
later gain powerful allies as Presidents John F. Kennedy and Lyndon B.

Johnson filled vacancies during the 1960s. A court with a center of gravity well to Burger's left would move further in that direction during his tenure, leaving him to rail in sometimes solitary protest against his colleagues' endorsement of new rights for criminal defendants.

Burger threw himself into the ideological combat. His nemesis was the equally combative Bazelon, who had become a nationally recognized advocate for the rights of the mentally ill. In 1954, before Burger joined the court, a majority opinion by Bazelon, in *Durham v. United States,* had adopted a new criminal insanity test, and its application became the subject of a prolonged, bitter clash between the two judges. The traditional test for criminal insanity was to establish that the defendant knew right from wrong; some jurisdictions also required defendants to show that they had acted under an "irresistible impulse." In Bazelon's view, these tests, adopted by courts in the nineteenth century, failed to take into account the insights of modern psychiatry; for example, he said in the *Durham* opinion, the "irresistible impulse" test "gives no recognition to mental illness characterized by brooding and reflection." Under the so-called Durham rule, a defendant would be excused from criminal responsibility if a jury found that the unlawful act was "the product of mental disease or mental defect."

The *Durham* decision was controversial, with leading members of the bench, bar, and psychiatric profession joining the debate on both sides. To its supporters, it was an admirable fusion of modern law and psychiatry. To its critics, it placed too much reliance on expert psychiatric testimony without giving juries sufficient guidance on the meaning of the term "mental disease or mental defect" and without requiring the defendant to prove that the mental illness actually caused the illegal act.

No other circuit ever adopted the Durham formulation, and the D.C. Circuit would formally abandon it in 1972, after issuing more than 150 opinions applying, explaining, and modifying the original decision. Burger found the Durham rule deeply objectionable. In his view, it supplanted the central question of individual responsibility and placed the courts in thrall to psychiatrists and their vague, unreliable theories. He assigned himself the task of marshaling the votes to overrule it, embarking on a dogged, even obsessive campaign that did not make his life on the court any easier. "I have spent my whole mature life as roughly in the 'pusher-forward' category, and now find myself a 'holder-backer' most of the time just to maintain what seems to me a reasonable balance and thoughtful progress in the law," he wrote to Blackmun in early 1957. "Being a holder-backer is far less fun."

Blackmun was sympathetic to Burger's concerns about the insanity defense. At Mayo, he enlisted an expert consultant with whom Burger could discuss his theories of criminal insanity, and he faithfully read the opinions that Burger regularly sent him. But he never threw himself into Burger's crusade. Nor did he respond to Burger's increasingly frequent and acerbic critiques of the Supreme Court. From the appeals court, Burger watched with dismay as the Supreme Court under Chief Justice Earl Warren issued one decision after another expanding the rights of criminal defendants and curbing the authority of police and prosecutors. His letters to Blackmun described the justices as "phonies" and "mediocrities."

As the two friends approached their fiftieth birthdays, and as Burger immersed himself in the work of the appeals court, it now became Blackmun's turn to feel restless. He had been at the Mayo Clinic for nearly eight years, and while he had enjoyed the work greatly and cherished his relationships there, he was beginning to wonder whether it was time to move on. "Right now, I feel like going back into private practice," he wrote Burger in late 1957. "Do you have any suggestions?"

Within a year, an unexpected opportunity presented itself. Judge Sanborn, approaching his seventy-fifth birthday, told Blackmun that he was planning to take senior status on the Eighth Circuit. The move would open a vacancy, and he wanted Blackmun to be his successor. Federal judges do not ordinarily anoint their successors, but Sanborn was well connected and thought he could bring about Blackmun's appointment. In any event, he would make it clear that his assumption of senior status was contingent on his approval of his replacement.

It was a fork in the road, as significant as the chance Blackmun had passed up two decades earlier to go to Washington and join the New Deal. His initial response was predictably diffident. "I appreciate your

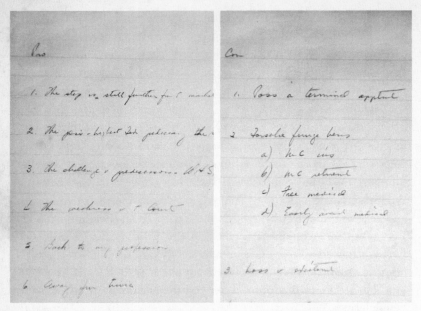

As Blackmun considered whether to seek an appointment to the U.S. Court of Appeals for the Eighth Circuit in 1959, he weighed the pros and the cons.

comments more than I can tell you, but I strongly feel my lack of experience and of qualifications," he wrote to Sanborn. "At this early moment, I do not know what to say other than to mention again, as I have so many times in the past twenty-six years, how grateful I am for your personal interest and confidence. Your friendship has been one of the main and dominant factors in my life, and your judicial work and attitude have always been examples of which I know few parallels."

Sanborn pressed ahead. He told Blackmun that he had consulted Warren Burger on how to proceed. "Don't question your qualifications," he said in a handwritten note. "You have everything that is needed to make an outstanding Circuit Judge. Go over the matter with Warren and perhaps he can arrange a meeting with the Attorney General. It seems to me that politics ought not to have too much influence and anyway they can't do much until there is a vacancy which depends on me."

Alone with his thoughts, Blackmun picked up a yellow legal pad and listed the pros and cons of the decision. By the time he finished, there were seventeen of each. Among the considerations in favor of becoming a judge were these: "away from trivia," "better use of my talents," "a little travel," "different kind of pressure and reduction of it," and "service to U.S. and public." On the negative side: "possibly a terminal appointment," "loss of excitement," "loss of contact with important people," "loss of stature locally," and "loneliness." It is unclear whether the last concern was personal or professional: whether he feared missing the collegiality of the Mayo Clinic doctors or being away from his family during the one week a month that he would spend with the other Eighth Circuit judges hearing arguments in St. Louis. With three daughters approaching college age, he was also worried about having to live on a judge's salary of $25,500 a year, a considerable pay cut from the $43,000 he was earning as Mayo's general counsel. On a separate sheet, he made some financial calculations. "Conclusion: We can continue to maintain our standard of living, but no more," he decided.

Burger quickly became the unofficial manager for a campaign in which Blackmun had yet to enlist formally. He wrote Blackmun as soon as Judge Sanborn had informed him of the plan. "I am overjoyed by a note from JB [the two referred to Sanborn by his first and middle initials] which is a step toward which I have been working for a long time. Happily the other 'principals' are I think at least receptive. My problem will be to get Blackmun in the right mood!" Burger added: "You are a gem among friends—indeed, the rarest jewel of all."

He did not conceal his own sour mood about life on the D.C. Circuit. "If I really liked the Court as I did the Department of Justice work I would be a better advocate for *urging* you on," he wrote a few weeks later. "As it is I can say with 100% conviction only that you are ideally equipped to be an appellate judge—a better one, I assure you, than I."

In early February 1959, Sanborn was the Burgers' houseguest in Washington while he attended a bar association meeting. He and Burger paid a call on Lawrence E. Walsh, the deputy attorney general, to inform the Eisenhower administration of Sanborn's willingness to take senior status if he could be confident that his successor "would not weaken the court." Burger's participation in such a meeting as a sitting judge was unusual. Asked by Walsh to suggest candidates, Sanborn named Blackmun and three others. Two weeks later, Walsh called Blackmun to ask whether he would accept the appointment if offered. Blackmun said he would. In a detailed, six-page narrative of his appointment that he dictated several months later, Blackmun never identified the moment of decision or explained why the seventeen "pros" on his list outweighed the seventeen "cons." Clearly he was flattered, more than a little intrigued, and, having recently turned fifty, ready for a new venture. Although months passed before his nomination went to the Senate, on August 18, the telephone call from Walsh was the only contact Blackmun had with the administration until he received congratulations from Walsh and Brownell after he was confirmed.

The American Bar Association rated Blackmun "exceptionally well qualified," an evaluation it had given to only 8 of the 275 candidates its Standing Committee on Federal Judiciary had rated in the previous three years. Although Blackmun's nomination was in no way controversial, the approach of the 1960 presidential election was already causing the confirmation process in the Democratic-controlled Senate to stagnate. Nineteen judicial nominees were awaiting confirmation, some for many months. An editorial in the *Minneapolis Star* on September 10 called for speedy action on the Blackmun nomination: "This particular delay will cost Minnesota an important appointment and—what is more important—the nation the services of an outstanding judge unless there is a sudden burst of activity on behalf of Blackmun by Minnesota's senators and the Senate Judiciary Committee."

Two days later, Senator Humphrey called Blackmun at home. It was a Saturday, and Blackmun was on the roof clearing leaves and painting the gutters. Humphrey asked him to come to Washington as soon as possible for a hearing before a Judiciary subcommittee—a hearing that would last twelve minutes. The subcommittee recommended the nomination to the full committee, and at two-thirty in the morning of September 15, 1959, in the closing hours of the congressional session, the

Senate confirmed Blackmun unanimously. He took his seat on the bench in St. Louis and heard his first arguments on November 12, his fifty-first birthday.

It was a challenging time to be a federal judge; many areas of American law were in flux. Under Chief Justice Earl Warren, the Supreme Court had made a number of sweeping pronouncements that would need translation by the lower courts in the crucible of actual cases. *Brown v. Board of Education,* decided only five years earlier, was one example. It was now up to the lower courts to respond to the recalcitrance of school districts and the fitful pace of desegregation. Missouri and Arkansas provided the Eighth Circuit with a steady diet of school desegregation cases. Harry Blackmun's expectation that the appeals court would offer a low-stress, low-visibility environment for the next phase of his legal career quickly proved unfounded.

Of the 217 opinions Blackmun would write for the Eighth Circuit, two in particular illustrate his stance during an era of rapid legal change. In *Jones v. Alfred H. Mayer Co.,* the question before the court was whether, in the days before the passage of fair housing laws, a property owner could refuse to sell to a black person. A black man to whom a white St. Louis developer refused to sell a home had brought a lawsuit based on the Civil Rights Act of 1866. This little-used statute, enacted in the aftermath of the Civil War, gave to "all citizens" the same right to "inherit, purchase, lease, sell, hold, and convey real and personal property" as is "enjoyed by white citizens." The issue was whether the law applied only to government action or, in fact, also covered acts of private discrimination. The answer was not completely clear. While the Supreme Court's older precedents indicated that Congress lacked constitutional authority to prohibit private discrimination of this sort, there were also suggestions from more recent cases that if the Court revisited the issue, it might find otherwise.

Blackmun's sympathies were with the plaintiff, Joseph Lee Jones, but he felt constrained to follow precedent. "A change of course" could well be in the wings, Blackmun said in the opinion he wrote for the Eighth Circuit in 1967, observing further that it would "not be too surprising if the Supreme Court one day" found that the 1866 law, examined anew, did apply to private discrimination. But that prospect, by itself, "falls short of justification by us as an inferior tribunal." He concluded, reluctantly, that the suit must fail.

The case drew wide attention and, as Blackmun expected, the Supreme Court agreed to review it. Now he was in the unusual position, for a lower-court judge, of hoping to be reversed; that, he told his colleagues, had been the point of the way he constructed the opinion. To his Eighth Circuit colleague Gerald W. Heaney, he said: "I did my best to serve the issues up on a tray, figuratively, for the Supreme Court to take. I hope they will. This is the kind of situation where one does not mind being reversed. Perhaps I should be more willing to strike out for the frontier and be less influenced by Supreme Court decisions which remain on the books."

To another colleague, M. C. Matthes, he wrote: "I did my best in the opinion to lay the issue out on the table in a quavering state and to spell out precisely how the opposite decision could be reached. The implication was that we were bound by existing Supreme Court utterances. I am fairly convinced, personally, that fair housing is an important factor in the elimination of the ghetto."

Blackmun's hope was realized. In an opinion by Justice Potter Stewart, the Supreme Court reversed the Eighth Circuit decision, ruling by a vote of 7 to 2 both that Congress, in the 1866 law, had intended to prohibit private discrimination and that the Thirteenth Amendment, the amendment that abolished slavery, had supplied the legislature with the authority to do so.

In another decision on the cutting edge of evolving constitutional law, Blackmun wrote an opinion for the Eighth Circuit abolishing corporal punishment in the Arkansas prison system. The question, in *Jackson v. Bishop,* was how to apply the Eighth Amendment's prohibition against cruel and unusual punishment to the conditions within a prison. Arkansas rules authorized officials to beat inmates with a leather strap, up to five and one-half feet long, known as the "bull hide." Three prisoners brought a constitutional lawsuit seeking an injunction. An earlier suit had resulted in a decision permitting use of the strap once "appropriate safeguards" were in place. Did that ruling provide inmates with sufficient protection against abuse?

Early in his judicial career, Blackmun established a practice that he would follow throughout his tenure on the Eighth Circuit and on the Supreme Court. Before a case was argued, he would review the briefs submitted by the parties and any memos prepared by his law clerks. He would then dictate a memo to himself, summarizing the arguments and giving his preliminary responses. Offering his unvarnished personal reaction to the debates swirling around him, these notes are among the most valuable documents in the Blackmun case files. His preargument memo in the prison case was no exception.

"It is obvious from the record that any so-called safeguard is entirely unworkable," he wrote to himself, observing that the rules already in effect had been "flagrantly violated." The strap "inflicts such pain and is so barbarous that it is abhorrent to public opinion. This kind of thing the testimony shows breeds hate." But how to approach the constitutional analysis? There were few precedents for applying the Eighth Amendment to prison conditions. "Constitutional standards are evolving and are not static," Blackmun wrote. "We must look at present day concepts and opinions." Noting that nearly every state had abandoned corporal punishment in prison, and that fourteen had explicitly outlawed it, he added: "A court's conscience is necessarily the product of prevailing public opinion." He said his "sympathies, at the moment, are in favor of going all the way" to forbid corporal punishment entirely. "This would be an interesting case to work on from the historical point of view. I would not mind having it."

Blackmun did get the assignment, and his opinion closely tracked his memo. Noting that "corporal punishment generates hate toward the keepers who punish and toward the system which permits it," he observed: "We have no difficulty in reaching the conclusion that the use of the strap in the penitentiaries of Arkansas is punishment which, in this last third of the 20th century, runs afoul of the Eighth Amendment."

The opinion in *Jackson v. Bishop* was widely noticed and favorably received by the judicial and wider legal community. Judge Robert Van

Pelt, one of the judges who had heard the argument with Blackmun, wrote him that "the opinion constitutes a milestone in Eighth Amendment decisions and is an opinion of which you will always be proud." Several months later, after the Arkansas attorney general announced that he would not appeal, Blackmun received a congratulatory letter from Edward L. Wright, a prominent Little Rock lawyer and president-elect of the American Bar Association, who had argued the case as the court-appointed counsel for one of the inmates. "The good effect of the decision will be vital for generations," Wright said.

Blackmun replied: "That opinion was not the easiest to prepare. I suppose this in part is due to the fact that one necessarily becomes somewhat emotionally involved in the record." On the face of it, this was a puzzling reaction to the lawyer's compliment. There is nothing to indicate that the decision was difficult; to the contrary, Blackmun had welcomed the assignment and had proceeded to translate his immediate response to the case into an opinion that his colleagues joined enthusiastically. It is unclear whether Blackmun nonetheless perceived that he had struggled with the decision or whether he thought it would be unseemly to acknowledge that on such an important issue, he had scarcely struggled at all.

But a struggle was taking place on the Eighth Circuit, one with long-lasting consequences for Harry Blackmun. The subject was capital punishment.

By the mid-1960s, there was growing legal ferment over the death penalty. It appeared to Blackmun and many others that the Supreme Court would soon take up the issue, and there was a strong possibility that the Court would find that the existing death penalty laws violated the Eighth Amendment's prohibition against cruel and unusual punishment. That day had not arrived, however, and the courts of appeals had little choice but to decide, on the basis of the available precedents, the cases that reached them.

"I am told we have a good one coming up from Nebraska, the Pope murder case, where a death sentence has been imposed," Blackmun wrote to Burger in March 1966. This might be the case to go up to the Supreme Court, he speculated. The seemingly inexplicable triple murder had galvanized the Midwest. The defendant, Duane Pope, was a twenty-two-year-old college football star who, a few days after his graduation from McPherson College in Kansas, crossed the state line to Big Springs, Nebraska. There he robbed the Farmers State Bank and shot three employees, including the bank's seventy-seven-year-old president, to death. Then he headed west by bus and by plane, gambling in Las Vegas and attending a bullfight in Tijuana, before turning himself in. A federal jury rejected his insanity defense and sentenced him to death under the capital punishment provision of the bank robbery statute. His appeal raised questions about the way the trial court had handled jury selection and about the psychiatric evidence.

Federal appeals courts usually assign cases to be heard and decided by panels of three judges, but in *Pope v. United States,* the Eighth Circuit decided that all seven active judges should hear the appeal. "I have a faint suspicion that the job of writing the opinion will come my way," Blackmun told Burger in August. "Maybe if I disagree with the rest of them I shall avoid that task." There was no disagreement, however. All seven judges voted to uphold the death sentence, and the assignment went to Blackmun. Although he opposed capital punishment, hardly an unusual position in Minnesota, which had repealed its death penalty in 1911, the *Pope* case was not a challenge to capital punishment as such. In any event, in the absence of Supreme Court precedent to the contrary, Blackmun viewed the death penalty as a matter for the legislature, not the courts, to decide.

During Pope's trial, the government's expert witness had testified that the defendant was schizophrenic. While the defense had objected to the jury instructions on insanity, which required proof of "irresistible impulse," the instructions were proper under the circuit's precedents, and the jury had voted to convict. There appeared to be no grounds for overturning that judgment. At the end of his twenty-five-page opinion, Blackmun added a paragraph expressing his doubts about the death penalty and suggesting that executive clemency rather than execution might better serve the ends of justice in Duane Pope's case. In a cover letter to his fellow judges, Blackmun wrote, "You may perhaps feel that my closing comments about capital punishment and executive clemency should be omitted. If you do, please say so."

Two of the other judges, Floyd R. Gibson and M. C. Matthes, accepted this invitation to raise objections. In separate responses, they called Blackmun's closing comments about capital punishment "gratuitous." The word stung, although the context suggests that neither judge intended the term as an insult and neither meant to provoke a fight. Gibson, in fact, made a point of describing the rest of the opinion as "masterful." Explaining his objection to the capital punishment remarks, he said that because the jury's findings were "in accord with the statutory authorization, I do not think it is proper for us to comment upon this permissible decision." Matthes made the same point: "So long as there is such statutory authorization, I question the propriety of courts theorizing whether the death penalty should be abolished."

Despite having invited criticism, Blackmun was deeply wounded when he received it. "I strongly feel that the characterization by two of you that that paragraph is 'gratuitous' is unfair," he wrote in a letter he circulated to the full court. "I equate the adjective 'gratuitous' with 'uncalled for' and I am not ready to concede that the comment was uncalled for. The paragraph was written out of a feeling of sincerity and conviction on my part." Nevertheless, he said, he would remove the passage.

Now the other two judges took offense. "Unfairness" was "an accusation never before made during my twelve years of judicial life," Matthes observed. "I am somewhat concerned that you would rely upon the innocuous term 'gratuitous' as a premise for impugning my fairness." For his part, Gibson noted that he was "only expressing my difference of opinion with you on the issue of capital punishment. I recognize that you have a right to your opinion and views, but I also feel that I must be accorded the same right."

The court's collegiality appeared on the verge of unraveling. At this point, Judge Donald P. Lay intervened with a private letter to Blackmun. "Perhaps it is none of my business, but I cannot help but express regret over the correspondence between you and Charlie Matthes," he said. "I would hate to see any personal dissidence among two of the nicest guys on the court." The dispute was just "a matter of unintended misstatements," Lay believed. One of the court's most liberal members, Lay told Blackmun that he would file a concurring opinion in the *Pope* case and, speaking in his own voice, without involving the other judges, would add a final paragraph: "The ends of criminal justice would be served by a life sentence for Duane Pope. I fully recognize that clemency is not within the power of the judiciary, yet the overall circumstances of this case and the need of humaneness in laws of criminal procedure require me to speak."

As Blackmun was working on the *Pope* opinion, he had shared portions of the case with Burger. Now, with the decision about to be issued, he told Burger what had happened. "I got into a real hoedown about capital punishment," he wrote in February 1967. "I did not realize that emotions ran so deep. The opinion will be filed this week without the paragraph, but with Judge Lay filing a separate concurrence in which he makes passing mention of it."

Months later, the episode appeared to have become more, rather than less, painful to Blackmun. "I continue to kick myself for withdrawing my comment about capital punishment," he wrote in a letter to Burger in September. "In retrospect, I suppose it was expediency, namely, to avoid a hoedown in the court. Yet, I was right about it and one never should compromise when one is right. I gained nothing by it except misunderstanding and, if that was to come anyway, I might as well have held my position."

Simultaneously, Burger was nursing his own wounds. In a long letter to Blackmun on Labor Day 1967, the eve of his sixtieth birthday, Burger wrote: "You know the old saw about the most terrible hour in life being the one in which a man looks back over the book he has written and compares it with the one he intended to write. In charity I spare myself that torture. But in one respect I can face it. As a kid I had the inclination to protest what I thought was wrong. It got me some bloody noses, some rejections, some isolation. But as I look back there are no regrets about walking away from a fight or a problem."

Nor could he walk away today, Burger continued, from the battles he continued to fight on the D.C. Circuit. "In the present context if I were to stand still for some of the idiocy that is put forth as legal and constitutional profundity I would, I am sure, want to shoot myself in later years. These guys just *can't* be right. So there is nothing to do but resist. The question for careful judgment is when, where, etc."

In reply, Blackmun sent birthday greetings and a five-page, single-spaced letter filled with soothing, encouraging words. "You and I are very different in many ways," he told Burger:

> You have a great number of things which I lack. You have the ability to make an excellent impression, to be heard and to be acknowledged. You work extremely well under pressure. You think well on your feet. You are an excellent advocate. You know your way around, procedurally. You impress in every possible way. You stand out in a group. And all this is merited and deserved.
>
> On the other hand, you and I are very much alike in certain ways. I think we both abhor the phony and usually we can detect it. We have the same basic loyalties. Despite our humble backgrounds we are not impressed with or desire the material things of life, beyond a point. . . .
>
> I do not need to tell you what your friendship and confidence have meant to me over half a century. You know this. You have always been a rock on which I could rely and your steadfastness of decision has been an anchor. And your constant availability when in need has meant so much. . . . I am grateful to you for all this. We have had some interesting experiences together and I can't think of any of significance that I am really ashamed of. . . . Yes, we could have stayed in Saint Paul and Minneapolis and achieved some legal prominence and been a financial funnel, but to what end? . . .
>
> All in all, I am convinced that you and I have no reason for regrets. You have achieved much and have had fun doing it. Compare yourself with 99% of the guys who went to high school with you, or law school for that matter. It has been a good sixty years.

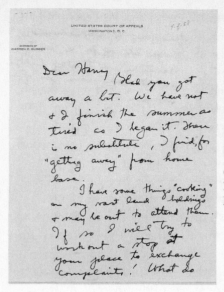

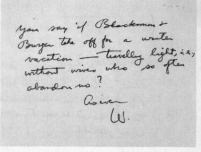

One of Burger's many letters urging Blackmun to join him on a trip to Europe, just the two of them

One of the most striking aspects of the correspondence between the old friends is Warren Burger's repeated importuning of Harry Blackmun to join him on a European trip, just the two of them. Although the two families sometimes vacationed together in Florida, Blackmun resisted Burger's overtures to go on a Warren-and-Harry trip to Europe. It was not for lack of trying—hectoring, teasing, pleading—on Burger's part. In 1962, Burger proposed a trip to Lisbon: "If I could get you to realize (a) we are mortal (b) we are not getting younger & (c) we need to have at least a once a year binge while we stay on this job, I could get you to push me into doing something like this! . . . There's a very wise book with a title 'Revolt of the Middle Ages' and it is not essentially history. If there isn't such a book I'm thinking of writing it, but I need to acquire some background. Join me!"

The next year Burger tried again. For $20 a day, he said, they could spend a month traveling through Belgium, Denmark, Germany, France, and Spain. By eating only two meals a day, they could lose weight at the same time. They could each buy a Mercedes at a discount. "I have meant to tell you of a discovery I made a few years ago. It is a very profound one: we are not going to live forever. I have kept this to myself because I do not wish to disturb my contemporaries unduly until they are properly prepared. Worse than that we are not going to be young forever. I was old at 18 and have tried to get more flexible since then. In certain areas I have had some success, but not all." In a postscript, Burger provided a list of "all you need": "(a) $1,200 (b) one dress shirt & suit four wash & wear shirts (c) 2 wash & wear slacks one sport coat & sweater (d) 2 underwear & pjs (e) raincoat (f) no hat (g) passport (I'll vouch for you)."

When Blackmun turned him down with a "maybe next year," Burger wrote again. He was "depressed and even saddened" by what he acknowledged as "selfish disappointment." Blackmun was making a serious mistake, according to Burger. "I say saddened because I have a profound conviction that each of us, and 'both of us,' needs an 'escape' kind of holiday right now, and I mean right now. What may be the many and diverse cause of our discontent, frustrations, and confusions is less important than that we do something about them now. To me it is almost like postponing a cancer operation. I have been very depressed about a number of things for a long time. And as you well know, being a quasi-medic by osmosis, depression does not usually cure itself; it needs treatment. The best treatment I know is to climb a mountain and watch some of them at least dissolve in the clean clear air and improved vision which comes from distance."

In the tone of a rejected lover, Burger wondered whether Blackmun's response was "just a Harvard man's way of saying 'I have made up my mind, dammit, now go away and don't bother me'?" This emotional letter concluded: "Believe me, old friend, you are making a mistake—perhaps as large a one as I made in letting myself be 'conned' into becoming a Judge. But I will subside and lick my wounds, hoping meanwhile that some divine unguent is available to each of us if we fail ourselves in this way."

Burger followed his letter with a telephone call. Alarmed, Blackmun replied by letter:

You were obviously deeply troubled and I tried to "read between the lines" to imagine its source and to see whether there
was any way in which I could be of at least a little help. I do not
want to be presumptuous but if I can be of assistance I want to
be. If you want me to hop a plane and come to Washington for a
couple of days I will be glad to do so. . . .

   I feel as though I am letting you down. This is the last thing I
would want to do to you. You must realize that. . . . I will call
you some night this week for I am concerned about you. I will
try to reach you on Thursday at home. We will lick whatever is
bothering you, I know.

But Burger's despair deepened. The following week, abandoning
his typewriter and scrawling on seven pages of a legal pad, he wrote:
"I do concede that I ask too much sometimes of others. Not many are
in this select club, but when they let me down I confess I am deeply,
abnormally hurt & in these rare cases—or as to these few persons—it
must, in the context, be a secret hurt. . . .

   "Alas, how many hurts have I inflicted all unknowing on someone
expecting love, confidence, trust, encouragement? I would fear to know.
Probing ever so gently at one of these things I suffered once I was startled to learn that others need not be too concerned for me since I—as
was well known to everyone—was strong, decisive, determined etc. etc.
and impervious to the 'slings and arrows' of both friend and foe. . . .
My ensuing reaction was how completely I had failed to reveal myself to
someone who should have known better what fragile porcelain can re-
side within a man."

   Clearly Burger's lonely battles on the D.C. Circuit were taking their
toll on him. There was a hint, as well, of deeper problems, perhaps
related to family rather than to work. With his maudlin tone and self-
consciously poetic imagery, Burger depicted himself as the misunderstood hero of a running melodrama in which he persisted in trying to
cast Blackmun. "You, too, are a 'romantic idealist' *with oak clusters!*" he
told his friend, despite a tendency to "err on the side of too thick a

bottle and too tight a cork." He then concluded: "Please don't be concerned. I needed to take the 'inner cork' off even if for only a few minutes. It is safely restored & will be released as need dictates."

Blackmun replied with relief: "Of course, you are a romantic idealist and perhaps an incurable one and you always have been. You and I both are. . . . Don't ever let this characteristic be changed. It is one of your great strengths and fundamentally makes you what you are and no apology whatsoever need be made for this. . . .

"We all have our frailties but you should never, never be concerned about yours. You have the corresponding strength which makes the presence of both features attractive and desirable. I concede that I have erred on the side of too thick a bottle and too tight a cork." Then Blackmun referred to a death-row inmate whose sentence he had upheld in an opinion for the Eighth Circuit the previous year. "Victor Harry Feguer died on the gallows in Fort Madison, Iowa, last Friday. And you say people call you a hanging judge."

Burger went to Europe alone that summer, to attend a judicial conference at The Hague. Having nearly recovered his equilibrium, he could employ, in a letter to Blackmun, a wry tone that contained just a tinge of bitterness. "No, indeed, I am not mad. Just damned sad. It surely will look funny as Hell when we finally get to that tour with sturdy nurses pushing our wheel chairs and we two fiddle with our hearing aids. I can just hear it: 'What did you say? Girls, what girls, I don't see any girls.' (Who said that?) No, I am too philosophical to be mad at a 'natural mistake'—natural in the sense that each one of us knows his own problems best."

Even in the Eisenhower years, Burger had been mentioned as a potential Supreme Court nominee, but during the presidencies of Kennedy and Johnson, both Democrats, such chatter receded. With the election of a Republican, Richard M. Nixon, in 1968, Burger's name was in play once again. Chief Justice Earl Warren had already announced his retirement, and the Senate had blocked Johnson's efforts to install his friend Abe Fortas, an associate justice since 1965, in the position. Burger told Blackmun he was not greatly interested in the chief justiceship because he regarded the Supreme Court as almost beyond repair. "What can one man do to stop the nonsense?" Burger wrote to his friend on March 31, 1969. "RN can only straighten that place out if he gets four appointments and draws on the State and Federal bench for the replacements. Few lawyers can accomplish the job of reading up now on what the extent of the subversion of the law has been."

Burger was being more than a little coy. Far from discouraging speculation that he might be the next chief justice, he was, in fact, cultivating his contacts in the new administration. He and Nixon had known each other casually from shared labors in Republican Party vineyards decades earlier. During the presidential campaign, Nixon quoted from a law-and-order speech that Burger had given in Wisconsin and had subsequently made sure to circulate in Washington. During the early months of the administration, Burger sent the White House suggestions for nominees to the lower courts. On May 21, 1969, it was his turn. President Nixon nominated him to be chief justice of the United States.

Blackmun's letter of congratulations to his old friend had an elegiac tone. "The sun has come up on another day," he wrote the morning after the announcement. "It is a beautiful one here and a fine omen for what lies ahead." He continued: "The last half of May 21, 1969, was a great, great day, not only for you but for all your friends, both personal and professional, those known and unknown, those once known and now forgotten, who share with you the day and the accomplishment and the investment of responsibilities. It is a great day for America for reasons which I need not list but which you and I have discussed so many times on Dayton's Bluff and elsewhere in Saint Paul and in Washington and in Rochester. This is no less so just because you happen to be the central figure involved.

"I know the kind of person you are and the kind of man and lawyer you have been. I find nothing wanting."

Blackmun concluded: "My support is yours for the asking at all times."

3

OLD NUMBER THREE

"I AM FILLED with plans, ideas, and programs," Warren Burger wrote to Harry Blackmun. "I want your ideas."

It was June 1969, a week after Burger became chief justice. His initial impressions of life at the Court were negative. The chief justice's office was cramped; at the same time, space elsewhere in the building went begging. "Two great Conference rooms unused and the C.J. in quarters a Law Clerk would reject!" He was determined to make changes. "But I realize I must move with some caution & deliberation & I must *pace myself*. I never sought this job—never really would want it—but now it is here & *we will do it.*"

If there were warning signs in this communication—chambers that had been adequate for every chief justice since Charles Evans Hughes would not do for Warren Burger?—Blackmun did not appear to notice them. Instead, he responded eagerly to the declaration that *"we will do it,"* taking Burger at his word that the new chief justice really meant "we." Blackmun sent back an eight-page, single-spaced memorandum addressing nearly every aspect of the Court's operations, from how to handle law clerks to whether the Supreme Court term really needed to end in June, to the desirability of providing every justice with a limousine and driver. "City traffic is on the increase," Blackmun said. "A Justice deserves to be relieved of struggling with it on the way to and from work. The most inconsequential automobile accident, when he is driving, can be most embarrassing."

Among his suggestions was one to end the tradition of announcing opinions from the bench. Nearly every other court issued its opinions through the clerk's office without ceremony, he pointed out. The Supreme Court's bench announcements, at which justices summarize their opinions for whoever happened to be in the courtroom audience, were an "anachronism" and a waste of the justices' time, Blackmun said. More generally, he added: "I wonder if there is not a great deal of obsolescence in routine."

Perhaps Blackmun was simply trying to demonstrate his usefulness to the new chief justice, but some of these suggestions were curious. He had no personal desire for a limousine; he was to become so closely identified with the little blue Volkswagen Beetle he drove into the Supreme Court garage every day that when he died, his family rented one for the funeral procession. And far from shunning the spotlight that falls temporarily on justices as they announce a majority or a dissenting opinion from the bench—a practice that Chief Justice Burger did not, in fact, abolish—Justice Blackmun would use, to the fullest, the opportunity to speak in his own voice, beyond the confines of the printed page.

During the summer between Burger's investiture and the start of the Court's 1969 term, in October, the two men were in constant communication. As one of his first law clerks, Burger hired a *University of Minnesota Law Review* editor whom Blackmun had interviewed and recommended. Back in Minnesota, Blackmun became a kind of self-appointed spokesman for Burger; as he addressed various audiences, he would depict his friend in terms that softened Burger's harder edges. The Burger Court under its "active, energetic new chief" might not prove so different from the Court under Earl Warren, Blackmun told a group of FBI agents attending a training program in Rochester. "Don't assume that his attitude will be the opposite of Mr. Warren's," Blackmun said. "Despite what some newspaper articles say and what some commentators say, Mr. Burger's entire background, believe it or not, is in the liberal tradition and not in the conservative tradition." Blackmun predicted: "His era will not be a status quo one. He will incur criticism and opposition not unlike that of Chief Justice Warren but of a different kind. I think it will be an interesting period."

Burger himself was uneasy, girding for battle. Shortly before the term began, he wrote Blackmun from his vacation hotel on the Portuguese coast. He had been exhausted, sleeping twelve or fourteen hours a day, slowly regaining his equilibrium. He was prepared to stand up to the incumbent justices who, he knew, had not welcomed his selection. He told Blackmun that on his early visits to the Court, "I began to discover various booby traps, ambushes, and the like. This may have a ring of paranoia but I'll fill you in. More than one guy there will bear a close watch." He was studying the Court's recent work and finding it unimpressive: "Read all at once the quality of fantasy, lack of disciplined thinking emerges sharply from the 1968–69 work. Black comes out looking the best of all. Except for his 'absolutes' he is the most consistently disciplined intellect there—if two years of opinions is a fair basis, which it may not be. We must rest our hopes for a 'restoration' on Haynsworth, plus Black, of course, and then [Byron] White, [John Marshall] Harlan & Stewart in that order. It is really incredible to me how 9 men could have gone so far from reality for so long. Fortas was actually a far stronger & sounder judge than some others I could name. . . . Poor, sad Abe Fortas."

Fortas had resigned a few months earlier, in May 1969, following a financial scandal that erupted after the failure of his nomination as chief justice in 1968. Now the matter of Fortas's replacement was on Burger's mind. Nixon had nominated Clement Haynsworth, Jr., a federal appeals court judge from South Carolina whose confirmation hearing in the Senate Judiciary Committee was taking place as Burger wrote. The hearing was not going well, and Blackmun, monitoring the news from his home in Rochester, replied that "your man Haynsworth has been given a bit of a rough time." Nonetheless, Blackmun remained "positive he will be confirmed." Blackmun also agreed with Burger's high opinion of Fortas and Hugo L. Black, the eighty-three-year-old senior associate justice. "Black still rings loud and clear," he wrote.

Blackmun then turned to what Burger's new position might mean for their friendship. As appeals court judges, they had occupied the same rung of the judicial hierarchy for the past decade. Now they were no longer equals. "You have two of my cases up there for argument this fall," Blackmun wrote. "I shall never discuss any case of mine with you. I mention these two now—and there will be more— only because I know you will decide them precisely as you see them. Never feel any obligation or loyalty to me. In a way, this is the first time in our lives we have been in such a position. Whatever you do, there will be no hard feeling between the two of us and no need ever to explain or defend."

Although Blackmun had not seriously considered the prospect of his own potential nomination to the Supreme Court, his name had, in fact, been put forward even before Nixon took office. At the urging of one of the Mayo Clinic's senior physicians shortly after the 1968 election, Representative Albert H. Quie of Minnesota wrote to Bryce N. Harlow, an assistant to the president-elect, recommending Blackmun for any future Court vacancy. And in May, following the Fortas resignation, Quie wrote again, this time directly to the president: "In my opinion, the superior talents, scholarly attainments and juridical accomplishments of Judge Blackmun attest to his eminent suitability to serve in such a capacity." Another member of the Minnesota congressional delegation, Clark MacGregor, also enlisted in the effort; before long, Blackmun's name was in circulation. An article in the *Washington Star* on July 25, 1969, placed him as one of the top contenders for the vacancy and featured his picture. Burger sent a copy of the article to Blackmun with a handwritten cover note: "Harry, this is all to the good. Seeds need time to grow but they need planting! More later."

The Haynsworth nomination came later that summer, along with a bruising confirmation battle; the testimony included charges that the judge had displayed ethical insensitivity by participating in cases in which he had a financial interest. And on November 21 the Senate rejected Haynsworth's nomination by a vote of 55 to 45. The administration chose another federal appeals court judge from the South, G. Harrold Carswell, whose nomination also failed in the Senate, amid evidence of his hostility to civil rights. Days later, on April 9, 1970, Attorney General John N. Mitchell called Harry Blackmun and summoned him to Washington.

"I asked if there was any preparation I had to do," Blackmun wrote in an unpublished memoir of his nomination that he dictated for his files later that year. "He said no and that it only concerned the Supreme Court and whether I was willing to accept a nomination to the court. I observed that perhaps this was something that one did not turn down." Burger had clearly been in on the administration's discussions, because he telephoned soon after Blackmun concluded his conversation with Mitchell, well before word of his possible selection became public. With only minutes to spare after a long sprint through the parking lot, Blackmun caught an afternoon flight to Washington from Minneapolis. He was unable even to reach his wife before his departure. Dottie Blackmun's father had died the day before, and she was out of town taking care of the funeral arrangements.

On the plane he started to draw up another of his series of lists of pros and cons, as he had done eleven years before when deciding whether to pursue the appeals court opportunity. While the balance sheet in 1959 had been evenly divided between positive and negative, this time he found himself listing only "all the negatives to this." Among them were "my lifelong friendship with the chief justice, my political inactivity, my taking too long on opinions, my lack of appetite for Washington living, and my lack of acquaintanceship with Washington power." There were no corresponding positives. If the prospect of being named to the Supreme Court thrilled or even interested him, he gave no indication. "I suppose this was primarily a defense mechanism," he observed in the memoir.

Events were moving more quickly than Blackmun imagined. An assistant attorney general, William H. Rehnquist, had already been assigned to analyze Blackmun's court of appeals record and would turn in his favorable report on April 10. "I think he can be fairly characterized as conservative-to-moderate in both criminal law and civil rights," Rehnquist wrote. "He does not uniformly come out on one side or the other, though his tendencies are certainly more in the conservative direction than in the liberal. His opinions are all carefully reasoned, and give no indication of a preconceived bias in one direction or the other. No one could possibly accuse him of lack of scholarship, since his opinions are replete with citations and discussion."

Blackmun was in the process of signing the guest register at the Cosmos Club, a private men's club where he usually stayed on trips to Washington, "when a hand was laid on my shoulder." It was an FBI agent, who spent the next three hours interviewing him. The next day he met at the Justice Department with Mitchell, Rehnquist, and another assistant attorney general, Johnnie M. Walters, the head of the department's Tax Division. Walters asked whether any of Blackmun's daughters, then age twenty, twenty-two, and twenty-six, "could be typified as hippies." Blackmun showed the men his daughters' photographs, which allayed the administration's concerns about the family's younger generation. In fact, Susan, the youngest daughter, then in her junior year of college, was at the time a self-described hippie and political radical who regarded Nixon as the ultimate enemy and made her views clear within the family. Once, when Blackmun presented her with a pen that Nixon had given him, she responded: "Wow, a pen from Tricky Dick." Blackmun snatched the pen from her hand and left the room.

As the meeting in the attorney general's office stretched through the lunch hour, Blackmun was surprised at how much time the three senior officials were spending with him. "It became apparent, however, that all three were raw and bleeding from the Haynsworth–Carswell incidents and were deeply disappointed about the Haynsworth rejection and embarrassed about the Carswell one." In the afternoon Attorney General Mitchell took Blackmun to the White House to meet the president.

The meeting lasted forty-five minutes. As they talked, Nixon occasionally put his feet up on his desk. There was little small talk. Nixon asked Blackmun his net worth. "My hackles rose at this point and I must have shown it. I told him that apart from my house my net worth was probably about $70,000. Mr. Nixon's response was, 'We have reached the point where we have to put paupers on the Supreme Court.' I must have flushed again and perhaps evinced a little annoyance at this, for he followed through by saying, do not misunderstand me. What I mean is that anyone with substantial wealth is under disadvantage from the start. He then asked me to guess what he was worth when he left Washington at the conclusion of his Vice-Presidency. He answered his question himself. He said, $42,000, and observed that many in subordinate positions went away millionaires. One either is honest in government or is dishonest."

After requesting Mitchell's formal recommendation and receiving it, the president informed Blackmun that his nomination would be announced in four days. "He then stood up and the interview was over," Blackmun later wrote. "He took my arm, however, and led me to the window overlooking the Rose Garden. He said, Judge, when you come down here, you will be completely independent. That is the way it should be. I should warn you, however, that the 'Georgetown crowd' will do their best to elbow in on you. You will be wined and dined and approached. I suspect that two of the Justices have fallen victim to this kind of thing. Can you resist the Washington cocktail party circuit? My response was that I could and, in fact, that I had to in order to maintain my ability to work and my health. He then asked whether Mrs. Blackmun could resist it. I told him that I thought she could. He said it is very important."

No one had asked Blackmun to bring his financial records to Washington, so Assistant Attorney General Walters arranged to come to Rochester to examine the tax returns himself. The two men booked separate flights, timed to arrive simultaneously in Minneapolis. As it turned out, Senator Walter F. Mondale of Minnesota, an acquaintance of Blackmun's, was on the same plane as the judge, talking to another passenger, a local business owner whom Blackmun also knew. "Do you know Blackmun?" the man asked the Democratic senator. "Yes, he's another conservative," Mondale replied. As Blackmun recounted the moment in his nomination memoir, "I wondered whether to let him know that I was there so that he wouldn't later be embarrassed or whether I should try to play it out by ignoring everything. At that point Fritz turned and saw me and said, 'Oh, Judge, I have just been telling Ed what a great guy you are.' " The conversation was cordial, Mondale indicating that he would support Blackmun's nomination without, at the moment, making a public statement.

Arriving in Minneapolis, Blackmun offered the assistant attorney general a seat in his Volkswagen. They drove together to Rochester and met the next morning, a Saturday, to go over the tax returns. All was in order. "Those are the cleanest returns I think I have ever seen," the Tax Division chief told the prospective nominee. In the report he wrote Washington, Walters noted that he had studied only the tax returns, and not Blackmun's judicial opinions. "Judging from the orderliness I saw reflected in the judge and his tax returns, plus what I have been advised by others," the assistant attorney general nevertheless observed, "he no doubt is a very fine judge."

The only financial issue of potential concern to the newly sensitized administration was Blackmun's participation in two cases that involved the Ford Motor Company, even though he owned fifty shares of the firm's stock. The administration's lawyers and, eventually, both the American Bar Association's screening committee and the Senate Judiciary Committee concluded that his financial interest was so minimal as not to present a problem.

Following his meeting with Walters, Blackmun flew to St. Louis for what was to be his final argument as a judge on the Eighth Circuit Court of Appeals. Word was spreading of his imminent nomination. After the official announcement, on Tuesday, April 14, the central hall of the St. Louis federal building, where the court met, was filled with reporters and television cameras. "It reminded me of the description of the mob at the Bastille," Blackmun recalled. When the reporters asked him whether he was, as the White House press secretary had described him, a "strict constructionist," Blackmun replied that he did not operate according to labels but "tried to call them as I see them." The next morning he went to his St. Louis chambers to clean out his desk. Justice Byron White and former Justice Tom Clark called to congratulate him. On his way to pick up his ticket for the flight home to Minnesota, he stopped at a doughnut shop "and felt very lonely and mildly distressed."

The early signs pointed to a trouble-free confirmation—just what the administration was hoping for. The ABA gave Blackmun its highest rating. Hubert Humphrey, the former vice president and Minnesota senator whom Nixon had defeated in the 1968 election, also endorsed the nomination. Press coverage was generally favorable; Blackmun was described in such terms as "quiet and scholarly," "hard to label," "a judge's judge." While the Associated Press, in a wire story carried by hundreds of newspapers, stressed Blackmun's "striking similarity in view to his old friend, Chief Justice Warren E. Burger," the *Washington Post* had a different emphasis. "His opinions and reputation indicate that he is a conservative with an independent mind and sensitivity to new ideas," the *Post* article said.

Among the congratulatory messages was one from the defeated nominee Clement Haynsworth. It was addressed to "My Dear Mr. Justice," although Blackmun had not yet been confirmed. "I am certain that a great majority of the Senate is now prepared to consider your nomination objectively, and I earnestly believe they will make the hearing and the subsequent proceedings a pleasant experience for you," Haynsworth wrote. He added that during his own travail, "one of the nicest notes I received" was from Nancy Blackmun, Harry's oldest daughter. Haynsworth said he was sending Nancy a copy of his letter to Blackmun "to tell her that the wounds of last fall are all scarred over, so that my eyes are on the future and my emotional health quite unimpaired, and, finally, to assure her that she can look forward happily to the time when her father will be recognized as one of the more distinguished justices."

Judging by the tone of his responses to the congratulatory mail, the good news from Washington did little to lighten Blackmun's mood. "The roof, indeed, has caved in upon my family and me," he wrote to a law school classmate in a typical response. "What the future holds, I do not know. We shall struggle with it day by day." To another friend, he referred to "the crisis which has engulfed Dottie and my family and me."

His confirmation hearing, on April 29, 1970, lasted less than four hours. Blackmun had made the rounds of Senate offices the day before and spent a quiet night at the Cosmos Club, where "I read a little Tolkien." He relied on the club's doorman to find a tailor to patch the torn jacket of the one suit he had brought with him. Dottie Blackmun remained in Rochester. They had discussed whether she should join him for the hearing, but, he later recalled, "I concluded that I should walk this last mile alone."

The senators' questions were friendly, even perfunctory, and not a single witness testified in opposition to the nomination. Blackmun assured the Judiciary Committee members that he would not hesitate to disagree with Chief Justice Burger, "and he is the first person to be aware of this." Blackmun said: "At times undoubtedly our friendship will be strained mightily because of disagreement. I do not fear this."

Perhaps he heard his mother's voice as he spoke those words. Theo Blackmun, then eighty-five years old, had responded to the nomination by warning her son that his relationship with Warren Burger would now inevitably change. In an oral history recorded after his retirement, Blackmun recalled his response to her prediction. "Mother, it just can't. We've been friends for a long time."

"Well, you wait and see," his mother replied.

The Judiciary Committee approved the nomination unanimously, followed by a 94-to-0 confirmation vote in the Senate on May 12. It was two days short of a year since Fortas had resigned. Blackmun never forgot that he was the third choice for the seat and for many years thereafter would refer to himself as "old number three." He was sixty-one years old.

On the eve of his formal swearing-in, Blackmun received a welcoming letter from Burger. With his first term as chief justice almost complete, Burger's tone was upbeat, a marked change from the previous summer. The justices had proved to be "a congenial, considerate and dedicated group," he said, attributing the good relations on the

Blackmun with Burger and President Richard M. Nixon as he prepares to take his seat on the Supreme Court, June 9, 1970

Court to "perhaps a sense of relief that, while they would not have elected me, I was not as bad as some feared!" Nonetheless, Burger made it clear that he had an agenda to carry out; the implicit message was that Blackmun was now fully expected to join him in that mission. "The largest—or one of the largest problems I see ahead is to draw away from the attitude that everything unwise or wicked is unconstitutional and that if we but search, we will find some long hidden meaning in Due Process or Equal Protection or whatnot," Burger wrote. "All good ideas do not spring from the Constitution, and all dubious ones are not prohibited by it. It is not a code. We must not overload it and demand too much of it—more than it was built to carry." Then, turning from the doctrinal to the personal, he concluded: "It will be a great way for us to finish our judicial stint, and that law firm idea of 35–40 years ago now comes into fruition in a way we never dreamed of—at least until lately! Welcome to Washington."

The Blackmun family gathers for the swearing-in. Left to right: Blackmun's mother, Theo Blackmun; daughter Nancy; daughter Sally; Justice Blackmun; Rick Funk, Sally's husband at the time; Dorothy Blackmun, his wife; daughter Susie; Roger Karl, Susie's husband at the time; Betty Gilchrist, his sister.

For the official swearing-in, on June 9, Blackmun booked five rooms at the Dupont Plaza Hotel for himself, Dottie, and their family: three daughters, two sons-in-law, his mother, and his sister, Betty. The morning ceremony was brief, and Blackmun stayed at the Court to have lunch with his new colleagues. His old law firm, by then called Dorsey, Marquart, Windhorst, West & Halladay, sponsored a dinner in his honor that night for sixty guests at the elegant Madison Hotel.

Blackmun had already been given some Supreme Court homework. Immediately after the confirmation vote, the Court had sent him the files on twenty-two cases, all pending requests for certiorari, the formal term for a grant of review by the Court. Under the Court's rules, four votes are necessary for a case to be accepted for decision, and it was clear to Blackmun that he would be in a position to cast the deciding vote in most if not all of the pending ones. It was an unpleasant surprise. He had hoped to "ease into this with the opening of the 1970 term," he wrote to Burger after receiving the files, "but the 22 cases destroyed that hope." He added: "Obviously, they would not have come were I not the swing vote. It is somewhat shattering to start that way."

Blackmun's letter spelled out his personal expectations. "I want to be of help," he said to his old friend. For the first time in twenty years, the two would be living and working in proximity. "I look forward with more eagerness than I can express to a renewal of our old walking sessions when we at least talked things out and unloaded our gripes and frustrations," Blackmun wrote. "This possibility is, for me, one of the appealing aspects of this stressful period. I do not want our friendship ever to be an embarrassment to you. We shall have to guard this, lest it be misunderstood, but I hope we can renew to an extent those happy and comforting occasions of long ago."

The conclusion of the 1969 term (a Supreme Court term is identified by the year it begins, although a term lasts from October until the following June or July) proved messier than Blackmun expected. Burger had told him the summer recess would probably begin on June 15, but it was June 29 before the justices finished their work and freed their newest colleague to return home to Minnesota. Blackmun was shaken by the intensity and high stakes. "In my few short days in Washington, it is very apparent that the technique and the pace and the attitudes are different," he wrote on June 19 to Judge Pat Mehaffy, his closest friend on the Eighth Circuit. "I do not know whether I shall be able to survive."

Back in Rochester, Blackmun was a local hero. The city's chamber of commerce sponsored a Harry Blackmun Day, with a testimonial lunch at the Kahler Hotel. His twenty years in Rochester, he told the assembled guests, had been "a time of great contentment and satisfaction." At the conclusion of the proceedings, Dottie Blackmun bowed her head and wept. It was, Blackmun wrote the next day to his host, "one of the very few times when I have seen Dottie visibly moved."

On August 17, the *Minneapolis Star* published an editorial entitled "Justice Blackmun's Farewell." The newspaper clearly knew its native son well. "He is a tense man, combining a deep humility with

'WELCOME ABOARD, HARRY!'

This newspaper cartoon from 1970 captured Blackmun's own view of his predicament so perfectly that he kept it on the wall of his chambers for the rest of his tenure.

confidence in his scholarship," the editorial said. "It is never certain what a man will do once he reaches the high court. Nevertheless, given his mastery of the law, the tumult of the times and his own inner tensions, one wonders, as he leaves Rochester, how his Middle American background, with its tolerance based on personal relationships and its intolerance based on fear of change, will shape his approach to the work of the Supreme Court, where great questions turn as much on personal philosophy as on precedent."

The Blackmuns had considered keeping their Rochester house but decided against becoming absentee landlords. They sold the house and rented a three-bedroom apartment in a high-rise building in Arlington, Virginia, with a balcony and a view of the Washington Monument and the Lincoln Memorial. Warren and Vera Burger, also living in suburban Arlington, had made a different choice, acquiring a six-acre gentleman's farm they called Holly Hill. By now a confirmed Anglophile, Burger gardened and collected antiques and fine wines. His gift to Blackmun on joining the Court was a formal top hat. Blackmun's note of thanks on July 1 was a wry comment on the projected lifestyle the gift suggested: "I have now had a chance to examine it carefully. It is a very fine one and a wonderful target for snowballs. You will have to tell me how and when to employ it and how I go about borrowing from you the proper clothes to accompany it. Anyway, I am grateful. When I return, you should tell me what special items I need in wardrobe. I am just a country boy and while I have adequate tails and summer and winter dinner jackets and an old pair of suspenders, that is about the extent of it."

Burger replied: "I have your 'country boy' letter. I have no advice about tall hats, but it appears to me your wardrobe is in good order."

Difficult as June had been, the real work lay ahead. There were seventeen cases already scheduled for argument in the fall on which the eight-member Court had been deadlocked. Thirteen of these were being argued for the second time, and four for a third. In addition, five new cases raised difficult issues that were intertwined with the old ones. The other justices already knew these cases, or at least the issues, intimately, while Blackmun would be operating from a standing start. "One may surmise as to these that the Court is sadly divided," Blackmun wrote in a memo to himself summarizing the outlook for the coming term. "Thus it will be a difficult term for me."

On October 12, 1970, the term's first day hearing oral arguments, Burger sent Blackmun a warm handwritten letter. "When we had those dreams of 'doing it together' neither of us ever dreamed it would be this way or in this place," he wrote. "This is the first 'real day' here and it is a baptism of fire few new Justices have experienced. For me it is the beginning of a great career for you—and an association which, whatever the decisions, will be a source of constant strength to the Court, the country and the C.J. As ever, Warren."

Blackmun's first assignment came the next week in a case called *Wyman v. James.* It was a new case, not one of the reargued ones. The question was the constitutionality of a New York State law that required welfare recipients to permit periodic home visits by their caseworkers, on pain of forfeiting their benefits if they refused. The federal

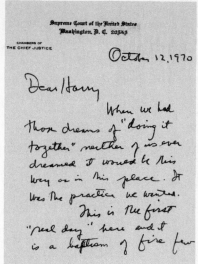

Supreme Court of the United States
Washington, D. C. 20543

CHAMBERS OF
THE CHIEF JUSTICE

October 12, 1970

Dear Harry

When we had those dreams of "doing it together" neither of us ever dreamed it would be this way or in this place. It was the practice we wanted.

This is the first "real day" here and it is a baptism of fire few new Justices have experienced. For me it is the beginning of a great career for you - and an association which, whatever the decisions, will be a source of constant strength to the Court, the country and the C. J.

As ever

Warren

Burger welcomes Blackmun to the Court—a dream come true.

district court in Manhattan had ruled that the home visit was a search within the meaning of the Fourth Amendment, requiring either the resident's consent or a search warrant supported by probable cause. Conditioning welfare benefits on acceptance of a search without meeting these requirements, the district court held, was thus a violation of the Fourth Amendment.

During the first week of arguments, Blackmun had seen how the Court's decision-making process worked. At the end of each week in which they heard arguments, the justices would meet alone in a closed-door conference, with no law clerks or other staff, to discuss and vote on the cases. (The word *conference* has two meanings at the Court. Lowercased, it refers to the meeting. But *Conference,* with a capital *C,* refers to the nine justices as a collective group. A memo to the other eight justices would thus be addressed "To the Conference.") The procedure at the meeting was highly formal. The chief justice sat at one end of a long table and the senior associate justice—Hugo Black—at the other. The others took assigned seats along the sides. The justices spoke and voted in order of seniority. Burger would summarize the

The justices pose with their new colleague for a formal photograph for the 1970 term. Standing, left to right: Thurgood Marshall, Potter Stewart, Byron R. White, Harry A. Blackmun. Seated, left to right: John Marshall Harlan, Hugo L. Black, Chief Justice Warren E. Burger, William O. Douglas, William J. Brennan, Jr.

case and, unless he chose to "pass," would announce his vote: affirm or reverse. The discussion and voting would then proceed to Black and on to the other associate justices: William O. Douglas, John M. Harlan, William J. Brennan, Jr., Potter Stewart, Byron R. White, Thurgood Marshall, and, finally, Blackmun. As the junior justice, he was the official doorkeeper, responsible for getting up from his seat to deal with the not infrequent interruptions as law clerks or other employees came to deliver messages. "Sometimes you're in the middle of expounding your views when you have to get up and answer that door, and your views evaporate and are lost in the confusion," Blackmun would recall.

As the discussion moved down the line, Blackmun took notes on a sheet of paper divided into four squares on the front and another four on the back, one for each of his colleagues. He would note his own vote inside a square belonging to a justice whose position he agreed with. He referred to the justices by their initials and to himself as X. After the justices voted, the chief justice would assign the majority opinions in cases in which he voted in the majority. If the chief was in dissent, the senior associate justice in the majority got to make the assignment. Whatever strategic purposes particular assignments might serve, the overall goal remained the same week in and week out: to apportion the opinion-writing duties roughly equally among the justices for each of the two-week argument sittings that the Court held from October through April. Votes were tentative, subject to the ultimate persuasiveness of the draft majority opinion and any dissenting opinions.

The vote in *Wyman v. James* was 6 to 3 to reverse the district court opinion and uphold the challenged provision of New York's welfare law. The dissenters, not surprisingly, were Douglas, Brennan, and Marshall, the Court's most predictable liberals. Douglas, still vigorous at seventy-two, had been named to the Court by Franklin D. Roosevelt at the age of forty. Blackmun knew Douglas only by reputation: brilliant, cantankerous, eccentric. He was determined to get along with Douglas but did not know whether he would be able to do so. Douglas spoke little in conference, and when he did, it was often to needle Burger. Blackmun later recalled that occasionally after Burger would describe a case at some length and announce how he intended to vote, Douglas would express the opposite opinion in as dismissive a way as possible. If Burger had voted to affirm, for example, Douglas would say when his turn came: "Chief, for the excellent reasons that you have spelled forth, I vote to reverse."

Brennan, a key strategist and architect of some of the Warren Court's most important decisions, was a former member of the New Jersey Supreme Court. A man of great personal charm, a Democrat, and the only Catholic justice, Brennan had been named to the Court by Eisenhower in an effort to appeal to urban Catholic voters in the 1956 presidential election. Marshall, born into a segregated world just four months earlier than Blackmun, was the first black member of the Court and a hero of the civil rights movement for his stewardship of the legal strategy that had resulted in the landmark decision *Brown v. Board of Education,* only sixteen years earlier. Since then, he had served as a federal appeals court judge in New York and as solicitor general of the United States, arguing the government's cases before the Supreme Court. Named to the Court by Lyndon Johnson in 1967, he had been the junior justice before Blackmun's arrival.

Of the other justices, Blackmun was slightly acquainted with White, who had attended the Eighth Circuit's annual judicial conferences over the years. But White was not an easy man to know, and Blackmun could hardly call him a friend. A former Supreme Court law clerk himself, White had been a college All-American football star and played professional football while attending Yale Law School. Although named to the Court by Kennedy, White was a conservative on most issues other than civil rights.

Blackmun felt little affinity for a fellow midwesterner, Potter Stewart, the son of a prosperous Republican family from Ohio who had been the youngest federal judge in the country when he was named, at age thirty-nine, to the Sixth Circuit Court of Appeals, in Cincinnati in 1954. Four years later, he became Eisenhower's last appointee to the Supreme Court. Moderately conservative in most areas of the law, Stewart was a strong defender of the freedom of the press. He had little respect for Warren Burger, a lack of regard that in Blackmun's view extended to himself. "I always had the feeling that he wasn't too sure about the rightness of my being on the Court," Blackmun would recall years later.

He was most in awe of Hugo Black and John Harlan. At eighty-four, Black had served on the Court since 1937—almost for Blackmun's entire legal career. A former senator from Alabama, Black was largely self-taught but extremely well-read. He expressed a purist's view of the Constitution, regarding its protections as absolute. Interpreting the First Amendment's injunction that "Congress shall make no law" abridging freedom of the press, Black would insist: "No law means *no law*." Early in Blackmun's tenure, Black visited his chambers to offer some advice: "Always go for the jugular. Never agonize in an opinion. Make it sound as though it's just as clear as crystal."

Harlan was a very different personality, with an affinity for nuance rather than absolutes. He was himself the grandson of a Supreme

Court justice, the first John Marshall Harlan, who in 1896 had earned a place in history as the lone dissenter from the Court's justification of "separate but equal" racial segregation in *Plessy v. Ferguson*. The younger Harlan was a Princeton graduate and Rhodes scholar who had been a leading member of the New York bar, with an active Supreme Court practice on behalf of corporate clients, before beginning his judicial career on the federal appeals court in Manhattan. His eyesight had failed almost completely by the time Blackmun met him, but at seventy-one he remained highly productive and engaged in the Court's work. More than anyone else on the Court, he appeared to appreciate the difficult position that Blackmun faced in filling a year-old vacancy. Blackmun recalled that after one day on which the justices had heard four reargued cases, all previously tied at four votes to four, Harlan put his arm around Brennan in Blackmun's presence and said: "Bill, why don't we let Harry go into conference with himself and the rest of us go back to our chambers and go to work on something else, because we know how our votes are, but he's the one that has to make his mind up on these cases."

Burger assigned Blackmun the opinion in *Wyman v. James*. Blackmun circulated a draft in six weeks and the other members of the majority quickly joined. The word *join*, Blackmun quickly learned, is used within the Court in unusual ways. A justice who wants to indicate formal agreement with another's proposed opinion sends the author a letter saying "please join me," using *join* as a transitive verb to convey the sense "count me in." Blackmun would later recall that when he received his first "join" memo from a colleague, "I didn't know what that meant. I thought it meant that that was a summons to go down to his office and join him for something, and he wanted to talk about the case." *Join* is also used as a noun. An offer to negotiate would frequently be phrased: "If you can make these changes, you can have my join." By contrast, an oblique, seemingly benign phrase—"I shall await further writing in this case"—is actually the formula for refusing to join, an indication that a dissenting vote is forthcoming.

Justices sometimes strayed from the simple "join me" formula, instead taking the occasion to lavish praise on the "excellent" opinion under consideration. Douglas tried to keep this practice in check, once explaining to Byron White that although he was enthusiastic about an opinion White was circulating, he would withhold a "flowery" comment "not because I lack enthusiasm for your product, but for two independent reasons: (1) if I am flowery vis-à-vis you, others might be upset if I'm not flowery vis-à-vis them, (2) I myself am always so grateful for the simple words 'Please join me' that anything else would be needless."

In his opinion in the *Wyman* case, Blackmun wrote that even if the home visit was properly viewed as a search, a proposition he doubted, "it does not descend to the level of unreasonableness" and consequently does not violate the Fourth Amendment. He paid great attention to the facts of the case, noting that the visits were preceded by written notice and were "a gentle means" and "reasonable administrative tool" for the state to make sure that the public assistance was used properly for the benefit of the dependent children, who were its focus. In a footnote, he observed that in this particular instance the need for periodic inspections appeared justified because the infant living in the home had suffered a fractured skull and a possible rat bite, signs of neglect or abuse. "The picture is a sad and unhappy one," he wrote.

On his copy of Blackmun's proposed opinion, Burger scrawled: "Harry—A great start & an event long looked forward to by me—clear & to the point and in an important case." Douglas circulated a dissent that Marshall and Brennan joined. Privacy of the home "is as important to the lowly as to the mighty," Douglas wrote, asking whether, if the case had concerned not a welfare mother "but a prominent, affluent cotton or wheat farmer receiving benefit payments for not growing crops, would not the approach be different?" But Blackmun's opinion, supported by the six-justice majority, was the opinion of the Court.

When it was announced on January 12, 1971, the decision in *Wyman v. James* was widely publicized, vividly bringing home to Blackmun the visibility that came with his new position. Taking the measure of the new justice, most of the commentators viewed the decision as proof that Blackmun would be the conservative law-and-order justice that Nixon had sought. The Associated Press observed that Blackmun "has demonstrated that not all conservative jurists speak with a Southern accent." Blackmun's hometown newspaper, the *Rochester Post-Bulletin,* ran the AP story under the headline BLACKMUN RATED MORE CONSERVATIVE THAN BURGER: TOGETHER THEY'RE TURNING THE COURT AROUND. In Washington, people started referring to Burger and Blackmun as the Minnesota Twins. To his surprise, Blackmun also received dozens of letters from the general public. Most praised the opinion, with some criticizing welfare recipients in abusive terms. "I have never regretted my vote in that litigation and would vote the same way again," Blackmun said in a brief written reminiscence of his early years on the Court. "The case served well as a starter." He noted that Justice Brennan had apologized for dissenting from Blackmun's first opinion, explaining to him that a new justice is traditionally assigned a unanimous decision for his initial opinion. "I had not known of the tradition and was not bothered by its non-observance," Blackmun wrote.

But other cases did not go so smoothly. *Baird v. State Bar of Arizona* and *In re Stolar,* two of the reargued cases held over from the 1969 term, concerned the requirement that Arizona and Ohio had imposed on would-be lawyers to answer questions about their political beliefs and possible Communist affiliations. Loyalty oath cases raising similar issues had been a staple of the Court's docket since the 1950s. Now these requirements for admission to the bar were being challenged on First Amendment grounds.

In the Arizona case, Sara Baird, a graduate of Stanford Law School, followed the instructions to list all the organizations she had belonged to since the age of sixteen. But she refused to answer whether she had ever been a member of the Communist Party or of any organization "that advocates overthrow of the United States Government by force or violence." At that point, the Arizona Bar Committee refused to process her application. In the Ohio case, Martin R. Stolar, who was already admitted to practice in New York, swore to the Ohio bar examiners that he had never been a member of the Communist Party or any socialist party. He was denied an Ohio license, however, for refusing to list the "names and addresses of all clubs, societies or organizations" he had ever belonged to and for refusing to state whether he had ever been a member "of any organization which advocates the overthrow of the government of the United States by force." Both the applicants had appealed and had lost in their state supreme courts.

Blackmun's law clerk, Daniel B. Edelman, who had come with him from the Eighth Circuit, recommended a vote to reverse, but Blackmun saw the cases differently. In his memo to himself in the Arizona case, he wrote: "I have to be a little afraid of my prejudices here, for I have always felt that an examining committee has certain rights of investigation and that one must not resist that investigation when he demands so extensive a right or privilege as that of practicing a profession." Blackmun recognized the "extraordinarily sensitive" nature of the issue, "yet I always get the impression that in cases of this kind the applicant is dodging something. He is not arguing innocently First and Fifth and Fourteenth Amendment rights as a matter of theory, but as a protective device. He wants the privileges of our government, and yet would overthrow it." Denial of a license did not infringe on would-be lawyers' freedom of belief or association, he wrote, because the applicants could continue to associate or believe as they wished, only without the privilege of practicing law.

Blackmun's vote, it turned out, was not decisive. There were five votes in favor of both the bar applicants: Justices Black, Douglas, Brennan, Stewart, and Marshall. As the senior justice in the majority, Black had the authority to make the assignment and assigned the opinions to himself. Blackmun, who dissented along with Burger, Harlan, and White, volunteered to write the dissenting opinions.

Black circulated his majority opinions less than a month after the oral arguments. But the Court could not issue the rulings without the promised dissents, and by year's end, Blackmun had not circulated anything. On January 11, 1971, after the justices returned from their Christmas recess, Black sent Blackmun a letter complaining about the delay: "I think it would not be inappropriate, without criticizing anyone on the Court, to state that I believe we are further behind in handing down opinions at this time of year than we have ever been since I became a Justice, more than 33 years ago."

Blackmun was crushed. He had been tested and found wanting by the justice he admired most. Further, he was deeply embarrassed. Black had circulated his letter to "Members of the Conference"—that is, to the full Court. Not only that, he had misspelled Blackmun's name as Blackman.

Blackmun replied the next day, also sending copies to the other justices. "The receipt of your note persuades me that it is time for me to point out something I should have stated at Conference before now and which I had assumed was obvious. Some of us are inclined to forget, I suspect, that this term thus far has been a very difficult one for me personally, and for reasons which are applicable to me alone." Blackmun explained that he was referring specifically to the seventeen reargued cases with which the other members of the Court were deeply familiar. He knew the Court was closely or evenly divided in these cases, he said. "This made the cases weigh particularly on me for I felt that in many of them my vote might be the decisive one. As a result, I have taken what may appear to the rest of the Court to be an excessive amount of time on these particular matters. I merely remind the Justices that each of these cases is a new decision for me, and is not ground which I am covering for the second or even the third time."

Blackmun concluded: "This note merely defends myself to a degree, and anticipates criticism which I feel might otherwise be forthcoming as the year moves along."

Black replied the same afternoon, spelling Blackmun's name correctly this time. "I appreciate very much the extra work that was put on you by the number of cases in which you have had to cast the pivotal votes," he said. "At any rate, if you obtained any idea of any kind or character that what I said was critical of you, please remove such thoughts from your mind."

Black's original letter had been a clear breach of the Court's informal social rules: justices may vigorously dispute one another's views but are expected to refrain from personal criticism. There was a context for his behavior. The elderly justice, his health failing and his world changing, was, in fact, in a rage. First Warren Burger and now his Minnesota twin had been foisted on a Court where Black, who as the Democratic whip in the Senate had been one of FDR's closest allies, had been proud to serve alongside Burger's liberal predecessor as chief justice, Earl Warren.

Another of the reargued cases, *Rogers v. Bellei,* appeared to drive the point home. The question in *Rogers* was the constitutionality of a provision of immigration law as it applied to persons born abroad "of parents one of whom is an alien, and the other a citizen of the United States." Under the Immigration and Nationality Act, such individuals were U.S. citizens at birth but would forfeit citizenship if they were not physically present in the United States for five continuous years between the ages of fourteen and twenty-eight. The provision was challenged by a thirty-one-year-old Italian-born man who had visited the United States five times during his adolescence and had even registered for the draft but lost his citizenship because he had not lived in the country for five consecutive years. A federal district court had declared the measure unconstitutional, largely on the basis of a 1967 Supreme Court decision, *Afroyim v. Rusk,* which held that Congress lacked the constitutional authority to strip citizenship from a U.S. citizen. The appellant in that case was a naturalized American whose citizenship was revoked for voting in an Israeli election. Black had written the 5-to-4 opinion over a dissent by Harlan.

After the *Rogers* case was argued for the first time, in January 1970, Black prepared a majority opinion on behalf of the Italian-born plaintiff, but the eight-member Court deadlocked and the case was scheduled for reargument the following November. Before the second argument, Black gave a copy of his proposed opinion to Blackmun. If Blackmun accepted it, it would become the majority opinion. If he rejected it, Harlan's position would prevail. Now he had to choose between two of the Court's leading figures: Black, the passionate old man, embodiment of an earlier age that, like Black himself, was beginning perceptibly to fade, and Harlan, who in his gentility, caution, and intellectual rigor personified the eastern legal establishment. After reviewing the briefs and Black's draft opinion from the previous term, Blackmun came down on Harlan's side, writing to himself in his preargument memo: "There is a good deal to be said for Mr. Justice Black's position, yet I have the general feeling that it is somewhat glib. . . . All in all, the statutory plan does not seem basically offensive to me."

On March 15, 1971, Blackmun returned Black's proposed majority opinion with the cover letter: "I am about to circulate my own attempt, which I am afraid is laborious and tentatively reaches the opposite conclusion. Actually, I found the case a most fascinating one on which to work." According to Blackmun's proposed opinion, the residency requirement was "reasonable" and the forfeiture of citizenship for failing to meet it was simply the loss of a statutory benefit to which there was no constitutional right in the first place.

Harlan was quick to join Blackmun's opinion, calling it "an outstandingly thorough and persuasive job." Burger, Stewart, and White also joined. Black's fury dripped from what was now a dissenting opinion. "Of course the Court's construction of the Constitution is not a 'strict' one," he wrote. "On the contrary, it proceeds on the premise that a majority of this Court can change the Constitution day by day, month by month, and year by year, according to its shifting notions of what is fair, reasonable, and right. . . . While I remain on the Court I shall continue to oppose the power of judges, appointed by changing administrations, to change the Constitution from time to time according to their notions of what is 'fair' and 'reasonable.' "

When Black wrote those words, in early April, the fate of another of his proposed majority opinions was still in Blackmun's hands. The question in *Palmer v. Thompson* was whether the city of Jackson, Mississippi, violated the constitutional guarantee of equal protection by closing its five municipal swimming pools—four of them set aside for whites and one for blacks—rather than integrate them. The city's motive was clear: to resist desegregation. But that did not make the action unconstitutional, Justice Black argued, because blacks and whites were equally affected. There was "no state action affecting blacks differently from whites."

Burger, Harlan, and Stewart had already joined Black's opinion. Before ultimately providing a fifth vote, Blackmun was beset by conflict. In addition, he felt the need to explain himself in a concurring opinion, a draft of which he circulated on April 27. "For me, this is perhaps the most excruciatingly difficult case of the present term," his concurrence began. "I frankly admit that I find myself close to dead center." He also referred to his "unduly long and uncomfortable struggle" and to his "judgment, inadequate and hesitant though it may be."

Returning Blackmun's draft, Burger urged him to "consider some 'muting' " of his description of how hard the decision was. "I suppose this is because I am always uncomfortable—and I think most readers are—with our speaking too much of the difficulties of close cases," Burger wrote. "I hope you will 'settle' for a simple statement that you find it a close & hard case." Burger then made his suggested changes directly on the opinion, crossing out the phrase "inadequate and hesitant" and inserting a substitute first sentence: "Cases such as this are invariably 'hard' cases because there is much to be said for both positions." Blackmun, who had already heard much the same advice from Hugo Black, accepted Burger's suggestions with only minor changes when the opinions were published, on June 14.

In another case that spring, Blackmun departed not only from Black but from Burger as well. *James v. Valtierra* questioned a California constitutional provision requiring the approval of voters in a local community before a state agency could construct a low-rent public housing project. The federal district court held that the provision violated the federal Constitution's guarantee of equal protection by placing a special burden on those who would utilize public housing. In his preargument memo to himself, Blackmun was inclined to agree. The provision "seems innocuous enough" on the surface, he wrote, but was actually "a thinly veiled attempt to avoid the availability of low-income housing." He noted that in the case before the Court, the voters in two California counties had defeated the public housing referendums: "This burden lies particularly heavy on those who require assistance, namely, the poor people."

At the justices' conference, much of the conversation concerned California's long tradition and wide use of referendums. "They say too much democracy violates the Equal Protection Clause. Let California run their own show," Burger said in support of the referendum, according to Blackmun's notes. But Blackmun was not persuaded. While Burger, Harlan, Stewart, and White joined Black's opinion upholding the referendum, Blackmun joined Marshall and Brennan in dissent. The vote, with Douglas not participating, was 5 to 3.

Difficult as the term was, there was an unexpected mountain to climb before it could end—the Pentagon Papers case. In mid-June, the *New York Times,* followed quickly by the *Washington Post,* had printed articles based on a secret archive of classified documents on the history of America's involvement in the war in Vietnam. Both newspapers were planning to publish lengthy series based on the forty-seven-volume archive, compiled under the direction of Robert S. McNamara when he had been secretary of defense under President Johnson. The Nixon administration quickly went into court, claiming that continued publication would reveal military secrets and threaten national security. The United States Court of Appeals for the Second Circuit, in New York, granted a temporary injunction, while the D.C. Circuit refused the administration's request. Both courts ruled on June 23. By the end of the following day, the *Times* and the government had both filed appeals seeking the Supreme Court's emergency intervention.

Four justices—Black, Douglas, Brennan, and Marshall—said there was no need to hold oral argument. In their view, the Court should simply declare that the First Amendment did not permit restraints on publication in the circumstances presented by this case; the injunction against the *Times* should be lifted immediately. But the four justices could not find a fifth to decide the cases summarily. Blackmun thought the administration should be given the opportunity to make its case. "My general reaction, contrary to that of some of the Justices, is that a litigant is entitled to his day in court," he wrote in a memo to himself on June 25. "The presumptions, of course, are against the Government, and the United States has a very heavy burden. Nevertheless, if it alleges national jeopardy, it should at least have an opportunity to prove it. . . . I fully anticipate that the Government will lose the case. I have, however, heard many arguments where the result seemed to be a

Re: TIMES - POST

My general reaction, contrary to that of some of the Justices, is that a litigant is entitled to his day in court. I recognize the demands of the First Amendment, but, unlike some others, I do not regard it as an absolute. If the proposed publication would be a means whereby the code is broken, or if it were otherwise demonstrated that publication would jeopardize national security, then, I think, restraint is in order. The presumptions, of course, are against the Government, and the United States has a very heavy burden. Nevertheless, if it alleges national jeopardy, it should at least have an opportunity to prove it.

For me, it is no answer to say that two district courts and two courts of appeals have generally decided the issues against the Government. The

Blackmun recorded his preliminary thoughts on the Pentagon Papers case, June 25, 1971: the government was entitled to its day in court.

foregone conclusion. That possibility should not deny the Government or any other litigant the right to be heard."

Along with Burger, Harlan, and White, Blackmun was willing to wait until October to hear the cases, with the Court enjoining further publication in the meantime. But Stewart, who also wanted to hear the cases on the merits, argued that the Court should take them up immediately. His position prevailed, and the argument was set for a special Saturday session the next day, June 26. Alexander M. Bickel, a Yale Law School professor, argued for the *Times*. Blackmun found Bickel's presentation the more impressive, but the government's argument by Solicitor General Erwin N. Griswold the more persuasive. "I feel the government has proved its case on the diplomatic area," he wrote in his notes after the argument. "The alleged stakes are high—real lives—prolongation of war. Can anyone know the consequences?"

The decision in *New York Times v. United States* was issued four days later, on June 30, 1971. In the view of six justices, the government had not proved its case and publication must be permitted to resume. An unsigned, three-paragraph opinion expressed their collective judgment, and each of the six—Black, Douglas, Brennan, Stewart, White, and Marshall—filed separate concurring opinions explaining their individual views. Blackmun, Burger, and Harlan dissented, each also writing separately. "The First Amendment, after all, is only one part of an entire Constitution," Blackmun wrote in his four-page dissenting opinion. "What is needed here is a weighing, upon properly developed standards, of the broad right of the press to print and of the very narrow right of the Government to prevent." Although Blackmun had modulated the draft prepared by his clerk Michael A. LaFond—adding the words "broad" to the right of the press and "very narrow" to the right of the government—the rewording did little to blunt the criticism that came his way. His vote solidified his reputation as a clone of the new chief justice, despite his dissenting vote two months earlier in the California public housing case. He received dozens of letters, many from ordinary people expressing dismay at his position. "I thought you were a 'strict constructionist,' " one man wrote from Tenafly, New Jersey. "If the first amendment means nothing to you what does the rest of the Constitution mean? Strict constructionist *bah*! More a strict Nixonist." And from Minneapolis came a postcard: "The 2 Nixon appointees from Dayton Bluff Elem. School jump thru the hoop like 2 trained poodles."

As the term ended, Burger sent Blackmun a handwritten letter. "You did not know what the President was getting you into but I am sure you have no regrets," he wrote. "Far from it, you have flowered under the combination of the pressures and the challenge and every friend is happy and proud. It has been a 'hard' year with more 'great cases' than in any year in the memory of Court watchers. Yet I will immodestly say we have carried our share. Others must decide how well we have done it, but I am not worried."

4

THE ROAD TO *ROE*

"HERE WE GO in the abortion field," Blackmun wrote to himself as he prepared for the argument in the Supreme Court's first abortion case in January 1971. The mix of anticipation and resignation in his words reflected an awareness he shared, with the other members of the Court, of the country's growing ferment—in state legislatures and in state and federal courtrooms—over whether the time had come to end the century-old regime of criminalizing abortion.

Four states—New York, Washington, Alaska, and Hawaii—had repealed all criminal penalties for abortions performed by licensed doctors, up to specified points in pregnancy. Thirteen other states had passed "reform" laws, expanding the circumstances under which abortion was permissible. But thirty-three states continued to outlaw nearly all abortions; in many of these states, there was little prospect for change. Abortion reformers were turning to the judicial system, intent on getting the issue before the Supreme Court. Among them was Dr. Jane E. Hodgson, a prominent Mayo Clinic–trained obstetrician in St. Paul who had just filed a Supreme Court appeal on her own behalf. She was challenging her prosecution in Minnesota for performing an illegal abortion on a woman who, early in pregnancy, had contracted German measles, a disease linked to a substantial risk of serious birth defects. In an article Dr. Hodgson had written for the Mayo alumni magazine, she explained that she had acted according to

No. 84 - United States v. Vuitch

Here we go in the abortion field. The case is

presence of a serious procedural question under 18 U.

be taken direct to this Court from a judgment of the Di

for the District of Columbia, dismissing an indictment

on the invalidity or construction of the D. C. statute?

Blackmun prepares for the argument in the Court's first abortion case, *United States v. Vuitch,* January 1971.

her view of the patient's best interests, and she predicted that "some day, abortion will be a humane medical service, not a felony."

It was far from clear to Blackmun or the other justices that the Supreme Court could resolve the rapidly escalating debate even if it chose to try. Several of the growing number of abortion cases then awaiting the Court's consideration—including Dr. Hodgson's appeal from Minnesota, *Roe v. Wade* from Texas, *Doe v. Bolton* from Georgia, and *United States v. Vuitch,* the case from the District of Columbia that the justices were about to hear that January—contained technical jurisdictional problems that appeared likely to prevent the Court from reaching, or ruling on, the underlying issues. In fact, when the appeal in *Roe v. Wade* had arrived at the Court the previous October, it was placed on a list of cases being held until the Court resolved the issue, in *Younger v. Harris,* of whether federal courts could intervene in state criminal proceedings. The *Younger* case, which had been pending since 1968, had already been argued twice and was still undecided as the Court prepared to hear the arguments in *Vuitch.*

None of the justices had ever confronted an abortion case. Blackmun had not expressed a formal position on the subject, although his ties to Mayo and to the medical profession generally were likely to have made him more aware than the other justices of the winds of change blowing through the health care establishment. At its annual meeting in 1968, the American Public Health Association had voted to support repeal of restrictive abortion laws, urging that "access to abortion be accepted as an important means of securing the right to space and choose the number of wanted children." The American Medical Association had recently replaced its long-standing opposition to abortion with guidelines for doctors in the small but growing number of states where abortion was legal in at least some situations. The AMA's House of Delegates voted in June 1970 to permit licensed physicians in those states to perform abortions as long as the procedure took place in a hospital and two other doctors had been consulted. Two months later, the executive board of the American College of Obstetricians and Gynecologists adopted a policy allowing its members to perform abortions at the patient's request, without the AMA's restrictions.

In his file on the *Vuitch* case, Blackmun included an article from the *Journal of the American Medical Association* on civil-liability issues facing doctors for performing an abortion, or in some cases for refusing to perform the procedure. The article reported on a New York case from 1968, two years before the state repealed its restrictive law and made abortion legal up to the twenty-fourth week of pregnancy. Under the old law, middle-class women with access to private medical care could occasionally, with the approval of hospital committees, get "therapeutic" abortions. A New York court had found a hospital negligent for refusing, on a 2-to-2 vote, to permit an abortion for a woman who had contracted German measles and whose doctor had recommended that she consider terminating the pregnancy. The baby was born with serious defects.

If the developing law of abortion was a largely unfamiliar subject, Blackmun was painfully familiar with the consequences of unintended pregnancy. Sally, his middle daughter, had become pregnant in 1966, at the start of her sophomore year at Skidmore College, in upstate New

York. She was nineteen years old. The family never seriously considered abortion as a possible course of action, although given his medical connections, Blackmun could probably have arranged for a safe abortion for his daughter. Instead, Sally dropped out of college and married her twenty-year-old boyfriend, only to suffer a miscarriage less than three weeks after the wedding. The marriage did not last. (She later graduated from college and law school, married again, and had two daughters.) In one variation or another, such family traumas were hardly uncommon at a time when reliable birth control was difficult to obtain, particularly for unmarried women; when half of all pregnancies were unintended; and when some one million women a year risked sterility or death to terminate unwanted pregnancies.

If such women were fortunate, they found their way to Dr. Milan M. Vuitch, a Serbian-born gynecologist who performed thousands of safe abortions in his Washington, D.C., clinic. He charged between $100 and $200. The procedure, of course, was illegal. In 1969, Dr. Vuitch was indicted for violating the District of Columbia's abortion law, which made it a crime for a physician to perform an abortion except "as necessary for the preservation of the mother's life or health." The law, enacted by Congress in 1901, carried a penalty of up to ten years in prison.

Dr. Vuitch, who was actively supported by the abortion-reform movement, filed a motion to dismiss the indictment: the law, he maintained, was unconstitutionally vague for failing to define "health" with sufficient precision to let doctors know whether they were complying with the law or violating it. Federal District Judge Gerhard A. Gesell agreed, dismissing the indictment and ruling that the law "fails to give that certainty which due process of law considers essential in a criminal statute." Gesell's finding was the first federal court decision declaring an abortion law unconstitutional. The federal government appealed the ruling directly to the Supreme Court, without first taking it to the court of appeals, a choice that created a jurisdictional issue on which the *Vuitch* case nearly foundered. It was not clear, as a matter of legal procedure, whether the Court had the authority to hear the direct appeal.

In his preargument memo, Blackmun considered the jurisdictional question at length and decided to oppose the direct appeal. "I am in favor of restricting direct appeal to this Court in every way possible," he wrote to himself. "We have enough to do, and the case is better prepared if it percolates through the normal structure." If a majority of the Court decided to reach the merits, moreover, he was "inclined to uphold the statute at this point" and permit the government to take Dr. Vuitch to trial. But his tentative approval of the law was conditioned on interpreting it in a way that permitted doctors to use their best judgment without fear of prosecution. "Certainly a good faith medical judgment must be a defense to any charge under the D.C. statute," Blackmun wrote. In other words, the law's health exception ought to be given a broad interpretation. Then he moved to an issue which, at that early point in the case, there was no reason to expect the Court even to address: the right to privacy. If the majority was not inclined to decide the case by giving a broad definition to the health exception, he wrote, "then I think I could go along with any reasonable interpretation of the problem on principles of privacy."

Although Blackmun did not explain himself further, he was clearly aware of, and keeping the door open to, a line of reasoning derived from the Court's decision six years earlier, in *Griswold v. Connecticut,* to strike down the state's prohibition on birth control. That decision was based on the recently articulated "right to privacy" that lawyers challenging abortion statutes were now beginning to incorporate into their arguments. But however far down the privacy road Blackmun might have been prepared to go, it would prove unnecessary at this early point to commit himself. Hugo Black circulated a draft majority opinion in which the Court asserted jurisdiction and ruled that the health exception should have the broadest possible meaning, justifying abortion for the protection not only of a woman's physical health but of her mental health as well. "Certainly this construction accords with the general usage and modern understanding of the word 'health,' which includes psychological as well as physical well-being," Black wrote, noting that the dictionary definition of *health* was the "state of being sound in body or mind." He added: "Viewed in this light, the term 'health' presents no problem of vagueness. Indeed, whether a particular operation is necessary for a patient's physical or mental health is a judgment that physicians are obviously called upon to make routinely whenever surgery is considered."

Blackmun's view of abortion—either as social policy or constitutional law—was deeply submerged in the *Vuitch* decision. Disagreeing with Black's conclusion that the Court had jurisdiction to decide the case, he had joined a dissenting opinion by Harlan that was addressed solely to the jurisdictional question. Brennan and Marshall had also joined the jurisdictional dissent. With the four justices avoiding the merits entirely, it was unclear, as the various opinions circulated, that there would be a majority for any single proposition. Neither Douglas nor Stewart had been willing to sign Black's opinion on the definition of *health*: Douglas viewed the statute as so vague that Black's linguistic effort could not save it, and Stewart contended that a proper interpretation of the law made any licensed, competent doctor who performed an abortion "wholly immune" from criminal prosecution. Thus only Burger and White supported Black's full opinion, on the jurisdictional issue and on the merits. For that reason, Blackmun told the other justices, he was willing to join the portion of Black's opinion that addressed the health exception, in order to help make a majority for a disposition of the case. "Assuming, as I must in light of the Court's decision, that the Court does have jurisdiction of the appeal, I join Part II of Mr. Justice Black's opinion and the judgment of the Court," he wrote in a brief concurring opinion. In deciding to follow Blackmun's example, Harlan provided a fifth vote for the broad definition of *health*. The tally thus was complete: five votes for jurisdiction (Black, Burger, White, Douglas, Stewart) and five for "health" (Black, Burger, White, Blackmun, Harlan).

On April 21, 1971, the decision in *United States v. Vuitch* was issued, with Black writing a two-part opinion for his two separate majorities, and the Supreme Court's first encounter with abortion was over. As a technical matter, the decision was a defeat for Dr. Vuitch. The statute was not void for vagueness; the district court's decision was overturned; and the prosecution could go forward. But the abortion-rights movement greeted the *Vuitch* decision, properly, as a significant victory. The decision treated abortion as a surgical option not fundamentally different from any other, and what seemed to matter most to the Court was that sufficient leeway be given to a doctor's professional judgment. As its reference, after all, the Court had cited not the Bible but Webster's dictionary. The next day, the justices met and voted to hear two more abortion cases: *Doe v. Bolton* and *Roe v. Wade*.

The two cases had arrived at the Court separately in the fall of 1970; each represented a point on the spectrum of the evolving abortion debate. *Roe v. Wade* challenged a Texas law that was typical of measures enacted by most states as the movement to criminalize abortion swept the country in the second half of the nineteenth century (Texas joined the movement in 1854). The slightly amended law now before the Court, dating to 1911, made it a crime for a doctor to perform an abortion except "for the purpose of saving the life of the mother." The penalty was a minimum of two and a maximum of five years in prison.

The Georgia law challenged in *Doe v. Bolton* dated only to 1968, when it replaced a law from 1876 nearly identical to the current Texas law. It was an example of the abortion "reform" statutes recently adopted by about one-quarter of the states. Georgia permitted abortion when, in the judgment of a woman's doctor, backed by two other physicians who had independently examined her, the pregnancy endangered her life or threatened serious, permanent injury to her health; when the fetus would "very likely be born with a grave, permanent, and irremediable mental or physical defect"; or when the pregnancy resulted from rape. The abortion had to be performed in an accredited hospital, with the approval of a special hospital committee. Furthermore, only Georgia residents were eligible, and the penalty for a doctor who performed an abortion under circumstances not permitted by the law was one to ten years in prison.

Both cases arose from lawsuits designed by the abortion-rights movement to test the statutes, and both suits had been notably, although not completely, successful in the lower courts. The federal district court in Texas had declared that the state's law was both unconstitutionally vague and in violation of the "fundamental right of single women and married persons to choose whether to have children." The district court in Georgia, while upholding the 1968 law's residency, hospitalization, and special hospital committee requirements, had ruled that the restrictive list of conditions under which abortion was permissible violated a pregnant woman's right to privacy and to "personal liberty."

In reaching these conclusions, both courts pressed well beyond the boundaries of existing Supreme Court precedents. The court in Texas relied on language in the *Griswold v. Connecticut* decision (1965), which did not discuss abortion but held that married couples have a constitutional right to use contraception. Specifically, the district court based its abortion ruling on a concurring opinion in the *Griswold* case that found support for a right to marital privacy in the obscure language of the Ninth Amendment: "The enumeration in the Constitution of certain rights shall not be construed to deny or disparage others retained by the people." The district court in Georgia, also relying on *Griswold,* cited not only the Ninth Amendment but also the *Griswold* majority's view that "penumbras of" and "emanations from" the guarantees of various provisions of the Bill of Rights served to protect a "zone of privacy" that was older than the Constitution itself. "For whichever reason, the concept of personal liberty embodies a right to privacy which apparently is also broad enough to include the decision to terminate a pregnancy," the district court said. But while striking down the statutes, neither court was willing to issue an injunction actually forbidding the states from enforcing them. For that reason, those challenging the statute decided to appeal. They appealed directly to the Supreme Court.

The authority of the federal courts to issue the type of injunctions the plaintiffs requested was only one of the thorny jurisdictional questions, far removed from the abortion question itself, that the two cases appeared to present. It was, in fact, the initial reason the Court had not acted earlier on the appeal in *Roe v. Wade.* The decision the Court had been waiting for, *Younger v. Harris,* was finally issued in February 1971, without definitively resolving the problem. At that point, the justices continued to defer action on both *Roe* and *Doe* until they decided the *Vuitch* case. The Texas case had another technical problem. The pregnancy that Jane Roe, the pseudonymous plaintiff whose real name was Norma McCorvey, had claimed when the case was filed in early 1970 had certainly ended—one way or another—by now. Why wasn't her case moot?

The Texas and Georgia cases were due to be scheduled for arguments late in the fall of 1971. But in September, just before the new term began, Justices Black and Harlan suddenly retired—each for reasons of rapidly failing health. Black died barely a week later, and Harlan died in December. The vacancies presented Chief Justice Burger with an administrative problem. Given the contentious political climate, with memories of the Haynsworth and Carswell nomination debacles still fresh, there was every reason to fear that the positions would not be filled quickly. Important cases were often deferred when the Court was not at full strength, and so Burger appointed Potter Stewart and Harry Blackmun to a committee he created to screen the pending cases and recommend which ones should go forward and which should be held for consideration by a nine-member Court. The committee decided to let the abortion cases go forward as scheduled. Years later, in 1986, when William H. Rehnquist faced the same issue as a new chief justice, Blackmun recounted the episode for him. "I remember that the old Chief appointed a screening committee, chaired by Potter, to select those cases that could (it was assumed) be adequately heard by a Court of seven," Blackmun wrote. "I was on that little committee. We did not do a good job. Potter pressed for *Roe v. Wade* and *Doe v. Bolton* to be heard and did so in the misapprehension that they involved nothing more than an application of *Younger v. Harris.* How wrong we were."

The cases were argued on December 13, 1971. Three days later, the justices met in conference to discuss the cases and vote on the outcome. Numerous published accounts, based on justices' papers and law clerks' recollections, have failed to resolve important ambiguities about just what occurred in the closed-door conference. Blackmun's cryptic notes from the discussion are not free of ambiguity, either; for one thing, he made no record of his own remarks. The docket sheets

he used for recording the conference votes in every case are, unchar-
acteristically, marked "tentative" for both *Roe* and *Doe*. Nonetheless,
his records indicate agreement among all seven justices that the Texas
law was, for one reason or another, unconstitutional.

Douglas said that any abortion statute was "vague under Due Process unless it gives M.D. acting in good faith absolute immunity
when he seeks to protect the life or the health of the woman." Stewart, Brennan, and Marshall also voted to strike down the Texas law.
White expressed the view that abortion must be permitted for
"health problems," as in the statute the Court had just upheld in the
Vuitch case. That was a sufficient basis for the decision, and there
was no need to move beyond it to the privacy issue, White said,
adding, "The state has some right to protect the fetus." No one expressed concern about the mootness issue. Burger said that having
been filed as a class action, the case was not moot because the Court
could make the assumption that the class of plaintiffs "still has pregnant members." On the merits, Burger said, "I have trouble not finding the Texas statute unconstitutional," although he wanted to see
"modifications" in the district court's opinion. Then he posed a separate question that did not have an immediate answer. In the case of a
married woman seeking an abortion, he asked, "Does the husband
have to consent?"

The outcome in the Georgia case was considerably less clear.
Burger was "inclined to hold the statute constitutional." The chief
justice's view comported with Blackmun's preliminary conclusion.
Blackmun's "general impression" was that the law was "pretty good
and strikes a good balance of the asserted interests," he observed in
the notes he made while preparing for the argument. His law clerk
George T. Frampton had summarized the Georgia case in a thirty-
nine-page memorandum on the eve of the argument, presenting an
equivocal view of the case. The district court's emphasis on the rights
of the pregnant woman was analytically weak, Frampton wrote, and
its conclusion was perhaps "supportable but difficult to reach because
of the strong recognition it accords the woman's right as against other
interests." He continued: "Perhaps a better way of approaching it is to

reason not that the woman's right is so strong but that to permit other criteria in these statutes [other than a doctor's view of the best course for the patient] is in the end to restrict medical judgment about what is best for each woman."

Douglas found the Georgia law "a better statute than Texas" but still "troublesome." He was "not sure" about what to do, he said, wondering whether the Court should send the case back to the district court for more findings on how the law operated. White said he would probably vote to uphold the law. "The state has some powers to recognize claims of the unborn child," he said. "The question is where it cuts in." Brennan, Stewart, and Marshall said they would strike down the law. The law "overrides a good faith determination by the attending M.D." was the way Brennan framed his objection to the statute.

Burger assigned the cases to Blackmun, who never knew exactly why. Certainly his medical background from his years at the Mayo Clinic made him a logical candidate. But the more likely reason was that Burger, whose political antennae made him better attuned than some other members of the Court to the inflammatory nature of the issue, believed he could count on Blackmun to deliver narrowly focused opinions that would discharge the Court's duty without doing or saying anything more than necessary. Unknown outside the Court, the assignment was controversial within it. Douglas—the Court's most senior member by seventeen years—objected that he and not Burger should have made the assignment in *Doe v. Bolton,* because Burger was not in the majority in the Georgia case. Burger replied that there was no clear majority for any single disposition of the case and that Blackmun should attempt to produce tentative opinions that would command a majority in both cases.

The inconclusive nature of the Court's discussion at conference gave Blackmun little guidance. The day he received the assignments, he wrote to Thomas E. Keys, the medical librarian at the Mayo Clinic, asking whether the library might have "anything about this history of abortion." Blackmun added: "Of course, if you suggest that I come out for a week's research in your hallowed precincts, I would be tempted." The

Mayo library staff immediately started doing research and sending bibliographic material to Blackmun.

Blackmun turned not only to Mayo but also to his family. As his youngest daughter, Susan, described the episode later in her father's presence, while addressing a dinner in his honor: "All three of us girls happened to be in Washington soon after Justice Burger had assigned the opinion to Dad. During a family dinner, Dad brought up the issue. 'What are your views on abortion?' he asked the four women at his table. Mom's answer was slightly to the right of center. She promoted choice but with some restrictions. Sally's reply was carefully thought out and middle of the road, the route she has taken all her life. Lucky girl. Nancy, a Radcliffe and Harvard graduate, sounded off with an intellectually leftish opinion. I had not yet emerged from my hippie phase and spouted out a far-to-the-left, shake-the-old-man-up response. Dad put down his fork mid-bite and pushed down his chair. 'I think I'll go lie down,' he said. 'I'm getting a headache.'"

As the year ended, a statement issued by President Nixon from his home in San Clemente, California, left little doubt how political the abortion issue had become or how visible the eventual Supreme Court decisions would be. Preparing for his upcoming reelection campaign, in 1972, Nixon announced that he was revoking his administration's recently liberalized policy on abortions at military hospitals. Under the two-year-old policy, every military hospital was to make abortion available. Now the hospitals were instructed to follow the law of the state in which they were located—in the great majority of the jurisdictions, abortions were still illegal. "While this matter is being debated in state capitals, and weighed by various courts, the country has a right to know my personal views," Nixon said. "From personal and religious beliefs, I consider abortion an unacceptable form of population control. Further, unrestricted abortion policies, or abortion on demand, I cannot square with my personal belief in the sanctity of human life—including the life of the yet unborn." The phrase "abortion on demand" was Nixon's way of expressing solidarity with opponents of abortion; no one, after all, referred in that manner to any other medical procedure, such as "appendectomy on demand."

The Nixon administration, meanwhile, had made several false starts in its effort to fill the two Supreme Court vacancies. The president still wanted a conservative from the South, but it was not easy to find a southerner whose civil rights record would be acceptable to the Democratic-controlled Senate. In 1956, Richard Poff, a Republican member of Congress from Virginia, had signed the "southern manifesto" opposing racial integration. Now he withdrew his candidacy when it became clear that he would not be confirmed without a protracted battle. The administration also looked seriously at naming a woman, a California appellate judge named Mildred Lillie, to the Court, but the American Bar Association committee that vetted potential judicial nominees found her "unqualified," by a vote of 11 to 1. Another tentative choice, Herschel Friday, a lawyer from Little Rock, Arkansas, who had represented that city's school board in its resistance to desegregation, received a tepid reception from the bar association committee and was also dropped.

Finally, in late October 1971, with the new Court term well under way, Nixon offered the two vacancies to two very different men: Lewis F. Powell, Jr., a distinguished sixty-four-year-old lawyer from Richmond, Virginia, who had been president of the ABA; and an outspoken conservative from the administration, William Rehnquist, a forty-seven-year-old assistant attorney general. The Senate confirmed Powell by a vote of 98 to 1, but Rehnquist proved to be a lightning rod for criticism during a contentious confirmation hearing. Nonetheless, he was confirmed by a vote of 68 to 26.

Blackmun did not know Powell personally, but he remembered Rehnquist warmly as the administration lawyer who had helped him navigate the confirmation process less than two years earlier. On December 10, the day Rehnquist was confirmed, Blackmun sent him a gracious letter. "I have refrained from writing heretofore because I did not wish to embarrass you or upset the delicate balance of these days that have been so critical for you," Blackmun wrote.

The justices attend the 1972 State of the Union address. Clockwise from top left: William H. Rehnquist, Lewis F. Powell, Jr., Harry A. Blackmun, Thurgood Marshall, Byron R. White, Potter Stewart, William J. Brennan, Jr., William O. Douglas, Chief Justice Warren E. Burger. Burger presented the photo to Blackmun with the notation: "For Harry A. Blackmun, What have we got to be smiling about?"

"But now that the ordeal—of having one's entire life bared by those who, it seems, seek to destroy more than they seek to be informed— is behind you, I extend my congratulations and warm welcome." He added, "As the junior here I have been through the familiarization process more recently than the others. If I may be of help in any way, please call upon me." To Powell he extended a similar helping hand. January 7, 1972, the day the two new justices took their seats, was a happy one for Harry Blackmun, who had jumped from ninth to seventh in seniority. What really mattered was that he was no longer the newcomer.

Now that the Court was at full strength, Burger asked whether there were any cases that should be reargued. "I nominate for reargument the two abortion cases," Blackmun replied. "It seems to me that the importance of the issues is such that the cases merit full bench treatment." But Burger never scheduled a vote on the proposal, leaving Blackmun to press ahead with his draft opinions.

At the same time, also without the participation of the two new justices, the Court was grappling with a new birth control case, *Eisenstadt v. Baird*. Bill Baird, a birth control and abortion rights campaigner, had distributed a supply of contraceptive vaginal foam, during a lecture on birth control to students at Boston University. As a result, he was convicted of violating a Massachusetts law that made it a crime for anyone other than a doctor or a pharmacist to dispense a contraceptive product. The federal appeals court in Boston had overturned the conviction on the ground that the statute violated "fundamental human rights" as understood by the Supreme Court in the 1965 *Griswold* decision.

At the conference, it was clear that there was a majority to uphold the appeals court's decision. Brennan drafted a majority opinion in which he used the case to extend the *Griswold* ruling—which had protected the right of married couples to use birth control—to apply to unmarried individuals as well. "If the right of privacy means anything, it is the right of the *individual*, married or single, to be free from unwarranted governmental intrusion into matters so fundamentally affecting a person as the decision whether to bear or beget a child," Brennan wrote in language that was obviously crafted to apply in the abortion context, to which it would quickly migrate.

For Blackmun, White, and Burger, this sweeping language went too far. Burger decided to dissent, while White, who had also initially voted to dissent, now agreed with the majority that the conviction should be set aside, but on narrower grounds. He was circulating a concurring opinion that made two basic points. First, because there was nothing in the record of the case to indicate the marital status of the student who received the foam, there was no reason to expound on the rights of unmarried people to obtain birth control. Second, since the product at issue, Emko vaginal foam, was available over the counter in any drug-store, for use without a prescription or a doctor's supervision, the state's interest in suppressing its distribution was highly attenuated. "Had Baird distributed a supply of the so-called 'pill,' I would sustain his conviction under this statute," White wrote. Blackmun was considering whether to join White's concurrence.

Burger remained adamantly opposed to the outcome and wanted Blackmun to avoid committing himself to White's opinion. On March 7, 1972, as the justices were hearing arguments in another case, he passed a note down the bench to Blackmun. His own dissenting opinion was almost ready, Burger said. "I am 'closing in' on *Eisenstadt* and I feel like Alice in Wonderland with the distortion of *facts* by the first two opinions. I hope when mine comes around you will take a closer look at Byron's opinion. Its implications are very disturbing to me. For me it is a borderline 'prescribing' case and a clear cut drug dispensing case well within the state's police powers. I hope you will scan BRW's opinion again. Whether you join mine or not is irrelevant."

As a communication from one justice to another on a pending case, Burger's note was unusual, a clear violation of the Court's social norms. In the Court's ordinary practice, drafts of opinions circulate among the justices and are left to stand or fall on their own persuasive powers. When justices do lobby one another, the discourse is highly formal, with personal appeals disfavored. Here, Burger was presuming on a personal relationship, his tone patronizing. Whether Blackmun perceived it in that way, the note failed in its intended purpose. By the time the decision was handed down, on March 22, Blackmun had joined White's concurring opinion. Burger was left in solitary dissent, complaining that both the majority and the concurring opinions "seriously invade constitutional prerogatives of the states."

Blackmun, meanwhile, was continuing to work on the abortion cases. In his view, the Texas case was easily disposed of. The Texas law was vague, just as the District of Columbia law in the *Vuitch* case, lacking a proper definition of *health,* had been vague. "I think that this would be all that is necessary for disposition of the case, and that we need not get into the more complex Ninth Amendment issues," he wrote to the other justices on May 18, 1972, as he circulated the first draft of an opinion in *Roe v. Wade*. Because he viewed *Doe v. Bolton* as the primary case, which would have to do the heavy work of defining the right to abortion, he was not yet ready to share his thinking on that case with his colleagues.

The *Roe* draft was only seventeen pages long, with most of the discussion devoted to the jurisdictional issues. Blackmun spent only three pages analyzing what he saw as the constitutional question: the imprecision of permitting abortion only for "saving the life of the mother." What did that exception mean? Did it permit a doctor to perform an abortion "only when, without it, the patient will surely die? Or only when the odds are greater than even that she will die? Or when there is a mere possibility that she will not survive? . . . Must death be imminent? Or is it enough if life is prolonged for a year, a month, a few days, overnight? Is a mother's life 'saved' if a post-rape or post-incest or 'fourteenth-child' abortion preserves, or tends to preserve, her mental health?" Blackmun concluded that the statutory exception was "insufficiently informative to the physician to whom it purports to afford a measure of professional protection but who must measure its indefinite meaning at the risk of his liberty."

In the final paragraph of his analysis, Blackmun acknowledged that there were deeper issues in the case. "We are literally showered with briefs—with physicians and paramedical and other knowledgeable people on both sides," he said. But there was "no need" to discuss a right to abortion "or even to consider the opposing rights of the embryo or fetus during the respective prenatal trimesters." The simple fact was that the statute was unconstitutionally vague.

The proposed opinion fell well short of what the liberal justices—Douglas, Brennan, and Marshall—had expected from *Roe v. Wade*. Days later, they were somewhat mollified by the more extensive draft Blackmun circulated in the other abortion case, *Doe v. Bolton*. In striking down the major provisions of the Georgia law, he cited the recently decided *Eisenstadt v. Baird* and other precedents, including *Griswold v. Connecticut* and *Loving v. Virginia,* a 1967 decision that invalidated that state's prohibition of marriage between people of different races.

The justice used the various cases in support of the broad proposition that "a woman's interest in making the fundamental personal decision whether or not to bear an unwanted child is within the scope of personal rights protected by the Ninth and Fourteenth Amendments." But this right was not "absolute," Blackmun continued, because "the pregnant woman cannot be isolated in her privacy." At some unspecified point in the pregnancy, "another being becomes involved and the privacy the woman possessed has become dual rather than sole." The woman's personal right, therefore, "must be balanced against the state's interest."

"It is not for us of the judiciary, especially at this point in the development of man's knowledge, to speculate or to specify when life begins," Blackmun wrote. The Court needed to do no more, he said, than "to note that the state's interest grows stronger as the woman approaches term." Eventually, the state's interest becomes "compelling."

His colleagues' tepid responses persuaded Blackmun that he could not complete work on the cases in the month that remained of the term. On May 31, he made a formal proposal, with Burger's support, for both cases to be reargued in the fall. He did so with reluctance, Blackmun noted, because reargument "would prove costly to me personally, in light of the energy and hours expended." What he did not say, but the others understood, was that once the cases were restored to the calendar for reargument, there was no guarantee that he would receive the assignment again. In fact, with two new justices in the mix, there was no guarantee that the outcome would be the same. Nonetheless, Blackmun said, "I believe, on an issue so sensitive and so emotional as this one, the country deserves the conclusion of a nine-man, not a seven-man court, whatever the ultimate decision may be."

The move was greeted with suspicion by the liberal justices, who counted Powell and Rehnquist as almost certain votes to uphold the statutes. Douglas was so angry that he threatened to break with protocol and publish an opinion dissenting from the reargument order, although he eventually backed off and simply noted his dissent when the order was issued, on June 26, 1972.

Blackmun's "chronology of significant events," a term-by-term list of notable developments that he began keeping when he joined the Court, hints at the tension of this period. Referring to Douglas, he wrote on June 9: "Abortion case reargument discussion—WOD will 'write.'" Ten days later, Blackmun noted: "WOD says he will *not* circulate his abortion comments!" Then he added: "Light at the end of the tunnel."

That appraisal was optimistic, but the summer recess did bring both relief and some clarity. Blackmun's clerk George Frampton continued to work on the Georgia case. Frampton and his co-clerk, John T. Rich, whom Blackmun had hired from the chambers of Burger's nemesis, Judge David L. Bazelon, of the D.C. Circuit, urged Blackmun to keep the *Roe* decision focused on vagueness but to amplify and clarify the basis for the constitutional right to abortion announced in *Doe*. Frampton argued that the opinion needed an expanded explanation of the right to privacy. "Since the opinion does use this right throughout, and since it is a new application of it, I think considerable explanation is required in addition to what the circulated draft contained—which was little more than one sentence plus a string cite in text," Frampton's memo said. (A "string cite" is a bare list of precedents, invoked without further analysis to support a given proposition.)

In late July, Blackmun visited the Mayo Clinic library, where the staff had set aside a place for him to work and compiled a stack of books and articles on the history and practice of abortion. In longhand on a lined pad, he took careful notes, numbering each factual assertion and marking the citation for each. From the *American Journal of Public Health* for March 1971, for example, he copied down: "Risk from legal abortion in first trimester is less than carrying pregnancy to term." That article, a copy of which Blackmun brought back to Washington, surveyed the rapidly changing abortion landscape in state legislatures, courts, and foreign countries. It concluded: "The action of the U.S. Supreme Court is crucial to the rate of progress, but, regardless of the outcome of cases pending before the court, the clock can never be turned back. Safe, legal abortion is now recognized as a fundamental right of women, a protection of maternal health and family welfare, and an assurance that every child is a loved and wanted child."

Blackmun also placed in his file an article by the public opinion expert George Gallup, reporting on a June 1972 poll on attitudes toward abortion. ABORTION SEEN UP TO WOMAN, DOCTOR was the headline the *Washington Post* gave to Gallup's syndicated column. "Two out of three Americans think abortion should be a matter for decision solely between a woman and her physician," the article began. It reported that "a record high" number of respondents favored "full liberalization of abortion laws." To the question whether "the decision to have an abortion should be made solely by a woman and her physician," 64 percent agreed, 31 percent disagreed, and 5 percent had no opinion. There was almost no difference in responses between men and women. Among college graduates, support for a right to abortion was 87 percent. A majority of Roman Catholics, 56 percent, also backed abortion rights. Among all demographic groups, only those whose formal education ended with grade school expressed a majority-view opposition to legal abortion.

The beginning of the 1972 term, in October, found Blackmun in a considerably better frame of mind. He did not yet know how the other justices, his two new colleagues in particular, would respond, but the issues in his own mind were now fairly clear. As he prepared for the October 11 rearguments, he jotted notes on a legal pad in the highly personalized shorthand he often used (which is translated here). He placed a separate thought on each line:

Could a state outlaw *all* abortions?
Logically, on the fetal life thesis it could.
But there are opposing interests, too, as usual.
These deserve to be weighed.
They are: right of the mother to life, health, physical &
   mental . . .
Translated this means 9th and 14th amendment rights.
Texas exception OK so far as it goes but it does not go far
   enough.

Then he scrawled alongside this list: "No absolute right to do with body as one chooses."

Finally, he made a rough outline for an opinion in the Texas case.

A. A fundamental personal liberty is involved here—right to receive medical care. Of course we are not talking of right to advice re contraception but of the right to action after conception. Whatever the answer, something fundamental is involved.

B. Much precedent for this sort of thing—*Griswold,* etc.

C. The state purpose rationale.
   1. No distinction between single and married.
   2. Not a regulation of private sexual conduct.
   3. No legislative intent to make pregnancy a penalty for misconduct.
   4. Texas not consistent in its concern with the fetus.
      a. The woman is not made an accomplice to the crime.
      b. The woman is free to go elsewhere for it *sans* penalty.
      c. Self-induced abortion not a crime.
      d. Fetus killing not a homicide.
      e. Fetus has no personal rights.
   5. Historically there was no barrier. Thus state has no traditional interest.

This last point, the history of abortion, reflected Blackmun's Mayo research, which persuaded him that the criminalization of abortion was a relatively recent phenomenon, without roots in the English common-law tradition.

Two days after the arguments, the justices met to discuss and vote. In advance of the conference, Blackmun made notes of what he planned to say. He brought with him an outline of the Georgia case, which in his mind was still the lead opinion. Even if he did not receive the assignment this time, he observed, "I would like the privilege of circulating what I have."

According to his notes, Blackmun said he was "pleased we deferred" the cases from the previous term. His week at Rochester had given him "an awareness of medical history I have not had before." He made it clear that he hoped for the assignment. "I have a lot of personal investment. I am revising and expanding the proposed opinions to command a majority." It was "not a happy assignment," he said; the Court itself "will be excoriated."

In his outline for a new *Doe v. Bolton* opinion, he summarized the privacy analysis he proposed to use: "The right of privacy as exemplified in the decided cases here. This is broad enough to encompass the decision whether to terminate a pregnancy. . . . But, despite the arguments, the right is not absolute. There is a point at which another interest is involved—life or the potential of life." Here, in the margin, he added the word "health," and then continued: "sufficiently involved to warrant state regulation. . . . I avoid any determination as to when life begins, ∴ [therefore] a balancing of interests." On the side of the page, he added "fetus ≠ a person within the constitution."

The concluding section of his outline was labeled "Mandate," its assumptions almost poignant in their naive optimism.

1. A majority of state statutes go down the drain.
2. It will be an unsettled period for a while.
3. But most state legislatures will meet in '73.
4. Any point in withholding the mandate? To 4/1.

The suggestion inherent in the last two points was that if the Court issued its opinion early in 1973 but delayed issuing the mandate—the formal judgment—for a few months, the states would have time to bring their abortion laws into compliance.

The October 13 conference was highly consequential. Lewis Powell, a courtly, soft-spoken Virginian, the embodiment of the legal establishment, surprised his colleagues by declaring his support for the right to abortion. He was "basically in accord" with Blackmun, Powell said, but he wanted the Texas case to be decided on more far-reaching grounds than vagueness. "Make it the lead case," he said, suggesting

As he redrafts his abortion opinions in October 1972, Blackmun's assumptions are overly optimistic: "It will be an unsettled period for a while."

that the abortion question be framed as "a medical problem broadly defined." Stewart, too, wanted a broad decision on the Texas law. He suggested following the reasoning of a decision issued, less than a month earlier, by the federal district court in Connecticut, striking down that state's Texas-style abortion law on privacy grounds. In that opinion, *Abele v. Markle,* Judge Jon O. Newman quoted from Justice Brennan's opinion in *Eisenstadt v. Baird* on the right to decide "whether to bear or beget a child" without government intrusion. In his quotation from the opinion, Judge Newman italicized the word *bear.*

During the discussion, the only two clear dissenters were White and Rehnquist. The new justice said little, but White spoke at length. Personally, his views on abortion were "liberal," he said. But as a judge, he "would not second-guess the state legislature" in balancing the rights involved. "We downgrade the state interest tremendously to OK abortion for convenience," White observed, according to Blackmun's notes.

Burger indicated that he was still uncertain about the Georgia case. "The Texas statute must fall," he said, but he was "not sure of the grounds" and would await the opinions. He assigned the cases, once again, to Blackmun.

Five weeks later, Blackmun circulated a proposed opinion in *Roe v. Wade*. Fifty pages in length and containing long sections on the historical and medical aspects of abortion, it was drastically different from the version shown to the other justices the previous spring. The discussion of the right to privacy had been lifted from the original draft opinion in the Georgia case and moved wholesale into the Texas decision. The major change was that the analysis was now explicit about the point in pregnancy at which the balance of interests tipped in favor of state regulation. "You will observe that I have concluded that the end of the first trimester is critical," Blackmun wrote to his colleagues in the cover letter transmitting his draft opinion on November 21. "This is arbitrary, but perhaps any other selected point, such as quickening or viability, is equally arbitrary." He concluded: "It has been an interesting assignment." With the Texas opinion now the lead case, *Doe v. Bolton* simply applied the principles in *Roe v. Wade* to invalidate the Georgia statute, including its residency requirement.

The process now moved quickly into its final phase. Douglas, his skepticism overcome, quickly joined both opinions. "You have done an excellent job," he wrote Blackmun on November 24. On the same day, Rehnquist advised Blackmun that he planned to file a dissent. His letter was gracious. "I have to take my hat off to you for marshalling as well as I think could be done the arguments on your side," he said.

The bond the two men had formed following Blackmun's nomination was deeper than any differences in personality and outlook. In March 1972, when the Court issued *Schneble v. Florida*, Blackmun sent Rehnquist a copy of the ruling, with the cover note: "Dear Bill: Inasmuch as this is your first published opinion for the Court, would you do me the honor of autographing the enclosed so that my great-grandchildren may be proud of it a century hence." Rehnquist replied: "Delighted!" On the first page of the opinion, he wrote: "To Harry Blackmun with the warm regard & admiration of his junior brother, Bill Rehnquist." Later, inviting the Blackmuns for a visit to his newly acquired vacation house in Vermont, Rehnquist signed his letter "Affectionately, Bill."

Blackmun heard next from Powell, who pronounced himself "enthusiastic" about the draft opinions. "They reflect impressive scholarship and analysis, and I have no doubt that they will command a court." Powell had one suggestion: to place the point at which the state's interest became dominant not at the end of the first trimester but some three months later in the pregnancy—at viability, the point at which the fetus could survive outside the womb. This was the point that Judge Newman had used in the Connecticut case, although it was not part of the official holding of his decision. The date made sense to him, Powell observed: "I rather agree with the view that the interest of the state is clearly identifiable, in a manner which would be generally understood, when the fetus becomes viable. At any point in time prior thereto, it is more difficult to justify a cutoff date."

Blackmun asked his new law clerk Randall P. Bezanson to analyze Powell's suggestion. The clerk was not enthusiastic. What would happen during the three months between the end of the first trimester and the point of viability? he asked the justice in a memo. Didn't the state have a growing interest in protecting the woman's health during that period? "Justice Powell's suggestion seems to view the relevant state interests too narrowly," Bezanson said. "While the first trimester is, as you admit, an arbitrary cutoff, I don't think that it is all that arbitrary, and I would not want to prejudge a state's interests during the 'interim' period between the end of the first trimester and viability at this time. I would stand by your original position."

In his formal reply to Powell on December 4, Blackmun said that while he had "no particular commitment" to the end of the first trimester, he preferred to stay with that point. "I could go along with viability if it could command a court," he said, but he doubted whether it could. "I would like to leave the states free to draw their own medical conclusions with respect to the period after three months and until viability," Blackmun concluded.

On the bench a week later, Powell passed Blackmun a handwritten note: "I will join your present opinion and so I leave entirely to you whether to address the 'viability' issue," he said. "It does seem to me that *viability* is a more logical & supportable time, but this is not a critical issue with me."

The discussion between Powell and Blackmun had been private. Blackmun decided to solicit the views of the others. Viability "has its own strong points," he said in a memo to the Conference on December 11, 1972. "It has logical and biological justifications. There is a practical aspect, too, for I am sure that there are many pregnant women, particularly younger girls, who may refuse to face the fact of pregnancy and who, for one reason or another, do not get around to medical consultation until the end of the first trimester is upon them or, indeed, has passed." Blackmun said he was "willing to recast the opinions" but did not want to alienate any member of his tentative majority.

Douglas replied quickly, in a one-sentence memorandum, that he still preferred the first trimester. More extended and significant responses came from Marshall and Brennan. "Viability is a better accommodation of the interests involved," Marshall said, noting that the way the opinion was now structured might be interpreted as leaving states free to "prohibit abortions completely" at any point after the first trimester. He suggested that the opinion state explicitly that "between the end of the first trimester and viability, state regulations directed at health and safety alone were permissible." Brennan's proposal was similar, but he urged Blackmun to be more explicit about the interests that the Court would allow the states to assert in regulating abortion. " 'Viability,' I have thought, is a concept that focuses upon the fetus rather than the woman," Brennan said. He recommended that the notion that the state could regulate on behalf of the woman's health as pregnancy advances and "abortions become medically more complex" be spelled out. Viability was not relevant to that determination, Brennan observed. "Then we might go on to say that at some later stage of pregnancy (i.e., after the fetus becomes 'viable') the state may well have an interest in protecting the potential life of the child and therefore a different and possibly broader scheme of state regulation would become permissible."

Burger responded, too, but did not address Blackmun's question.

Instead, he said, "I have more 'ploughing' to do on your memo but one thing that occurs to me is the possible need to deal with whether husbands as such or parents of minors have 'rights' in this area."

Blackmun said he would circulate new drafts by the end of the year, and on December 21, he did so. Now, in the Texas case, the state's regulatory leeway was tied directly to the progression of the pregnancy. In regulating abortion, the state has two "important and legitimate" interests, Blackmun said; the two are "separate and distinct": protecting the health of the woman and the "potentiality of human life." During the first trimester, when abortion is safer than carrying the pregnancy to term, "the abortion decision and its effectuation must be left to the medical judgment of the pregnant woman's attending physician." For the next stage, "the State, in promoting its interest in the health of the mother, may, if it chooses, regulate the abortion procedure in ways that are reasonably related to maternal health." Only at the "stage subsequent to viability" could the state, "if it chooses, regulate, and even proscribe abortion except where it is necessary, in appropriate medical judgment, for the preservation of the life or health of the mother."

In a footnote, Blackmun acknowledged Burger's concern about the rights of fathers. There was no need to address the subject, he said, because "no paternal right has been asserted in either of the cases" and neither the Georgia nor the Texas law mentioned it.

The opinion's discussion of the right to privacy as the basis for the right to abortion had changed little from the earlier drafts. The four paragraphs on the subject were still spare, even cryptic. "The Constitution does not explicitly mention any right of privacy," Blackmun began, but the Court's precedents have recognized "a guarantee of certain areas or zones of privacy." After listing fourteen precedents, including *Griswold v. Connecticut, Eisenstadt v. Baird,* and *Loving v. Virginia* (the interracial marriage case), Blackmun indicated that there was no need to locate the right to privacy in any particular constitutional provision. "This right of privacy, whether it be founded in the Fourteenth Amendment's concept of personal liberty and restrictions upon state action, as we feel it is, or, as the District Court determined, in the Ninth Amendment's reservation of rights to the people, is broad enough to encompass a woman's decision whether or not to terminate her pregnancy."

Toward the end of the opinion, Blackmun notably blunted the suggestion, earlier in his analysis, that the ruling was principally about women's rights. "The decision vindicates the right of the physician to administer medical treatment according to his professional judgment up to the points where important state interests provide compelling justifications for intervention," Blackmun, the former Mayo Clinic general counsel, wrote. "Up to those points, the abortion decision in all its aspects is inherently, and primarily, a medical decision, and basic responsibility for it must rest with the physician."

This was, perhaps, not a surprising focus for a decision that voided criminal abortion laws; after all, it was not the woman but the doctor who faced criminal liability under every existing law. In addition, the briefs filed with the Court from many corners of the medical establishment portrayed existing abortion laws as a threat to women's safety, a substantial public health problem. If anyone's "liberty" was threatened, it was that of doctors. Nonetheless, the Court's emphasis on the rights of doctors was striking.

Douglas, Powell, Brennan, Marshall, and Stewart joined Blackmun's opinion without reservation. White and Rehnquist said they would dissent. Now the Court waited for Burger. He would join both opinions, he had said, but was considering whether to write separately. As the Court's Christmas recess ended and state legislatures began to convene around the country, Blackmun and the others grew increasingly impatient. "Harry—Are *Doe, Roe,* etc. going to be announced tomorrow?" Potter Stewart asked in a note he passed to Blackmun on the bench on January 16, 1973. "Who knows?" Blackmun replied by the same route. "I doubt now that they will be announced tomorrow. He says he may write. I hope for Monday, the 22nd, at the *latest*. They *must* come down."

On receiving this note, Stewart scribbled at the bottom: "I wholeheartedly agree."

Blackmun's suspicions were growing that Burger was deliberately delaying the opinions for political reasons. The chief justice was due

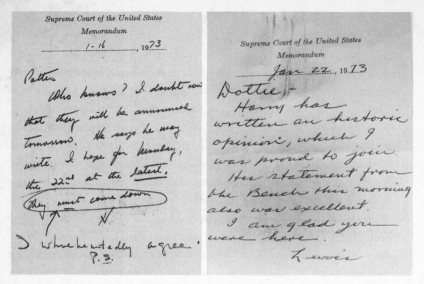

Burger's delay in circulating his concurring opinion in *Roe v. Wade* has held up the decision, and Blackmun and Potter Stewart share their growing impatience.

Lewis Powell wrote this note on the bench and had it hand-delivered to Dottie Blackmun after the courtroom announcement of *Roe v. Wade*.

to administer the oath of office at Richard Nixon's second inauguration, on January 20, and, as Nixon's first Supreme Court appointee, perhaps did not want to embarrass or upstage the president with a ruling in the abortion cases. The three-paragraph concurring opinion that Burger finally produced on January 18 contained a concluding observation: "Plainly, the Court today rejects any claim that the Constitution requires abortions on demand."

Blackmun's suspicions did not prevent him from consulting Burger about the announcement he planned to make from the bench. At one point in the eight-page script, Blackmun had written: "We have endeavored, too, to note the changes in attitudes" on abortion among medical organizations and courts. Burger reworded the passage so that it read, in part: "We cannot escape noting, too . . ." "We ought not to *look* for it!" he wrote on the copy he returned to Blackmun. Blackmun accepted the change.

Dottie Blackmun was in the courtroom audience on the morning of January 22, 1973. Lewis Powell had a messenger deliver to her a handwritten note: "Dottie—Harry has written an historic opinion, which I was proud to join. His statement from the Bench this morning also was excellent. I am glad you were here."

In his "chronology" entry for the day, Blackmun matter-of-factly wrote: "Abortion decisions down. LBJ dies." In many newspapers, the order of the two events was inverted, the death of the former president overshadowing the news from the Supreme Court. But the Catholic Church took full notice. The next day, Blackmun observed: "Abortion flak—3 Cardinals—Vatican—Rochester wires!" The decision was welcomed at the Mayo Clinic, where the chairman of the department of obstetrics and gynecology had signed one of the briefs against the Texas law. The day after that, Blackmun flew with Randall Bezanson, his law clerk, to Cedar Rapids, Iowa, Bezanson's hometown, to speak at a chamber of commerce dinner. He was met by several dozen antiabortion protesters. "Picketed!—police protection," the justice noted in his chronology. The rest of Harry Blackmun's life had begun.

5

FINDING HIS VOICE

CHRISTMAS AT THE Supreme Court, 1974: On November 1, Chief Justice Burger circulated a memo suggesting dates for the Court's annual Christmas party for the justices and employees. December 23 would be best, he said, with December 12 and 19 also possible. William O. Douglas sent back an immediate reply, circulating it to the other associate justices as well. "Dear Chief," he began. "The Christmas parties at Court have been getting so good I thought this year we might have three. One on December 12 could be initiatory and quiet. The one on December 19 could pick up momentum and the one December 23 could really explode!"

This was vintage Douglas: teasing, goading, making no effort to hide his contempt for Earl Warren's successor. And it was easy enough to poke fun at Burger's love of ritual, his insistence on trying to wrap a fractious band of individuals in the trappings of community. Justices' birthdays, for example, were celebrated over wine in the justices' dining room, the entire group answering the chief justice's summons regardless of whether the sixty-five- or seventy-five-year-old birthday boy was in a celebratory mood. Birthdays that fell during the summer recess—as did Burger's, on September 17, the anniversary of the date in 1787 when the delegates in Philadelphia signed their names to the Constitution—were marked en masse after the justices assembled for the new term. "All September and October birthdays will be noted at lunch Tuesday, Sept. 29," read one typical memo from the chief justice.

But while the aging Douglas was disdainful of these clumsy efforts at collegiality, his most junior colleague, William H. Rehnquist, wanted more. At fifty, Rehnquist was the youngest member of the Court by nearly ten years. Never before having served as a judge, he now missed being near the center of action at the Justice Department, and he chafed under the Court's remoteness and the isolation of the justices' daily routine. He was always looking for an excuse to foster some social life at the Court, or at least to leaven the atmosphere with a little cheer. At the end of the 1972 term, for example, Rehnquist had informed his colleagues that among some old papers in his chambers, he had discovered a poem entitled "To a Law Clerk Dying Young," written, he said, "by someone named A. E. Schmaussman, or Schmousman (the handwriting is not too good), who was apparently a law clerk here at one time." Finding the poem "very moving and emotional," Rehnquist "thought that a public reading of it would be a suitable occasion for a gathering." (There is no record of whether such a gathering ever took place or, indeed, of whether the poem itself existed.) The next year, Rehnquist had circulated a memo suggesting a variety of innovations. One was a coffee hour at the close of oral arguments each day, open to the justices and their law clerks. "I think that the practice which each of us appears to follow at the close of a day of oral argument— plodding back to his own individual salt mine—is bad for morale," Rehnquist wrote. He also complained that the justices' dining room "combines, to a degree that might be thought impossible, baronial elegance with dreariness." Burger's response to Rehnquist's suggestions was not encouraging. Everyone was too busy for a coffee hour. "My own attendance would be brief or rare, or both," Burger wrote to Rehnquist, adding: "I find it difficult to join my law clerks for lunch once every two weeks."

The Christmas party gave Rehnquist a new opportunity. "I have put together a very short skit which could be performed at the Christmas party," he informed the other justices by memo. "It is an attempted spoof of the three senior members of the Court—the Chief,

Bill Douglas, and Bill Brennan." He would recruit some of the law clerks to perform, he said, but added that "if any of you think such an effort would be inappropriate, I will forget about it."

While there is no record of what actually took place at the party, at least two of the senior justices were amused by Rehnquist's plan. "It's okay with me if you take on in caricature the three seniors here," Douglas told him. "My only request is that if you find frailties in this particular associate of yours, you attribute them to the other two." He added a handwritten postscript: "By my construction of the First Amendment you have absolute immunity." Brennan's response followed: "As so often is the case with me, I fully concur in the opinion of my Brother Douglas regarding the Christmas Party skit. This includes, of course, the attribution of the frailties to the other two."

The justices' informality with one another on the bench contrasted with the highly formal quality of communication among the chambers. During the four hours of oral argument a day—from ten in the morning until three in the afternoon, with an hour's break for lunch—the justices often amused themselves by passing notes commenting either on the courtroom proceedings or on events in the wider world. The days were long, not every argument was scintillating, and attention sometimes flagged. "Bill—You have been utterly quiet today! Is everything all right?" Blackmun asked in a note to Brennan. "I'm just bored. The previous argument was atrocious," Brennan replied.

Blackmun saved the notes that came his way. These small sheets torn from Supreme Court memo pads, with their handwritten scrawls, form a mosaic of Court life. "How would you like my job?" Burger asked in huge script, in a note to Blackmun during what must have been a particularly exasperating moment in the courtroom in early 1974. During the argument in an early sex discrimination case in 1973, Douglas sent this comment about Jane M. Picker, the lawyer for a teacher who was challenging a school district's policy of required, unpaid maternity leave: "How would you like to try to change this lady's position on any matter—where to have dinner for example?" And on October 10, 1973, as Potter Stewart's beloved Cincinnati Reds were losing to the New York Mets in the National League play-offs, his

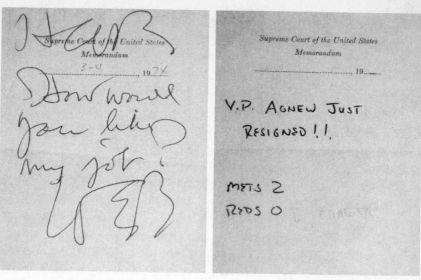

A trying moment in the courtroom: Burger to Blackmun

The headlines for October 10, 1973, passed along the bench by Potter Stewart

law clerk delivered this note, which Stewart then passed to Blackmun: "V.P. Agnew just resigned!! Mets 2 Reds 0."

Blackmun kept his attention focused on arguments by taking notes that were often pithy rather than extensive. In ordinary pencil, he would jot down the lawyers' key words, phrases, or concepts. In green, he recorded his own responses. "Here we go," he wrote in green as the argument got under way in the affirmative action case *Regents of the University of California v. Bakke,* in 1977. He gave grades to the lawyers according to scales that changed over time: sometimes letter grades, sometimes numerical grades, on a scale of 1 to 10, or 1 to 100. He also recorded physical descriptions of the lawyers in terms that were rarely flattering—they were intended not for publication but as aids to his memory. "Licks fingers," he wrote of one lawyer. Sometimes he simply noted "balding" or "hair." Of Archibald Cox, the Harvard law professor and former solicitor general who argued in the *Bakke* case, he wrote: "Hard of hearing. Overly 'smooth.'" Cox received a grade of 80. One of the highest grades he ever gave was to Alexander Bickel, the Yale law professor who argued on behalf of the *New York Times* in the Pentagon Papers case. Bickel received an "A minus" and the comment "likeable"—even though Blackmun voted against the newspapers' position. The few women who argued before the Court were usually described at least partly by their attire. "White dress, youngish, nice girl," he wrote of Dorothy Toth Beasley, an assistant attorney general from Georgia who argued for the state in the death penalty case *Furman v. Georgia*. In her first Supreme Court argument, he called Ruth Bader Ginsburg, a law professor and American Civil Liberties Union attorney, "very precise." By her fifth argument, Ginsburg was a familiar figure to the Court. "In red and red ribbon today," Blackmun noted.

He was annoyed when other justices chatted with one another while on the bench, as Brennan and White frequently did. Blackmun once passed a note to Burger threatening to walk out of the argument session "because I have had trouble hearing counsel *all* day over the din at the Bench. Three constant hours of it!" Burger replied that he would send a memo to the offenders, but there is no evidence that he ever did. Rehnquist, Blackmun's neighbor on the bench, was sympathetic and tried to offer practical suggestions. In response to one of Blackmun's complaints, Rehnquist replied by note, "I don't think it would be amiss for you to say, in an appropriate situation to counsel, 'Would you speak up—I can't hear you—we seem to have some intramural discussion here on the bench?' " Another time, Rehnquist offered a possible explanation for Brennan's behavior: "Some of the arguments are boring, and I think Bill has probably decided how to vote before he ever gets to the bench, but he could still (as could Byron) find something *quiet* to do so as not to interfere with those who want to listen and not to give impression of discourtesy to attorneys—do you think a mention to them might be beneficial." But although Blackmun complained for years—he included in his argument notes such comments as "This is a very *rude* tribunal"—he apparently never confronted the offending justices directly.

By the early 1970s, the Court was issuing decisions in 140 cases a year, up sharply from the fewer than 100 it had been deciding a decade or so earlier. (In recent years, the Court has decided between 70 and 75 cases per term.) Although Douglas complained that there was not enough work to do, most of the others felt hard-pressed to keep up. Blackmun typically arrived at the Court by seven in the morning. He had breakfast in the cafeteria with his law clerks every morning, always ordering one scrambled egg and two pieces of raisin toast. He stayed at the Court until seven at night, often working alone in a room reserved for the justices' use one floor below the main Court library. Usually he took a full briefcase of work home. In 1972, when Powell suggested an experiment by which the justices would pool their law clerks for the work of analyzing and recommending action on the thousands of petitions for certiorari, the formal name for requests for Supreme Court review, Blackmun was one of the first to enlist in the "cert pool." But as all the justices did, he continued to expect his clerks to provide a second layer of review within his own chambers. And he himself reviewed his clerks' work, not only correcting their spelling and punctuation but also checking the accuracy of the citations in the opinions they drafted for him. No other justice engaged in this level of detailed review.

Not only the pace of work but the range of subjects on the docket was dizzying. During one week in February 1974, to take a period at random, the Court decided fourteen cases, with opinions totaling 307 pages. Blackmun wrote majority opinions in three of the cases: one on the Freedom of Information Act (*Renegotiation Board v. Bannercraft Clothing Co., Inc.*), one on a welfare program for Indians living off reservations (*Morton v. Ruiz*), and one resolving a boundary dispute between two states (*Mississippi v. Arkansas*). The first was decided by a vote of 5 to 4, the second was unanimous, and the third provoked a solitary dissent from Douglas. Blackmun drew his narrow majority in the first case—Burger, Brennan, White, and Rehnquist—from across the Court's ideological spectrum.

One lesson for any new justice, in fact, was the fluidity with which coalitions formed and shifted and formed again, depending on the issue. It was extremely foolish ever to write off a likely opponent or to take a potential ally for granted. With so many cases under consideration at once, a colleague might, at any given moment, be both opponent and ally.

While Blackmun was working on *Roe v. Wade,* for example, he was also writing a majority opinion in a bankruptcy case that would become one of his best-known opinions from the period. His five-member majority in *United States v. Kras* included the two *Roe* dissenters, White and Rehnquist. On the opposite side were four strong allies from the abortion case, Douglas, Brennan, Stewart, and Marshall. The question was whether a federal law violated the constitutional guarantee of due process or equal protection in requiring the payment of a $50 fee as a condition for filing for bankruptcy, even from a person who claimed to be too poor to pay. Robert W. Kras was an unemployed welfare recipient living with his wife, mother, and three children, one of whom suffered from cystic fibrosis. He had an income of $366 a month and debts of over $6,000, which he sought to erase under the protection of the federal bankruptcy system. In his challenge to the filing fee, the federal district court in New York had ruled in his favor, declaring the law unconstitutional on the basis of a recent Supreme Court decision (*Boddie v. Connecticut*) that had struck down a mandatory fee in the Connecticut courts that kept some welfare recipients from filing for divorce.

Blackmun was skeptical. "I cannot escape the feeling that there is some merit in the principle that those utilizing bankruptcy should pay for it," he said in his preargument memo. Kras had filed suit rather than avail himself of the opportunity to pay the filing fee in installments, $1.28 a week for nine months, Blackmun noted. He suspected that the case had been manufactured by civil rights lawyers in the service of an agenda, an effort to use a sympathetic plaintiff to induce the Court to make poverty a basis for special constitutional protection.

At the conference after the argument, Blackmun found that Powell shared his suspicions. It was "a phony lawsuit," Powell said; Kras could pay the fee by giving up three packs of cigarettes or one movie a week. The vote was 5 to 4 to overturn the district court's judgment. Burger assigned the case to Blackmun.

In writing the opinion, Blackmun thought it was important to explain why the bankruptcy fee was constitutional when the Court had held less than two years earlier, in *Boddie v. Connecticut*, that the filing fee for divorce was not. The state had a monopoly over divorce, he wrote, while "bankruptcy is not the only method available to a debtor for the adjustment of his legal relationship with his creditors." Picking up on Powell's comment at conference, Blackmun went on to note that Kras could have paid the fee in weekly installments for "less than the price of a movie and little more than the cost of a pack or two of cigarettes."

Byron White, a member of Blackmun's narrow majority, told him there was no need to discuss the *Boddie* precedent or to say anything more than that the fee did not amount to invidious discrimination against the poor. Blackmun objected. The lower court had decided the case on the basis of *Boddie*, he told White, and "my inclination has been that we must meet the issue head on." White, unpersuaded, said he would write a separate, "chicken-narrow" concurring opinion, thus threatening to deprive Blackmun of a majority rationale. Then Thurgood Marshall circulated a stinging dissent. "It may be easy for some people to think that weekly savings of less than $2 are no burden," Marshall wrote. "A pack or two of cigarettes may be, for them, not a routine purchase but a luxury indulged in only rarely. The desperately poor almost never go to see a movie, which the majority seems to believe is an almost weekly activity." Stewart and Douglas also filed dissents; Brennan signed each of their opinions, as justices often do when their views are expressed by more than one dissenting opinion.

White then told Blackmun that "I have decided not to write separately in *Kras* and will join you just to settle the dust at least temporarily." With evident satisfaction, Blackmun wrote on the bottom of White's letter: "I suspect TM's opinion pushed BRW this way."

Blackmun was even more gratified when, more than a year later, he received a letter from Edward R. Korman, the government lawyer who had argued in defense of the statute. Korman, who later became a federal judge, wrote that he had been curious whether Kras would be able to pay the fee. "I discovered that on February 22, 1973, a little more than a month after the decision, Mr. Kras paid the $50 filing fee in full," Korman said. Blackmun replied: "The payment of the fee really does not surprise me very much. I always had a feeling that there was something wrong with this case and that, when known, it would serve to counteract the critical comments evoked." The particular criticism Blackmun had in mind was in the most recently published volume of Douglas's memoirs, *Go East, Young Man,* in which the author, cribbing from the dissenting opinion that Potter Stewart had filed in *Kras,* described the case with the comment: "Never did I dream that I would live to see the day when a court held that a person could be too poor to get the benefits of bankruptcy."

Blackmun forwarded Korman's letter to both Stewart and Douglas. "It is so seldom that we get a follow-through on cases," he wrote in a cover note. "Because each of you has given me a hard time on this one (Potter's dissent; Bill's comment on page 175 of his last book), I thought you might be interested in knowing that Mr. Kras, within six weeks of the rendition of our decision, paid the $50 filing fee in cash, in full." Blackmun concluded: "So it goes."

Not long afterward, indigency presented itself in another context: abortion. There had been a steady flow of abortion cases since the ruling in *Roe v. Wade.* A 1976 decision, *Planned Parenthood of Missouri v. Danforth,* rejected Missouri's requirement that a married woman receive the written consent of her husband before obtaining an abortion that was not necessary to save her life. During the consideration of *Roe* and *Doe,* the question of the husband's role had been raised repeatedly by Burger. He now joined White and Rehnquist in dissent from Blackmun's majority opinion. Blackmun wrote that while a "devoted and protective husband" had an obvious interest in his wife's pregnancy, "Inasmuch as it is the woman who physically bears the child and who is the more directly and immediately affected by the pregnancy, as between the two, the balance weighs in her favor."

The three cases that reached the Court the term following the *Danforth* case were different in kind from the other post-*Roe* cases. The question was not the degree to which a state could regulate abortion but whether it had to pay for abortions for women who could not afford them. Each of the three cases presented a variant of the issue.

Beal v. Doe, a case of statutory interpretation, questioned whether the federal Medicaid law required participating states to pay for poor women's abortions that were not medically necessary. In *Poelker v. Doe* the issue was whether a St. Louis municipal hospital that provided childbirth services for indigent women could refuse to offer elective abortions. *Maher v. Roe,* which Blackmun considered the most important of the trio, raised the constitutional question of whether a state— Connecticut, in this instance—had to make abortions available as part of the medical care provided to poor women, even if no statute required the state to do so. In all three cases, lower courts had ruled for the indigent women. Preparing for the arguments in early January 1977, Blackmun wrote that, clearly, states generally had discretion in how to spend their welfare dollars. But Connecticut's purpose in refusing to pay for abortions was not legitimate, he said. Instead, the state was trying to "do indirectly what *Roe* says it cannot do directly." He characterized as "drastic and disingenuous" the suggestion that a poor woman could simply find the money.

In all three cases, Blackmun found himself in the minority. One of his allies in *Roe v. Wade,* William O. Douglas, had retired in November 1975, disabled by a stroke, and had been replaced by John Paul Stevens, a federal appeals court judge from Chicago whose views on abortion were unknown. Stevens voted to reverse all three rulings. It was "important not to overrule *Roe,*" Stevens said in the conference on the Connecticut case. He also recognized that "the impact of *Roe* is eaten away" if an entire category of women could not get access to abortions. "But the state has an interest" in discouraging abortion, he observed, "and *Roe* so recognized."

Potter Stewart, a strong ally during *Roe*'s consideration, was now on the other side as well. Although *Roe* identified a constitutional right, Stewart said, the ruling placed no duty on states to subsidize abortion; besides, it was "probably constitutionally permissible for the state to have a policy of preferring birth over abortion." Another ally in *Roe,* Lewis Powell, said the constitutional issue was "not easy" but was significantly different from the question in the earlier case. "*Roe* concerns absolute deprivation and a criminal penalty," he said.

"Nothing is prohibited here. We pushed the Constitution to the outer limit in *Roe v. Wade*. The state has a substantial interest in trying to preserve life." Further, Powell said, it was "hard to see the end of the road" if the Court made access to abortion a constitutional right. "Do we finance the right to travel, free speech?" he asked. Burger's was perhaps the least surprising defection. That the state cannot stop abortions does not mean the state must pay for them, he said, according to Blackmun's notes from the conference discussion. Initially, Burger had voted to affirm the decision in the St. Louis public hospital case, requiring such hospitals to provide abortions. Blackmun was skeptical. "He will shift over, I forecast," he wrote in his notes of the discussion on *Poelker v. Doe*. Two weeks later, Burger announced a change of heart. "Further review of the record persuades me to vote to reverse," he said.

Along with Blackmun, Brennan and Marshall dissented in all three cases. Blackmun filed his dissenting opinion in *Beal v. Doe*, with a footnote making it applicable to all three cases. Of all his writing about abortion so far, this five-paragraph opinion constituted Blackmun's most pointed description of the plight of a woman seeking an abortion and unable to get one. "For the individual woman concerned, indigent and financially helpless, as the Court's opinions in the three cases concede her to be, the result is punitive and tragic," he wrote. "Implicit in the Court's holdings is the condescension that she may go elsewhere for her abortion. I find that disingenuous and alarming, almost reminiscent of 'Let them eat cake.'" Then he added: "There is another world 'out there,' the existence of which the Court, I suspect, either chooses to ignore or fears to recognize. And so the cancer of poverty will continue to grow. This is a sad day for those who regard the Constitution as a force that would serve justice to all evenhandedly and, in so doing, would better the lot of the poorest among us."

Throughout the 1970s, the Court was also dealing with capital punishment. The confrontation Blackmun had foreseen on the Eighth Circuit Court of Appeals arrived at the beginning of his second term, in the fall of 1971, with the Court's agreement to hear challenges to the death penalty statutes of Georgia, Texas, and California. As the Court was considering which of numerous appeals to accept, *Aikens v. California* appeared to be the lead case. In his preparation for the conference at which the justices would decide whether to hear *Aikens* or any of the others, Blackmun laid out his views. "At this point I still adhere to the concept that ordinarily punishment, including even the death penalty, is a matter for the legislature and not for the judiciary," he wrote in a memo to himself in September 1971. "It is in the former that public policy is expressed. It is there that this great crusade should be directed." He concluded, "It is, of course, easy for the Court to conclude that these are legislative policy matters rather than judicial Eighth Amendment ones. One could say that the Court is being cowardly about this. I think, however, that this is the sound approach. I doubt if we are ready to abandon the death penalty for treason or for spying, and if we are not ready to abandon it across-the-board, then we encounter grave logical difficulties."

Along with cases from Georgia and Texas, *Aikens* was argued on January 17, 1972. Nothing in the intervening months had changed either the opposition to the death penalty that Blackmun had long held as a citizen or the contrary position he felt he had to maintain as a judge. Preparing for the arguments, he had written to himself that "were I a legislator, I would vote against the death penalty. It does not mean, however, that if a State in its wisdom chooses to impose the death penalty for high crimes such as treason and certain types of murder such as killing by malice aforethought, I could say that such is violative of the Eighth Amendment. I would disagree with the policy, but I cannot throw it out, at this point at least, on constitutional grounds."

Before the *Aikens* case could be decided, it was rendered moot when the California Supreme Court invalidated the state's death penalty law and applied the nullification retroactively to every inmate on death row. The appeal from Georgia, *Furman v. Georgia,* then became the case through which the Court would render its judgment. On June 29, 1972, the Supreme Court ruled in favor of the prisoner, William Henry Furman, and, in doing so, it struck down every death penalty statute in the country. Five justices—Douglas, Brennan, Stewart, White, and Marshall—agreed that capital punishment, at least as it was then being carried out, violated the Eighth Amendment's prohibition against cruel and unusual punishment. The outcome relieved Blackmun of the burden of casting the deciding vote.

In his dissenting opinion, he ignored the advice Burger had given him the previous term, in the Mississippi swimming pool case, *Palmer v. Thompson,* not to wear his heart on his sleeve. His opinion began, "Cases such as these provide for me an excruciating agony of the spirit. I yield to no one in the depth of my distaste, antipathy, and, indeed, abhorrence for the death penalty, with all its aspects of physical distress and fear and of moral judgment exercised by finite minds." As a legislator or as a governor, he went on, he would stand strongly against capital punishment. But "the authority should not be taken over by the judiciary in the modern guise of an Eighth Amendment issue." Blackmun concluded, "Although personally I may rejoice at the Court's result, I find it difficult to accept or to justify as a matter of history, of law, or of constitutional pronouncement. I fear the Court has overstepped. It has sought and has achieved an end."

As the opinions were circulating, Blackmun had received a supportive note from another dissenter, Lewis Powell, who had joined the Court only about six months earlier, in January 1972. The note displayed a bit of the diplomatic skill that had served Powell well in his long career. He would be filing his own dissent, the new justice explained. "I am not joining your opinion in the capital cases only because of its manifest personal character. As you know, I have the greatest admiration for what you have said so eloquently."

Furman v. Georgia opened a new chapter in the Court's long encounter with the death penalty. Of the thirty-seven states with death penalty laws that had been invalidated by *Furman,* thirty-five acted within two years to pass laws designed to meet the Court's principal objection: the absence of standards to confine the jury's discretion and to prevent capital sentences from being imposed in an arbitrary manner. By 1975, when the Court agreed to hear challenges to the new laws in Georgia, Florida, Texas, North Carolina, and Louisiana, there were already several hundred people on death row under those recently enacted statutes.

The Court made *Gregg v. Georgia* the lead case. This new law, adopting a model used by a number of states, provided a list of ten "aggravating circumstances." A jury had to identify, beyond a reasonable doubt, the existence of at least one of these factors before the death sentence could be imposed. The allowable circumstances included a murder committed for money, the killing of a police officer or judge, and a murder that endangered many lives or was committed in a particularly heinous manner. Against such factors, the jury could weigh any mitigating circumstances or, if it found no mitigating element, could make a binding recommendation of mercy. Appeal of a death sentence to the Georgia Supreme Court was automatic; the higher court was directed to ensure that the sentence was not disproportionate to sentences imposed for comparable murders.

With only Brennan and Marshall dissenting, there were seven votes in *Gregg v. Georgia* to uphold the state law, but no single majority opinion, when the decision was issued on July 2, 1976. Stewart, Powell, and Stevens joined in one opinion and White, Burger, and Rehnquist in another. Blackmun drafted an opinion of his own. As in his *Furman* dissent, he said that while he would be willing to accept the challengers' arguments against capital punishment "were I a legislator or a member of the Congress of the United States," he did not believe that it was his role as a judge to nullify the choice made by a large majority of the states. Ultimately, though, he decided against filing the opinion. He had already made his position clear in *Furman v. Georgia* and had no appetite for prolonging the conversation. He simply filed a one-sentence statement: "I concur in the judgment."

While each encounter with the death penalty was clearly an unhappy one for Blackmun, he found some sources of satisfaction during the mid-1970s. Some were public and some, given the secrecy of the Court's deliberations, remained unknown outside the building. In his term-by-term "chronology of significant events," Blackmun customarily mentioned only a handful of cases. But one case he did single out for special mention was *Huddleston v. United States,* a 1974 decision interpreting a federal firearms law. The case itself was of minor consequence, but Blackmun was thrilled to be able to convert an initial

5-to-4 majority into an 8-to-1 vote of confidence, with only Douglas dissenting. The question was whether a law that made it a crime to issue a false statement "in connection with the acquisition of any firearm from a licensed dealer" applied to the redemption of one's own gun from a pawnshop. William C. Huddleston had pawned three rifles owned by his wife. When he went to redeem the weapons, the shop's owner, a federally licensed firearms dealer, required Huddleston to fill out a federal "firearms transaction record" that asked whether he had ever been convicted of a crime punishable by a sentence of more than one year. Huddleston answered no, but he had, in fact, been convicted six years earlier of passing bad checks, a California offense carrying a sentence of up to fourteen years in prison. Having been found guilty of the false statement, he based his appeal on the argument that Congress did not have pawnshop redemptions in mind when it referred to the "acquisition" of a firearm.

In his preargument memo to himself, Blackmun noted that while the law was "not a model of construction," Congress clearly intended to reach all transfers of firearms and just as clearly had the power to do so. The appeal was "a hopeless cause," he wrote. But four of his colleagues did not agree. After the argument, Douglas, Stewart, Rehnquist, and Powell all voted to reverse Huddleston's conviction.

Blackmun, assigned the opinion by Burger, circulated his draft on March 7, 1974. Stewart promptly abandoned his plan to write a dissenting opinion. "I think you have written a most thorough and persuasive opinion, and I do not plan to write in dissent," Stewart told Blackmun. Then Powell gave similar good news: "Although I voted the other way at Conference, upon a more mature consideration and in light of your excellent opinion, I am persuaded to join you." Rehnquist joined the opinion as well. The 8-to-1 decision was issued on March 26.

One of Blackmun's most significant and lasting contributions to constitutional law also took root during this period. The subject was advertising, long dismissed by the Court as mere "commercial speech," deserving of little, if any, protection under the First Amendment. In 1972 the American Civil Liberties Union had filed a Supreme

Court appeal on behalf of a newspaper editor in Charlottesville, Virginia, who published an advertisement for an abortion referral service in New York, where the legislature had recently legalized the procedure. "Unwanted pregnancy—let us help you," read the advertisement in the *Virginia Weekly*, promising "immediate placement in accredited hospitals and clinics at low cost." Virginia charged the editor, Jeffrey C. Bigelow, with violating a state law that made it a crime to "encourage or prompt the procuring of abortion" by means of a lecture, an advertisement, "or in any other manner." Bigelow was convicted and fined $500. The Virginia Supreme Court affirmed his conviction, rejecting his First Amendment challenge on the ground that a "commercial advertisement" such as this one "may be constitutionally prohibited by the state."

Roe v. Wade was pending when Bigelow's appeal reached the Supreme Court, so the Court deferred action. After *Roe* was decided—making abortion legal in Virginia, of course, as well as in New York—the justices sent the case back for reconsideration by the Virginia Supreme Court. After noting that neither *Roe v. Wade* nor *Doe v. Bolton* had discussed advertising, the Virginia court reaffirmed Bigelow's conviction, and he filed a new Supreme Court appeal.

Blackmun was immediately sympathetic to the arguments on Bigelow's behalf. The case was "easy," he wrote in his preargument memo: "Commercial speech is not *per se* more lowly than other forms." Under the Court's precedents, however, commercial speech clearly did occupy a lowly rung in the hierarchy of First Amendment protection. Blackmun sketched out a framework for modifying, if not directly overruling, those precedents. The First Amendment "should prevent states from prohibiting advertisements of products or conduct that is clearly legal at the place advertised," he wrote. False or misleading advertising could be regulated, "not because it is commercial or pecuniary in purpose but because it prevents commercial injury and without it commerce would be impossible." He said he would vote to "reverse and do so on a little broader base than the absolute minimum we could get away with here."

When the case went to conference on December 18, 1974, Rehnquist

December 30, 1974

PERSONAL

Re: 73-1309 - Bigelow v. Commonwealth of Virginia

Dear Harry:

I am having grave second thoughts on this case after more study and reflection.

If, as I think we agree, a state can prohibit advertising medical services, especially by non-doctors, why can't it limit advertising of a particular medical service in which the quotient of public interest is very high -- higher certainly than on tonsil-lectomy, appendectomy or hair transplants.

I now note that both you, Thurgood Marshall and I had question marks on our votes to reverse.

Burger has second thoughts on First Amendment protection for advertising.

and White cast the only two votes to uphold the conviction. The Virginia Supreme Court's decision would be reversed, and Burger assigned the case to Blackmun. But on December 30, Burger sent Blackmun a letter marked PERSONAL. "I am having grave second thoughts on this case after more study and reflection," Burger wrote. "If, as I think we agree, a state *can* prohibit advertising medical services, especially by non-doctors, why can't it limit advertising of a particular medical service in which the quotient of public interest is very high—higher certainly than on tonsillectomy, appendectomy or hair transplants." Burger said he was now considering a vote to affirm "on the narrow ground that a state probably has power to restrict advertising medical services, at least to licensed M.D.'s in Virginia. Let's discuss."

If the two ever had such a discussion, there is no record of it. Blackmun circulated a draft of his opinion on May 7, 1975, and by the next day had "joins" from Marshall, Powell, Stewart, and Brennan, who told him: "I think your handling of the difficult question in this case is exemplary and I am delighted to join your opinion." It took another month for Burger, along with Douglas, to join as well.

There seems little doubt that Blackmun was initially animated in *Bigelow v. Virginia* by its connection to abortion. There is no indication that he was thinking ahead to the next case. Once the decision was issued, on June 16, 1975, First Amendment protection for advertising became a reality. The next case came soon enough, and there was no turning back. The following term presented another Virginia case, this one a challenge to a state law that prohibited pharmacists from advertising the prices of prescription drugs. Pharmacists who might be tempted to advertise risked having their licenses suspended or revoked by the Virginia State Board of Pharmacy. A consumer group challenged the law on the ground that it kept prices high by preventing willing pharmacists from communicating useful information to willing listeners. The federal district court in Richmond had declared the law unconstitutional, and the state had appealed.

In his preargument memo on November 10, 1975, Blackmun saw the new case, *Virginia State Board of Pharmacy v. Virginia Citizens Consumer Council,* as a natural extension of the earlier one. "The emphasis in *Bigelow* was on the public and its right to receive information," he wrote. "Here, there is an interest in the general public in knowing what prescription drugs cost, in the consumers to make an informed choice where to purchase, in physicians in knowing what the drugs cost before prescribing them." Finally, he noted: "I have no great difficulty in concluding that the principles enunciated in *Bigelow* are applicable here and that this statute must fall."

Once again, Blackmun got the assignment. Among the other justices, Powell was concerned about the implications of opening the door to the advertising of professional services. "The next step, as no one appreciates better than you, will involve commercial advertising by the traditional learned professions: medicine and law," Powell wrote in response to the opinion Blackmun circulated in March 1976. It was important to indicate why that step was not inevitable, he said. While pharmacy is a profession, "and not an unimportant one," a pharmacist's role is "profoundly different" from that of a doctor and a lawyer. "Today the typical function of a pharmacist is pouring pills or tablets from a large bottle into a small bottle," Powell said. He attached a paragraph that made the point to his satisfaction: doctors and lawyers "do not dispense standardized products; they render professional *services* of almost infinite variety and nature." Blackmun readily accepted Powell's insert, which became footnote 25 of the opinion. When the decision was issued, on May 24, 1976, Rehnquist was the only dissenter. Back in March, in a handwritten note to Blackmun announcing his plan to dissent, he had observed: "But I say, in tribute to you, that I didn't think as good an opinion could be written in support of your result as you have written." Rehnquist added in a postscript: "You may *not* quote me."

Powell's concerns were well placed; it was only a matter of months before the question of advertising by attorneys reached the Court. Two young lawyers in Phoenix, John R. Bates and Van O'Steen, alumni of the local legal aid society, had opened a legal clinic with the goal of offering moderately priced services to middle-class clients who could not afford high legal fees but who did not qualify for legal aid. They challenged the Arizona State Bar's prohibition on advertising, by placing a commercial announcement in the *Arizona Republic* that promised "very reasonable fees" and gave examples: $175 for an uncontested divorce, $95 for a name change, $225 for an adoption. The bar brought disciplinary proceedings that resulted in a one-week suspension for each partner. Relying principally on footnote 25 from Blackmun's *Virginia Pharmacy* opinion, the Arizona Supreme Court rejected a First Amendment challenge and upheld the prohibition.

Preparing for the argument in January 1977, Blackmun saw little distinction between advertising prescription drug prices and advertising prices for routine legal services. "Let it develop," he wrote to himself. His opinion in *Bates v. State Bar of Arizona* contained caveats: it gave First Amendment protection only to "truthful advertisement concerning the availability and terms of routine legal services." Claims about the quality of legal services could easily be misleading, he said. The decision did not extend to the solicitation of clients, and it left the details of regulation up to the state bars. Nonetheless, Blackmun's commercial speech majority shrank nearly to the vanishing point. Burger, Stewart, Rehnquist, and Powell dissented, with Powell particularly disturbed at the failure of his footnote in *Bigelow* to have drawn a defensible stopping point. "Even the briefest reflection on the tasks for which lawyers are trained and the variation among the services they perform should caution against facile assumptions that legal services can be classified into the routine and the unique," he wrote in dissent. For his part, Burger predicted that the ruling "will only breed more problems than it can conceivably resolve."

Burger never yielded in his opposition to lawyer advertising. More than a year later, when the Court convened for the start of the 1978 term, he circulated copies of a letter on the subject that he had received from Admiral Hyman G. Rickover, the aging, much honored father of the nuclear Navy. Rickover had sent Burger a recent advertisement from the *Wall Street Journal* placed by a Navy lawyer who was leaving the general counsel's office and seeking to represent "contractors and others with claims against any agencies of the U.S. Government."

"The idea of a Government attorney announcing his resignation from Government service and simultaneously soliciting claims business against his former client is appalling," Rickover told Burger, who, without further comment, invited the justices' attention to "an interesting item."

Blackmun and Burger were on opposite sides of an issue that neither had even had occasion to consider barely a year earlier. Unlike Lewis Powell, who lost the argument and moved on, Burger, as was his custom, would not let go; he continued to needle; he began to include warnings about the evils of lawyer advertising in his speeches. And it was typical of Blackmun to hold fast to territory that he had staked out and to become deeply invested in its defense. What had begun almost imperceptibly was now becoming too obvious to deny. The common ground the two old friends had shared was crumbling away.

6

BIG STORMS

THE STRAINS BETWEEN Harry Blackmun and Warren Burger intensified with each passing term. There appeared to be no basis on which they could constructively discuss, let alone overcome, their doctrinal differences. By the 1980s, the gap between them would be all but unbridgeable. Years later, Blackmun would identify the tense weeks in the summer of 1974, when the Court confronted the Watergate crisis amid an internal crisis of its own, as a signal event in the dissolution of the friendship.

Blackmun himself had watched the moral unraveling of the Nixon administration with dismay. In August 1973, addressing the prayer breakfast at the American Bar Association's annual meeting in Washington, he had taken the prophet Nehemiah as his text and drawn an explicit parallel with current events. In 446 B.C., Nehemiah had returned from the Babylonian exile to find Jerusalem in ruins. Under the "pall of Watergate," Blackmun told his audience, "the times are not dissimilar." He continued: "There is a sadness all about us. . . . The very glue of our governmental structure seems about to become unstuck." And he asked: "Which will prevail—the 'better angels of our nature,' to use Mr. Lincoln's words, or something far, far less?"

Events in the eleven months since the ABA meeting had hardly been reassuring. First there was the Saturday Night Massacre in late October 1973, when Nixon ordered the dismissal of the Watergate special prosecutor, Archibald Cox, rather than turn over the White House tapes that Cox had been seeking (as possible evidence of a conspiracy to obstruct justice by covering up the origins of the Watergate burglary). Now another Watergate special prosecutor, Leon Jaworski, had renewed the demand for the tapes, and the president was resisting by claiming executive privilege. A federal district court judge, John J. Sirica, enforced a subpoena for sixty-four tapes. As the president remained defiant, the Supreme Court took the case directly from the district court on an expedited basis and heard argument on July 8, 1974. William Rehnquist, having so recently been a member of the Nixon administration, did not participate. The justices met in conference the next day, fully aware that the president's fate, if not the country's, was in their hands.

Although there were differences among the eight participating justices on how to approach the issues, all agreed that the president's claim of executive privilege was unsustainable and that he would have to turn over the tapes. Burger assigned the opinion to himself and, promising to meet a self-imposed July 15 deadline, promptly began circulating drafts of various sections with a cover letter telling his colleagues that "I will welcome—indeed I invite—your suggestions." Lewis Powell and Potter Stewart found the drafts analytically weak and became determined to produce alternatives. Burger's draft statement of the facts (the preliminary section of any opinion that summarizes the history of the case and identifies the legal issues), which the chief justice circulated on July 10, was not inaccurate so much as garbled and confusing. Powell and Stewart recruited Blackmun to write a revised statement of the facts, and he quickly produced a straightforward chronology.

His cover letter notwithstanding, Burger clearly did not expect and did not welcome having the core opinion-writing function snatched from his hands. He was not mollified by the cover letter that Blackmun attached to his draft of July 12:

Dear Chief:

With your letter of July 10, you recommended and invited suggestions. Accordingly, I take the liberty of suggesting herewith a revised statement of facts and submit it to you for your consideration.

Please believe me when I say that I do this in a spirit of cooperation and not of criticism. I am fully aware of the pressures that presently beset all of us.

Sincerely, Harry

Immediately after receiving Blackmun's draft, Stewart sent a memo to Burger, with copies to the Conference, calling it a "fine job." The memo was a signal, and not a subtle one, that Blackmun's version would become part of the opinion of the Court. Similar rewriting efforts would consume the justices for the next two weeks.

On July 24, the day *United States v. Nixon* was issued—under Burger's name as the sole author—one of Blackmun's secretaries left him a message from his youngest daughter. "Susie called to give you this message: 'Thanks.'"

Years later, Blackmun reflected on the impact that the evolution of the case had on Warren Burger. "It must have been as difficult a summer as he's ever lived professionally," he recalled. "It was the kind of situation that was ready-made for resentment and misunderstanding." Blackmun said he assumed that Burger "always resented" the events of that summer—specifically, Blackmun's alliance with the group that took the case away from Burger—and that "from then on we grew apart." He added, "I think I knew Warren Burger intimately, maybe in some ways better than he knew himself."

An observation rather than an explanation, this cryptic comment was as close as Blackmun came to acknowledging what had happened to the friendship. A combination of discretion and, perhaps, sentiment restrained him from saying more. When asked for public comments about Burger's life and career, he always adopted a nostalgic tone and always found accomplishments to praise. Undoubtedly, he did feel nostalgia for the decades of intimacy and promise the two had shared, going back to Dayton's Bluff and continuing through their years on the courts of appeals. Further, the justices viewed the Supreme Court as a family, and Blackmun was too much a gentleman to put the family's troubles on display.

But he was much less restrained in the privacy of his chambers. That much is clear from the notes he wrote to himself, the comments he jotted on drafts of Burger's opinions, and, in particular, the disrespectful way his law clerks felt free—or even encouraged—to refer to the chief justice. "Needless to say, I think the Chief's comments on this case are ridiculous," Richard K. Willard wrote to Blackmun on a memorandum Burger had circulated in a 1977 labor case. Commenting on the draft of a Burger opinion in a 1986 case, *Cabana v. Bullock,* Pamela S. Karlan told Blackmun: "The Chief's opinion has come around. Like the Bourbons, he forgets nothing and learns nothing."

On Blackmun's seventieth birthday, in 1978, his law clerks drew up a letter that purportedly came from Burger, complete with the bold "WEB" scrawl at the bottom, declaring a holiday for the Blackmun chambers in honor of the occasion. The letter parodied Burger's idiosyncratic penchant for using quotation marks to emphasize words and phrases on a seemingly random basis. "I have 'recently' been educated to the fact that your Leader's birthday 'is' scheduled for Sunday, November 12, 1978," read the letter, addressed to "Mr. Justice Blackmun's 'Clerks,' such as they are, Secretaries, and Staff." It concluded: "I, for my part, will be glad to consider joining any 'narrowly-drafted' message of birthday congratulations."

Blackmun's notations on Burger's opinions were caustic. "The expert in psych!" he wrote on Burger's draft of an opinion in a 1979 case on involuntary commitment to a mental hospital. (He also gave the opinion a grade of "C-minus.") "A regular law review article!" he wrote on a Burger opinion in a 1978 administrative law case that was filled with citations and legal analysis. "WEB did not write this," Blackmun added. He often filled the margins of Burger's opinions with question marks.

The notes Blackmun took for himself during the justices' conferences included such comments as "CJ keeps yapping" (from 1975)

The object in pencil!

C

Mr. Justice White
Mr. Justice Marshall
Mr. Justice Blackmun
Mr. Justice Powell
Mr. Justice Rehnquist
Mr. Justice Stevens

From: The Chief Justice

Circulated: APR 1 2 1979

Recirculated: _____

1st DRAFT

SUPREME COURT OF THE UNITED STATES

No. 77-5992

Frank O'Neal Addington,
Appellant,
v.
State of Texas.

On Appeal from the Supreme
Court of Texas.

[April —, 1979]

MR. CHIEF JUSTICE BURGER delivered the opinion of the Court.

We noted probable jurisdiction of this appeal to determine what standard of proof is required by the Fourteenth Amendment to the Constitution in a civil proceeding brought under

The notes Blackmun made on Burger's draft opinions—here, in a case on involuntary psychiatric commitment—show his growing disdain for his old friend.

and, under Burger's name, "talk, talk" (from 1979). "The CJ cannot control the conference," he wrote in 1980.

Blackmun's "chronology of significant events" offers, in words, the equivalent of a series of stop-action photos that document the deterioration of a friendship, although the context is ambiguous for a number of the entries. "Stress with the CJ," Blackmun wrote, without further explanation, on December 16, 1977, at a time when he was recovering from prostate cancer surgery and the contentious *Bakke* affirmative action case was under consideration. "I place three cases for discussion, CJ pre-empts all," reads an entry for the beginning of the 1980 term.

Burger's response to the election, in 1980, of Ronald Reagan and George H. W. Bush seemed, to Blackmun and several of his colleagues, to be excessive. "CJ takes over as usual in a big way," he noted in describing a visit to the Court by the president-elect and the vice president-elect on November 19, 1980. On January 9, 1981, he wrote: "CJ 'instructs' on proper inauguration wear. I say business suit under overcoat and robe. BRW [Byron White] says a Pittsburgh Steelers cap with earmuffs. WHR [Rehnquist] says stocking cap." Ten days later: "WHR tells me transition team had asked him to swear in White House staff Wednesday A.M. He said he was on bench [in] the A.M. but could come after 3 P.M. They called back to say CJ had preempted! He says he is furious." Finally, on January 23: "CJ ill—too much inauguration."

In addition to matters of personal style, there were substantive sources of stress. As noted in chapter 4, Blackmun suspected that in the winter of 1972–1973, Burger had deliberately delayed circulating his concurring opinion in *Roe v. Wade,* at a time when Blackmun thought speed was essential, in order to spare Richard Nixon embarrassment at his second inauguration. Having assigned Blackmun to write for the Court in *Roe,* Burger did little to support the opinion and eventually joined its critics, surely another source of resentment. *Roe* had been a baptism by fire, and Burger did little to help Blackmun endure the flames.

Another source of continuing irritation was the issue of lawyer advertising. Blackmun took a lasting proprietary interest in his majority opinion in *Bates v. State Bar of Arizona,* the 1977 case that extended First Amendment protection to commercial announcements by lawyers. Burger's public criticism of the precedent grew increasingly shrill. At the annual meeting of the American Bar Association in 1985, the chief justice denounced advertising by lawyers as "sheer shysterism." Blackmun saved the front-page article from the *Washington Post* on Burger's speech, as well as an editorial the *Post* published the following week that criticized the chief justice and praised lawyer advertising, declaring that "its benefits are worth preserving."

For his part, Burger appeared oblivious, at least during the early years, to the erosion that was taking place. While Blackmun believed that Burger resented his role in the Nixon case, there was no evidence of resentment in the birthday greeting that Burger delivered to him on November 12, 1974, barely four months after that decision. "I'd hate to think about being here if we weren't both here," Burger said. He signed the note, "As ever, Warren." On June 10, 1976, marking Blackmun's sixth anniversary on the Court, Burger's handwritten letter began: "Even though the 'fun goes out' this time of the Term, these have

Burger marks Blackmun's sixth anniversary on the Court.

been great years." He continued, referring to the Eighth Circuit appeals court: "Right now I suspect there are days when you yearn for the peace and quiet (?) of CA8, but now, on this sixth anniversary, *I'm* glad you've been here. And anyway, there is no peace and quiet & if we must be in the storms & turmoil, it's more fun to be in the Big Storms! Many more. As ever, Warren."

Burger and Blackmun could not have known it, but a particularly big storm was about to engulf the Court, and engulf them as well. Throughout the 1970s, a public debate had been growing over affirmative action in higher education. Did the special consideration that many colleges and universities gave in admitting members of minority groups violate the equal protection rights of white students? Although the Court made an initial attempt, in 1973, to address the issue in *DeFunis v. Odegaard,* it dismissed the case as moot the following year, because the white student who had challenged the University of Washington's affirmative action program for admission to its law school was on the verge of graduating from the law school (to which a lower court had ordered him admitted) and could not have been personally affected by a ruling. But in 1976, the University of California appealed a ruling by the California Supreme Court that invalidated a special minority admissions program at the medical school of the university's Davis campus. The suit had been brought by Allan Bakke, a white applicant who had twice been rejected and who claimed that the university had unconstitutionally discriminated against him by reserving sixteen of the one hundred places in the entering class for minority students.

Bakke's argument elicited a great deal of public sympathy, and the rigid nature of the medical school's minority set-aside put affirmative action in the worst possible light. Thus, when the Court took up the University of California's petition in January 1977, William Brennan and Thurgood Marshall, both staunch supporters of affirmative action, nonetheless cast strategic votes against hearing the case. Burger and Blackmun voted to deny for a different reason: they were content with the lower court's ruling. In a memo to himself, Blackmun noted that he was "sufficiently satisfied by the result reached by a liberal state court of high repute and by the briefs in opposition filed by organizations highly regarded for their sensitivity on civil rights issues." He named B'nai B'rith and the American Jewish Committee; both had expressed the Jewish community's long-standing antipathy toward the quotas that, until recently, had kept Jews out of many elite institutions. In Blackmun's view, the case presented more "an issue of social policy" than a question to be decided by judges. His hope—"perhaps a forlorn one"—was that "with the passage of a few more years the Nation will mature in its attitude and practice in this area of admissions policy, and that all will come to accept the fact that applicants are to be evaluated and judged, with fair measuring procedures, according to ability and promise of accomplishment."

But Stewart, White, Powell, Rehnquist, and Stevens voted to hear the case, *Regents of the University of California v. Bakke,* which was put on the Court's calendar for the 1977 term. By the time the argument

The Dominant Factors

A. The need for > minority justice in t perfors, includ such
The numbers so indicate, as to enrollment
The after paucity of minority profls

B. Past discrimin
Cann b denied to for yrs Meharry & Howard were it
the MC setn, despite recent efforts

Blackmun organizes his thoughts on the eve of the argument in the *Bakke* affirmative action case, October 1977.

took place, in October, Blackmun had significantly modified his views. The Court's action in granting the case deprived him of the luxury of musing about the passage of time, and required him to think through the issue as a legal matter. He was ready to give his approval, however reluctantly, to the Davis program. The case was, after all, about admission to medical school, and Blackmun was aware of the medical profession's history of racial discrimination. On October 7, 1977, a week before the argument, he composed a handwritten outline of a possible opinion. Stressing "the need for more minority participation in the professions, including medicine," Blackmun noted that it "cannot be denied that for years Meharry & Howard were it." Meharry Medical College, in Nashville, and Howard University's medical school, in Washington, D.C., had been established to train black doctors when other medical schools excluded black students. "Admissions policy has to have some flexibility," Blackmun wrote. Moreover, the judiciary had "no special knowledge" of educational policy; rather, "its posture is to protect against unfairness. Is the Davis approach unfair?" It was not, he said, because "race is used to enhance the fairness of the system. . . . We have seen that mere neutrality is often not enough."

No clear assignment came out of the conference the justices held after the argument. A week later, Burger circulated a memorandum proposing that the Court affirm the California Supreme Court on as narrow a ground as possible. The Davis program's rigid use of race must fall, Burger said, but the Court should assert this point "without putting the states, their universities, or any educational institutions in a straitjacket on the matter of broader based admissions programs." He suggested that the program could be struck down not for being unconstitutional but as violating the mandate of a statute—in this case, Title VI of the Civil Rights Act of 1964, which bars racial discrimination by educational institutions that receive federal money. The challenging constitutional questions should be left for another day, the chief justice believed. "If it is to take years to work out a rational solution of the current problem, so be it. That is what we are paid for." The Court should not permit "the mildly hysterical media" to drive its schedule, he added.

At the end of December, Burger circulated a thirty-five-page draft opinion—not to the full Court but only to Stewart, Rehnquist, Stevens, and Blackmun, whose votes he was counting on. On Blackmun's copy, Burger wrote: "Harry—I emphasize that this is almost right off the longhand draft, hence inescapably flawed in detail, style, organization, etc. The purpose, as indicated above, is to find out whether something along these lines will 'fly' with four others. Obviously any who agree generally are warmly invited to use their blue and red pencils. Happy New Year." Blackmun used only an ordinary pencil on the draft to make notes to himself. "I could not join this," he said.

The winter of 1977–1978 was a difficult time for Blackmun, as he underwent surgery at the Mayo Clinic for prostate cancer and missed the December arguments. The cancer had not spread and was deemed highly curable, but at sixty-nine years of age, Blackmun needed weeks to recover. When he returned to the Court in January, he struggled to catch up and did not respond to the growing number of proposed opinions that were circulating in the *Bakke* case. In addition to Burger's draft, there were proposals from White, Stevens, Rehnquist, Brennan, and Powell. Blackmun took detailed notes on each of the draft opinions, as well as on the arguments made by the dozens of organizations that had filed briefs on the two sides. He began to draft his own opinion by hand.

Finally, on May 1, 1978, he informed the Conference that he had reached a decision. He would vote to uphold the admissions policy. "I think the Davis program is within constitutional bounds, though perhaps barely so," he said in a thirteen-page memorandum. It was now clear that the Court was split 4 to 4. Four justices (White, Brennan, Marshall, and Blackmun) found the Davis program constitutionally permissible. Four others (Stevens, Burger, Stewart, and Rehnquist) would hold it impermissible under Title VI and order Bakke admitted to the medical school. Powell, writing for himself, took a different view. There was no difference between Title VI and the Constitution's guarantee of equal protection, he said. The Davis program violated both, and Bakke must be admitted, as the California Supreme Court had ruled. However, that court was in error in declaring that race could never be considered as part of the admissions process. A system that did not set aside a fixed number of places, but that considered race as a "plus" factor for the sake of diversity, could be constitutional, he concluded. On May 2, Burger circulated a memo: "Given the posture of this case, Bill Brennan and I conferred with a view to considering what may fairly be called a 'joint' assignment. There being four definitive decisions tending one way, four another, Lewis' position can be joined in part by some or all of each 'four group.'" There would thus be five votes to admit Bakke and invalidate the Davis program, and five votes to support the general principle of a properly tailored affirmative action policy.

Because several justices were preparing opinions (there would be a total of six opinions in the end), it would take nearly two months before the Court issued the decision. Blackmun was working on his opinion when his law clerk Keith P. Ellison brought him an article on the case from the November 1977 issue of *The Atlantic Monthly*, written by McGeorge Bundy, a former Harvard dean and national security adviser under Presidents Kennedy and Johnson who was then president of the Ford Foundation. Ellison said he was reluctant to add to Blackmun's pile of *Bakke*-related reading matter but that this article, "which has been acclaimed by some as the best piece to appear on the subject, does, I think, merit your attention."

Bundy's article, "The Issue Before the Court: Who Gets Ahead in America?," made a strong case for affirmative action. "To get past racism, we must here take account of race," Bundy said. "There is no other present way." Bundy also quoted Alexander Heard, the chancellor of Vanderbilt University: "To treat our black students equally, we have to treat them differently." Blackmun made check marks in the margins of the article and marked it "Read 5-6-78." He continued working on his opinion. "In order to get beyond racism, we must first take account of race," he would eventually write, echoing Bundy. "There is no other way. And in order to treat some persons equally, we must treat them differently. We cannot—we dare not—let the Equal Protection Clause perpetrate racial supremacy." The six-page opinion contained no footnotes. Whether Blackmun was even aware, by the time it was issued, on June 28, 1978, that he had borrowed those words is unclear. In any event, the thought behind the words was now, beyond a doubt, his own. Burger's initial effort at controlling the case having failed so completely, the chief justice did not write separately. Along with Stewart and Rehnquist, he simply signed his name to an opinion, filed by John Paul Stevens, that found the Davis program to have violated the "crystal clear" meaning and "colorblind" mandate of Title VI. "It is therefore our duty to affirm the judgment ordering Bakke admitted to the University," the Stevens opinion said.

Affirmative action was not the only big storm engulfing Harry Blackmun and the Court in the late 1970s. Blackmun had predicted that the states would respond quickly to the *Roe v. Wade* decision, and he was right—but not in the way he expected. Instead of amending their laws to accommodate the new regime of legal abortion, state after state enacted measures designed to blunt the impact of the ruling, by making access to abortion burdensome for both women and their doctors. For teenage girls, there were requirements of parental consent or notification. For grown women, there were waiting periods, necessitating multiple trips to doctors' offices or clinics, and "informed consent" provisions, which obliged doctors to show their patients pictures of fetuses in various stages of development. If consent of the husband could not be required—and *Planned Parenthood of Missouri v. Danforth* (1976) held that it could not be—then a state would ensure that the husband be notified before an abortion could take place. The battle over abortion was turning into a kind of legislative guerrilla warfare, with states erecting new barriers as quickly as the Court could strike recently enacted ones down.

There was another surprise as well. Blackmun had not imagined that he alone would come to personify an opinion in which he had spoken for a 7-to-2 majority and that was the product, after all, of a collaborative effort. Letters addressed to Blackmun poured into the Court by the tens of thousands, many invoking God's wrath and denouncing Blackmun as a baby killer. He read a number of the letters and saved them all. For a private man, a churchgoing Methodist who viewed himself not as an advocate for a cause but as the recipient of an assignment, who had discharged a collective duty, it was a disorienting experience. "I have never before been so personally abused and castigated," he wrote to Alquinn L. Toews, director of chaplain services at the Rochester Methodist Hospital, who had sent him a supportive letter several weeks after the Court had issued *Roe*.

The Reverend Vern Trocinski, a Catholic priest on the faculty of the College of Saint Teresa in Winona, Minnesota, was a personal friend with whom Blackmun had spent an evening in Rochester a week after *Roe* was decided. The two discussed the ruling. The priest wrote a week later to say that while "I do treasure our friendship deeply," he continued to have "a very difficult time" with the decision and now felt an "obligation church-wise and civil-wise to speak out in defense of the unborn."

Blackmun replied at length, indicating his own struggle to navigate a world that, for him, had changed profoundly. "Please give me the benefit of understanding in one respect," he asked his friend.

The Court's task is to pass only upon the narrow issue of constitutionality. We did not adjudicate that abortion is right or wrong or moral or immoral. I share your abhorrence for abortion and am personally against it. Yet, every state in this nation, by statute, permits abortion under at least some circumstances. . . .

One of the things that has saddened me these last two weeks is the reappearance of some denominational cleavage. This I deeply regret. I understand the critical letters, but I do not understand the vilification and personal abuse which has come to me from some quarters. It is hard to believe that some clergymen and sisters can indulge in such abuse and still profess to be workers in the vineyard. Perhaps I just do not understand. In any event, this kind of thing seems to go with this unwelcome job I seem to have inherited.

The academic response to *Roe v. Wade,* meanwhile, ranged from tepid to withering. Within a few months of the decision, the *Yale Law Journal* published a scathing critique by John Hart Ely, a former law clerk to Chief Justice Earl Warren and a rising star in legal academia. In the article, "The Wages of Crying Wolf: A Comment on *Roe v. Wade,*" Ely asserted that "*Roe* lacks even colorable support in the constitutional text, history, or any other appropriate source of constitutional doctrine." The opinion "is bad because it is bad constitutional law, or rather because it is *not* constitutional law and gives almost no sense of an obligation to try to be."

Coming from a liberal supporter of abortion rights, the article drew a great deal of attention in academic circles for its authorship as well as for its caustic tone. Blackmun read it and asked his law clerk James W. Ziglar to analyze Ely's argument. Ziglar was reassuringly dismissive. "Ely goes to great lengths to distinguish *Roe* from all the supposedly good things which the Warren Court did," he wrote. "In general, this article seems to be little more than an attempt to give liberals a way of reacting adversely to the abortion decision while maintaining a firm hold on their dedication to such decisions as *Miranda.*" He added, "Surely, this article won't be cited as the definitive work by anti-abortion forces."

That prediction turned out to be well wide of the mark. By 1985, "The Wages of Crying Wolf" had become the fifth-most-cited article published in an American law review during the previous forty years. A 1991 analysis of legal literature showed it to be the third-most-cited article ever published in the *Yale Law Journal*. Both the Reagan administration and the administration of George H. W. Bush invoked it in Supreme Court briefs seeking to persuade the justices to overturn *Roe*. But Ziglar's appraisal did prove correct in one respect: liberals in the legal academy embraced Ely's criticism, too. Still, there were a handful of exceptions: two Harvard law professors, Laurence H. Tribe and Philip B. Heymann, published separate law review articles in the months after Ely's article appeared, rebutting his assertion that *Roe* was untethered to legitimate constitutional analysis. Heymann wrote in the *Boston University Law Review* that *Roe* and *Doe* were "amply justified" by precedent and represented "incremental developments in constitutional doctrine" rather than the "quantum jump" that Ely derided. But Heymann's praise for *Roe* was hardly unqualified. While the basis for the decision was "far more solid than it at first appears," he wrote, that foundation was "never adequately articulated by the opinion of the Court."

Law review battles aside, it was Ely's critique that shaped the academic discourse. This debate—conducted almost entirely by men, at a time when women accounted for less than 3 percent of the law schools' tenured ranks—helped make it acceptable, even fashionable, to express disdain for the opinion even in liberal intellectual circles. The result was that in its earliest years, *Roe* lacked the enthusiastic support in the academic world that might have provided intellectual armor in the battles to come.

In 1977, Ely, perhaps intending a peace offering, wrote to commend Blackmun on his dissenting opinion in the trio of cases that found no duty, on the part of the states, to pay for abortions for poor women. These were the cases that had provoked Blackmun to observe, as noted in chapter 5, that "there is another world 'out there.'" Ely wrote: "I was critical of *Roe v. Wade* when it came down, but you certainly hit the nail on the head in your dissent in the abortion decisions of June 20. I frankly have trouble understanding how even the most strident anti-abortionist could regard it as a victory to have denied the right to poor people while retaining it for the rest of us. Surely blocking that kind of discrimination is just what the Court should be about."

Blackmun's response to Ely was cool. "It was good to hear from you about the recent third round of abortion decisions," he wrote. "I am aware, of course, of your criticism of *Roe v. Wade*." He then closed the letter by sending regards to a mutual acquaintance on the Harvard Law School faculty, to which Ely had recently moved. This was to be the only correspondence between *Roe*'s author and its most influential critic.

Within the Court, the other members of the *Roe* majority offered Blackmun support in ways that reflected their own personalities. As the first anniversary of the decision approached, the cantankerous Douglas tried humor, passing a note to Blackmun during an argument: "I am getting anniversary letters on abortion. They are much nastier than last year's. The best one is from a man who prays that my pacemaker will fail." Powell sent Blackmun clippings of two letters to the *Washington Star-News* that reflected favorably on a year's experience with legalized abortion. One was from an emergency-room nurse who described spending the years before *Roe* treating women for the dire consequences of illegal abortions. Suddenly, she wrote, those emergency cases stopped appearing. "What happened? Why it was directly coincident with the opening of clinics where this procedure could be done legally under the best medical circumstances. It has been that way ever since. . . . In the midst of the present anti-abortion clamor, people seem to have lost sight of the real reason liberalized abortion laws were passed in the first place. That reason is a purely medical one."

In forwarding the letters, Powell wrote, "These should be gratifying to you, especially when much of what you receive through the mail is so irrational." Then he added in a handwritten postscript, "I continue to think your opinion is a great one."

But there was a limit to what the others could do. *Roe v. Wade* was a burden that Harry Blackmun would bear alone. Fate—and Warren Burger—had dealt him an extraordinary hand. He was to be linked forever to a cause that had scarcely been his own. His concern had been medical autonomy, the ability of doctors to serve their patients according to their best judgment, without fear of criminal prosecution. Inside the Court, the debate that mattered had been over the proper role of federal judges, not about the moral absolutes—the rights of women, the rights of fetuses—that now increasingly framed the public conversation. And much of the public debate bore no connection to the way the case had looked to the Court. One common premise seemed to unite those who lionized Blackmun and those who demonized him: he had single-handedly ushered the country into the era of legal abortion. It was a premise that, as far as he was concerned, was refuted by the opinion's very first line: "Blackmun, J., delivered the opinion *of the Court*" (italics added).

Blackmun struggled to fit into a world that had changed drastically and unexpectedly. On the one hand, he saw himself as a passive participant, almost an accidental bystander at a cataclysm. To one letter writer, he described *Roe* in later years as something that "happened to me early in my years here." On the other hand, as attacks on the decision mounted both outside the Court and within it, he would come to embrace *Roe* with a fierce attachment and a deep personal pride. Much later, on a copy of an article in *Washingtonian* magazine suggesting that "the real story of *Roe v. Wade*" was that William Brennan was the unseen hand behind the opinion, Blackmun affixed a Post-it note: "This is hogwash."

While Blackmun never completely resolved the contradiction inherent in his response to *Roe v. Wade,* the world's view that he was the creator of abortion rights in America gradually, perhaps inevitably, shaped his self-image. Certainly, he saw himself from the beginning as *Roe*'s primary defender. The state funding cases of 1977 were a warning that not all the members of the *Roe* majority had read the decision as expansively as he did. In addition, the battle was shifting to include the other branches of government. Since 1976, Congress had attached a measure, known as the Hyde Amendment, to the annual appropriation for Medicaid, the joint federal-state program providing government-financed health care for the poor. Sponsored by Henry J. Hyde, an Illinois Republican who was one of the leading antiabortion members of the House of Representatives, the amendment prohibited the use of federal money for abortions in the absence of conditions that varied from year to year, depending on the strength of antiabortion forces in the House. In some years, funding was provided only if the abortion was necessary to save the woman's life. In other years, the exception included pregnancies resulting from rape or incest, or those that were certified by two doctors as likely to result in "severe and long-lasting physical health damage" to the woman. Under any of the formulations, poor women who needed abortions were treated differently from those who needed most other medical procedures. In 1980, the issue reached the Court in a case called *Harris v. McRae*. The Carter administration was appealing a ruling by a federal district court in New York that the Hyde Amendment for fiscal 1977, withholding funding except for lifesaving abortions, was unconstitutional.

In his preargument notes, Blackmun said that the Hyde Amendment was "more egregious" than the funding restrictions at issue in the earlier cases, which involved "non-therapeutic," or elective, abortions. Nonetheless, he expected the 6-to-3 majority from the 1977 cases to prevail and to uphold the Hyde Amendment. Lewis Powell, who had written the majority opinions in 1977, believed there was "no fundamental right to a funded abortion—that has to apply here & is the quicksand those cases laid," Blackmun wrote.

During the argument, on April 21, 1980, Blackmun noticed Congressman Hyde, with his distinctive thatch of white hair, prominently seated in the courtroom. "Is that Hyde in the center chair?" he asked Burger in a note he passed down the bench. "Don't know!" Burger replied. Blackmun did not believe the chief justice. "CJ denies knowing Cong. Hyde who sits in the hallowed front row center!" he wrote in his argument notes.

The conversation in conference went much as Blackmun had expected. Burger said that if he were a member of Congress, he would vote against the Hyde Amendment, but that as a matter of law, Congress was free to refuse to pay for treating mental illness, drug addiction, or any other category of medical care. Congress's "real motives are not open to judicial review and we cannot get into it," according to Burger, who voted to reverse the district court.

Brennan took the opposite view: "What is involved here is hostility to abortion." He voted to affirm, as did Marshall and Blackmun. Stewart—saying that *Maher v. Roe,* the 1977 case that decided the constitutional issue for the states, controlled the outcome—voted to reverse. To White, the case was "not nearly so clear" and "much harder" than *Maher,* but he also voted to reverse, as did Powell, who declared there was "no constitutional right to any medical care." Rehnquist also voted to reverse, saying that "the right to privacy cannot be expanded indefinitely."

For Blackmun, the surprise was the newest justice, John Paul Stevens, who had voted with the majority in the 1977 cases. He still believed that *Maher v. Roe* was correct, Stevens said, but "the interest here is a *federal* interest, not state. That is unique." Stevens spoke passionately. He called the Hyde Amendment a "perversion" of Congress's spending power. "We make federal policy by holding a revenue bill hostage. Reprehensible!" Stevens noted. "A significant number of women will suffer severe medical harm," an outcome that "cannot square with *Roe.*" The vote to uphold the Hyde Amendment was 5 to 4. Even though he was on the losing side, Blackmun saw that he had gained an able, committed ally.

Stevens, the only justice named to the Court by President Gerald R. Ford, had succeeded Douglas in 1975. He had clerked on the Supreme Court during the 1947 term for Justice Wiley B. Rutledge and had then become a prominent lawyer in Chicago, specializing in antitrust law, before Nixon named him to the federal appeals court there, the Seventh Circuit, in 1970. Blackmun's first encounter with Stevens had proven rather unsettling. When Stevens came to a speech Blackmun was giving at DePauw University in Greencastle, Indiana, in May 1971, the two spoke briefly. Blackmun, mistaking Stevens for another Seventh Circuit judge, Robert A. Sprecher, later wrote to Sprecher to thank him for coming. Sprecher, who in fact had not been there, passed the letter to Stevens. Stevens then wrote to Blackmun to tell him that it was "thoroughly understandable that you should have confused me with

Judge Sprecher in view of our comparable status and the fact that his name came up in our conversation with the gentleman who introduced himself to you just after I did." Stevens went on to explain how he happened to be in Greencastle. He had flown his own plane there from Chicago that afternoon, in perfect flying weather, because flying was "a favorite method of relaxation, which sometimes makes it possible for me to view some of our problems from a different perspective." Blackmun was abashed at his mistake. "I am very embarrassed about my confusion," he wrote to Stevens. "Something like that just should not happen."

Stevens would remain the junior justice for six years, marking a long stretch of stability on the Court through the late 1970s. In June 1981, Potter Stewart announced his retirement, after twenty-three years on the Court, although he was only sixty-six years old. Ronald Reagan named Sandra Day O'Connor, a state appellate judge from Arizona and a former majority leader of Arizona's State Senate, to succeed him.

O'Connor's views and her record on abortion were studiously ambiguous. Arizona had a powerful antiabortion lobby, from which she had kept her distance. In fact, she had cast a preliminary vote in the State Senate in 1970 in favor of a bill to repeal Arizona's criminal abortion statute. And in 1974, the year after *Roe,* she voted against a measure to prohibit abortions in some Arizona state hospitals. At her Senate confirmation hearing in September 1981, the National Right to Life Committee testified against her, and she had to walk through antiabortion pickets to get into the Judiciary Committee hearing room. She was overwhelmingly confirmed nevertheless, making history as the first woman to sit on the Supreme Court.

The arrival of a female justice had not been completely unforeseen, either outside the Court or within it. The previous November, Potter Stewart, already contemplating his retirement and the prospect that a woman might be named to fill the vacancy, had urged the Conference to eliminate the traditional reference to justices as "Mr. Justice" and to substitute the gender-neutral "Justice." Over Blackmun's protest, the justices voted to make the change. "It seems to me that of late we tend to panic and to get terribly excited about some rather inconsequential

> **Supreme Court of the United States**
> **Washington, D. C. 20543**
>
> CHAMBERS OF
> JUSTICE HARRY A. BLACKMUN
>
> November 17, 1980
>
> Dear Chief:
>
> If you are maintaining a permanent record on the vote to eliminate the use of "Mr.," please record me as in opposition.
>
> It seems to me that of late we tend to panic and to get terribly excited about some rather inconsequential things. I regard this as one of them. We are swayed by the anticipatory remarks of a federal appellate woman judge to the use of "Madam." So far as I am concerned, I think it would have been far better to let the present system, in force for many decades, continue until a woman is on the Court and her particular desires are made known. We seem to be eliminating, step by step, all aspects of diverseness, and we give impetus to the trend toward a colorless society.

Blackmun protests the Conference's decision to drop the traditional "Mr. Justice."

things," Blackmun wrote to Burger after the vote. "So far as I am concerned, I think it would have been far better to let the present system, in force for many decades, continue until a woman is on the Court and her particular desires are made known. We seem to be eliminating, step by step, all aspects of diverseness, and we give impetus to the trend toward a colorless society."

His linguistic bad humor aside, Blackmun reached out to O'Connor once she arrived, donating the services of his staff to help her set up her files. "I think you should patent your 'system' and offer it to incoming Justices for a not insubstantial price," O'Connor's secretary, Linda Blandford, wrote in a note of thanks. "It would be the best investment a Justice could make when coming to the Court."

Nonetheless, Blackmun was wary of his newest colleague—especially in light of Reagan's strong antiabortion stance in the 1980 presidential campaign. The test came the following year, when the Court accepted its next abortion case, *Akron v. Akron Center for Reproductive Health, Inc.* The Ohio city had adopted an ordinance to regulate, and discourage, abortions by imposing, among other requirements, an informed consent provision and a twenty-four-hour waiting period. Rex E. Lee, the U.S. solicitor general, filed a brief in support of the city of Akron that stopped just short of asking the Court to overturn *Roe*. Although Lee noted that the case did not directly raise the question of doing away with *Roe*, he said that the Court should use the new case to revise its approach to evaluating abortion regulations. Instead of applying "strict scrutiny"—the most exacting standard of judicial review, under which a regulation impinging on a fundamental right would be found unconstitutional unless it could be shown to be "narrowly tailored" to serve a "compelling state interest"—the Court ought to "give heavy deference to the state legislative judgment" on a case-by-case basis. Only a regulation that "unduly burdens the abortion decision" should be invalidated, Lee argued.

While the distinction between the two standards of review sounded technical, it would change the polarity of abortion litigation. Abortion would no longer be considered a "fundamental" constitutional right, one that the government could interfere with only for a "compelling" reason, and then only in the most "narrowly tailored" manner. In place of the legal presumption that any restriction on access to abortion was unconstitutional, with the burden on the government to prove otherwise, the administration's proposal would adopt the legal presumption that all regulations on abortion were to be considered constitutional unless proved otherwise. The change would shift the burden to the plaintiffs to prove that a state or local regulation posed an "undue burden" and should therefore be invalidated. And as ammunition for attacking the constitutional analysis in *Roe v. Wade,* Lee cited Ely's article "The Wages of Crying Wolf."

The Reagan administration's intervention elevated the *Akron* case from a relatively minor skirmish to a core attack on *Roe*'s continued validity. The case was "the real second round of the abortion controversy," Blackmun wrote in his preargument notes. The solicitor general's brief, he continued, was a body blow, proposing an approach that "provides no standards at all. . . . It either says abortion is not a constitutionally protected right, and is inconsistent with *Roe*, or says constitutional decision should be left to legislature, and is inconsistent with *Marbury*." Blackmun's reference was to *Marbury v. Madison,* the landmark 1803 Supreme Court decision that established the Court's power to invalidate legislation that it deemed contrary to the Constitution. Nonetheless, Blackmun predicted to himself, O'Connor would probably go along with the solicitor general. "Would not SOC be expected to go with the SG?"

During the oral argument on November 30, 1982, Blackmun made clear his displeasure with the administration. Only rarely did he ask questions from the bench, but this time he glared down at Rex Lee, held the administration's sand-colored brief in the air, and demanded: "Did you write this brief personally?"

"Very substantial parts of it," the startled solicitor general replied.

Blackmun's prediction about O'Connor proved correct. Although the Court struck down the Akron ordinance by a vote of 6 to 3, O'Connor joined White and Rehnquist in dissent. The two more-senior justices allowed her to speak for them in a twenty-three-page draft opinion that embraced the Reagan administration's "undue burden" standard and criticized, in forceful terms, the entire structure of *Roe v. Wade.* In her draft, O'Connor asserted that *Roe's* trimester approach, weighing the states' interest according to how far the pregnancy had advanced, "is a completely unprincipled and unworkable method of accommodating the conflicting personal rights and compelling state interests that are involved in the abortion context."

When Blackmun's law clerk Cory Streisinger complained to O'Connor's clerk Gary Francione about the dissent's caustic tone, Francione checked with O'Connor, who agreed to remove the word "unprincipled." The *Roe* structure, she now wrote, remained "unworkable" but was not "unprincipled." Streisinger reported back to Blackmun that O'Connor "realizes that her position in this area is vastly different from the one taken in *Roe v. Wade,* but she wanted to avoid anything that even indirectly appeared to be an *ad hominem* attack."

O'Connor made no changes in another part of her opinion, predicting that improvements in medicine would "in the not too distant future" move the point of fetal viability earlier in the pregnancy, from the beginning of the third trimester into the first trimester. "The *Roe* framework, then, is clearly on a collision course with itself," she wrote. When he read this passage, Blackmun put a question mark in the margin of O'Connor's draft. He may well have reflected that as *Roe* approached its tenth anniversary, it was certainly on a collision course with the Reagan administration's first Supreme Court appointee—and, predictably, with those who were likely to follow. The Court was aging. Brennan was about to turn seventy-seven. Burger and Powell, born two days apart, were seventy-five. Marshall and Blackmun himself were seventy-four. Five of the justices, then—all members of the original *Roe* majority—were well past normal retirement age. Sandra Day O'Connor was the future. She was fifty-three.

Still, *Roe* was safe for now. The administration's position, as well as O'Connor's dissent, had offended Lewis Powell. In his majority opinion in *Akron,* issued on June 15, 1983, he went out of his way to discourage future attacks on *Roe.* Powell invoked the rule of stare decisis (literally, "to stand by things decided"), the Court's doctrine of adherence to its precedents. *Roe* had been decided ten years earlier, Powell wrote, after having been "considered with special care." Since then, "the Court repeatedly and consistently has accepted and applied the basic principle that a woman has a fundamental right to make the highly personal choice whether or not to terminate her pregnancy." Stare decisis, Powell continued, "is a doctrine that demands respect in a society governed by the rule of law. We respect it today, and reaffirm *Roe v. Wade.*"

Even without a change in the Court's membership, instability loomed. As the *Akron* case was under consideration, Burger had contemplated filing a separate opinion that would qualify his continued support for *Roe.* He dropped that plan without explanation, telling Powell only that he would "wait for another day."

Justice O'Connor was also to have a profound impact on a question at the heart of the American system: federalism. The debate over federalism—the appropriate allocation of power between Washington and the states—had seemingly been resolved during Franklin D. Roosevelt's presidency, when a hostile Supreme Court finally yielded to the New Deal and gave Congress essentially unquestioned power over the national economy. For the next thirty-five years, the debate was quiescent, until William Rehnquist arrived on the Court in 1972, determined to reopen the question and move the balance more in the states' favor. His first opportunity came in 1975, in *National League of Cities v. Usery*, a state challenge to a recent amendment to the Fair Labor Standards Act, extending federal wage and hour protections to state and local employees. The issue was whether the states could raise a constitutionally based objection to the exercise of Congress's authority to regulate interstate commerce.

At the conference, it was obvious that Rehnquist had allies in his quest to rein in federal power. Powell called the matter "the most important case since I have been here." He added that "this Court is responsible for preservation of the federal system" and that federalism should operate "as a wide constitutional principle," with Congress regulating the states' internal affairs "only when necessary for federal interests." Burger assigned the case to Rehnquist, who wrote a broad opinion overturning a contrary precedent from 1968 and holding that Congress lacked authority to "displace the States' freedom to structure integral operations in areas of traditional governmental functions," such as what to pay their employees.

Blackmun provided a reluctant fifth vote for Rehnquist's majority opinion. He was "not untroubled," he said, but concluded that the Court was simply adopting a "balancing approach," not prohibiting federal regulation "in areas such as environmental protection, where the federal interest is demonstrably greater and where state facility compliance with imposed federal standards would be essential."

Not long after O'Connor's arrival, Blackmun's qualification was put to the test. Unlike her fellow justices, O'Connor had held an elected position; what was most significant was that it was a state office. She had been majority leader of the Arizona State Senate, the first woman in the country to have held so high a post in a state legislature. Her commitment to state sovereignty was deep and, in time, would play out across several areas of the Court's jurisprudence. Now, in her first term, her focus would be on a law that Congress passed in response to the energy crisis of the mid-1970s.

The Public Utility Regulatory Policies Act of 1978 required state utility regulators to consider adopting various energy-saving policies. In a suit brought by the state of Mississippi, a federal district court there found that the law violated the principles of state sovereignty endorsed by the Supreme Court in *National League of Cities*. The Reagan administration appealed. At the conference after the argument in January 1982, Powell and Rehnquist both expressed doubts about the law's validity, but O'Connor cast the only clear vote to uphold the district court's ruling. Burger assigned to Blackmun the majority opinion reversing the district court. Although the case, *Federal Energy Regulatory Commission v. Mississippi,* did not at first appear to be close, it turned out to be. Blackmun argued that because Congress could have directly taken over the regulation of private utilities, the public utility law "should not be invalid simply because, out of deference to state authority, Congress adopted a less intrusive scheme and allowed the States to continue regulating in the area on the condition that they *consider* the suggested federal standards." The states, Blackmun said, could give up their regulatory role if they chose.

O'Connor saw the case in a completely different light. The law served to "conscript state utility commissions into the national bureaucratic army," she wrote in a dissenting opinion, stating strongly that "state legislative and administrative bodies are not field offices of the national bureaucracy." The prospect that the states could give up regulating utilities "is an absurdity," she said, adding that if the majority's analysis "is sound, the Constitution no longer limits federal regulation of state governments." In April, Burger announced that he was changing his vote. O'Connor's opinion, he said, "persuades me that the Court goes too far." Powell and Rehnquist, who had at first been uncertain, were now also in dissent and Blackmun's majority, having shrunk to 5 to 4, was in peril. He and O'Connor engaged in a battle of footnotes. He said that her "apocalyptic observations, while striking, are overstated and patently inaccurate." In his "chronology of significant events" for April 16, 1982, he made a note: "FERC case blast at O'C."

Blackmun's majority held, but the episode fed his growing doubts, both about the Court's newest member and about his own position on federalism. Another test presented itself, in the form of *Garcia v. San Antonio Metropolitan Transit Authority,* argued in March 1984. The question in *Garcia* was whether Congress had the power to impose minimum wage and overtime provisions on public transit authorities. *National League of Cities* had given the states immunity from this type of federal regulation for their "traditional governmental functions." Was running a transit system such a role? A federal district court in Texas had said that it was, freeing the city of San Antonio, which had taken over a private transit system in 1959, from having to pay its transit workers according to federal standards. After the argument, the vote in conference was 5 to 4 to affirm that ruling. Along with Burger, Powell, Rehnquist, and O'Connor, Blackmun was in the majority, and Burger assigned the case to him. He was working on his opinion when his law clerk Scott R. McIntosh persuaded him that he was on the wrong side.

In a long memorandum, McIntosh argued that basing state immunity on whether a particular service is a traditional governmental function was neither "sound in theory or workable in practice." He said there were "serious problems with trying to provide a constitutional safe harbor for some governmental functions and not for others." Instead, the law clerk wrote, the test should be one of "nondiscrimination." Under this test, "federal regulation may extend to state functions as long as it applies uniformly to private as well as public activities and does not discriminate against the States and their subdivisions." McIntosh added: "I think that a discrimination standard fully protects States from the risk that the federal government will disrupt state programs in any meaningful way." Under that test, it was clearly permissible to regulate the wages and hours of public transit workers, because the same regulations applied to employees of private systems. If Blackmun accepted this reasoning, McIntosh said, he would still command a majority, because the dissenters—Brennan, Marshall, White, and Stevens—would certainly join him. The law clerk offered to produce a draft.

On June 11, 1984, Blackmun circulated the draft and informed the

Conference of his new position. He had spent "a lot of time" on the case, he said. "I have finally decided to come down on the side of reversal. I have been able to find no principled way in which to affirm." His new opinion did not overrule *National League of Cities;* instead, it purported to reaffirm its "central principle" that "the States occupy a special position in our constitutional system." The other justices might conclude that the case should now be reassigned or reargued, he realized.

With barely three weeks left in the term, the sentiment for reargument was strong, although Blackmun himself opposed it. Burger made the formal motion to reargue. "At this stage—almost mid-June— a 30-page opinion coming out contrary to the Conference vote on a very important issue places those who may dissent in a difficult position," the chief justice said. The Court issued a reargument order on July 5, posing the question to the parties in the most unambiguous terms: Should *National League of Cities* be reconsidered?

The reargument took place on the new term's opening day, October 1, 1984. At conference this time, with five votes in favor of overturning *National League of Cities,* it was the senior associate justice in the majority, Brennan, who assigned the case to Blackmun. On October 23, Blackmun circulated his new opinion. Eight years of experience under *National League of Cities,* he wrote, "now persuades us that the attempt to draw the boundaries of state regulatory immunity in terms of 'traditional governmental function' is not only unworkable but is also inconsistent with established principles of federalism and, indeed, with those very federalism principles on which *National League of Cities* purported to rest." Instead, it was the political process itself, with its "built-in restraints," that would protect the states from federal overreaching. In *National League of Cities,* "the Court tried to repair what did not need repair"; therefore, that decision was now overruled. The four dissenters indicated in unusually direct terms that they had no intention of laying down their arms. For her part, O'Connor wrote, she was confident that "this Court will in time again assume its constitutional responsibility."

During the following term, it was Blackmun's turn to be on the losing end of a vote change. The case was *Bowers v. Hardwick*. The question was whether the right to privacy recognized by the Court in the cases leading up to *Roe v. Wade* protected homosexuals from prosecution for their private sexual acts. Michael Hardwick, a gay man who had been charged with violating Georgia's criminal sodomy law, brought a successful constitutional challenge to the law in the federal appeals court in Atlanta. The Supreme Court initially voted not to hear the appeal brought by Michael Bowers, Georgia's attorney general, but an opinion by Byron White dissenting from the denial of certiorari eventually won the support of Burger, Marshall, and Rehnquist. With four votes, the case went on the docket. During the oral argument, on March 31, 1986, Blackmun jotted down a prediction of the likely outcome: 5 to 4, or perhaps 6 to 3, to reverse the appeals court ruling in favor of Hardwick.

He was surprised at the conference when Powell, whom he had counted as a sure vote for the state, expressed "mixed emotions" but nonetheless voted to affirm. "Sodomy in the home should be decriminalized," Powell said; to imprison a person for a private homosexual act would amount to cruel and unusual punishment under the Eighth Amendment. On his conference notes, Blackmun put an exclamation point next to Powell's remarks and added a notation drawing his law clerks' attention to the vote. "Clerks! Can this position hold," he wrote.

There were now five votes to affirm, striking down the Georgia law: Powell, Blackmun, Marshall, Brennan, and Stevens. According to Brennan, the case was not about homosexuality "but about privacy and consenting adults." Stevens was more troubled. "I have a bias," he said. "But we have to live with this." He noted that the American Psychiatric Association had removed homosexuality from its list of mental disorders. Why did Georgia not enforce the sodomy law against married couples? he asked. "Only prejudice supports the distinction." It was "a liberty case for me," Stevens said.

On the opposite side, Burger noted that he saw "no infringement on any fundamental right of privacy." Courts could speak of morality, he said, adding that England had condemned homosexuality "about 500 years ago" and "Georgia adopted the common law of England

200 years ago." Rehnquist, also voting to reverse, observed that "any criminal code embraces moral notions." White and O'Connor voted to reverse as well.

Brennan assigned the opinion to Blackmun. But on April 8, less than a week after the conference, Blackmun's doubts about Powell's position were realized. "Upon further study as to exactly what is before us, I conclude that my 'bottom line' should be to reverse rather than affirm," Powell wrote to the Conference. While the case posed Eighth Amendment problems for him, he said, it had not been argued or decided on the basis of the Eighth Amendment; Hardwick had never been put on trial. "I did not agree that there is a substantive due process right to engage in conduct that for centuries has been recognized as deviant, and not in the best interest of preserving humanity," Powell noted.

Blackmun's task now was to write a dissenting opinion, and he viewed the case as a natural extension of the abortion rulings. "We protect the decision whether to have a child because parenthood alters so dramatically an individual's self-definition, not because of demographic considerations or the Bible's command to be fruitful and multiply," he wrote. "The Court claims that its decision today merely refuses to recognize a fundamental right to engage in homosexual sodomy; what the Court really has refused to recognize is the fundamental interest all individuals have in controlling the nature of their intimate associations with others."

Blackmun decided to announce his dissent from the bench. The Court was about to conclude the term, with the case tentatively scheduled to be announced on Friday, June 27, 1986. His law clerk Pamela S. Karlan urged a slight delay. "I think Friday is a *bad* day to have the case brought down," she wrote on Tuesday, June 24. "A summer Friday and Saturday are probably the least likely time for people to take notice of what the Court has done. I would press, if I were you, for Monday instead." Blackmun sent a note to Burger that afternoon: "Dear Chief, May I ask that No. 85-140, *Bowers v. Hardwick,* go over from Friday to Monday? I shall be ready by then." Burger returned the note with "Done" written across the bottom.

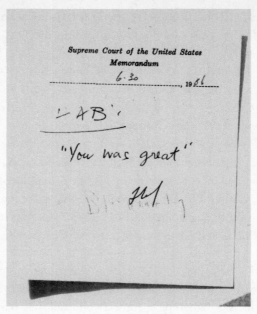

Thurgood Marshall congratulates Blackmun on the dissenting opinion he delivered from the bench in *Bowers v. Hardwick,* June 30, 1986.

Because June 30 was the final day of the term, it was clear to everyone familiar with the case that the decision would be announced that morning. The interest was intense. Blackmun read aloud from his dissenting opinion: "It is precisely because the issue raised by this case touches the heart of what makes individuals what they are that we should be especially sensitive to the rights of those whose choices upset the majority." He spoke for himself and the three other dissenters: Brennan, Stevens, and Marshall. When he was finished, Marshall passed him a note. It had been more than thirteen years since Marshall had accused his junior colleague of failing to understand, in the bankruptcy fee case, how other people lived. Now the aging civil rights hero wrote: "You was great."

7

DISSENTS

BY THE EARLY 1980s, the Burger Court was becoming increasingly dysfunctional, and Blackmun's exasperation with his old friend's management style was too great to bother concealing. The strains had been growing for years. In the late 1970s, Blackmun gave two off-the-record interviews to Scott Armstrong, the coauthor (with Bob Woodward) of *The Brethren,* a highly critical, best-selling account of Burger's leadership that infuriated the chief justice. Blackmun also authorized his former law clerks to talk to Armstrong and Woodward. Blackmun never revealed his cooperation to the other justices, more than one of whom had opened doors, or file drawers, to the authors.

Clearly, Blackmun was not the only member of the Court to chafe under the Burger regime. Problems had been apparent for years. In June 1975, as the end of the term approached with decisions in several particularly contentious civil rights and criminal cases still to be announced, William Rehnquist had sent Burger a letter, with copies to the Conference, that used a seemingly benign literary reference to convey a pointed complaint about Burger's handling of the Court's internal affairs:

Dear Chief:
I had a feeling that at the very close of today's Conference we may have fitted Matthew Arnold's closing lines in "Dover

Beach" wherein he refers to those "Swept with confused alarms of struggle and flight / Where ignorant armies clash by night." I therefore take the liberty of stating my understanding that at our Conference Monday morning, immediately after coming off the bench, we are planning to discuss all cases held for opinions scheduled, in Conferences held today or earlier, to come down next week.

A case that consumed the Court for much of the 1981 and 1982 terms, *Immigration and Naturalization Service v. Chadha,* offers dramatic evidence both of Burger's foundering leadership and of the severe fraying of the bond between Burger and Blackmun during their years together on the Court.

Jagdish Rai Chadha was a native of Kenya who had overstayed his student visa in the United States and, after a hearing in 1974, was found eligible for deportation. Under federal immigration law at the time, the attorney general had the power to show mercy by canceling deportation proceedings for aliens of "good moral character" who would suffer "extreme hardship" if deported. Chadha applied for and won such a reprieve and was on his way to becoming a permanent legal resident. But there was one more hurdle to overcome. Congress had attached a "legislative veto" provision to the immigration law, giving itself the power, by a vote of either house, to overturn the attorney general's decision to cancel deportation proceedings. In late 1975, the House of Representatives vetoed the attorney general's decision not to deport Chadha; the House Judiciary Committee's immigration subcommittee, after reviewing 340 cases in which the attorney general had canceled deportation, decided that Chadha and five others had not demonstrated sufficient "hardship" to qualify.

When Chadha was ordered deported the next year, he challenged the validity of the congressional intervention. The Constitution, he argued, gave Congress only one way to exercise its legislative authority: by passing a bill in both houses and presenting it to the president for a signature or veto. In the constitutional structure, there was no room for a "legislative veto," Chadha claimed. A federal appeals court agreed, declaring that the legislative veto violated the constitutional separation of powers.

The case was not one to captivate the general public, but for government insiders, it presented a question of surpassing importance. Since 1932, Congress had attached legislative veto provisions to more than two hundred statutes, some requiring action by both houses and some, as in Chadha's case, deeming action by one house to be sufficient. Political scientists had long viewed this arrangement as a constitutional accident waiting to happen, but the issue was of more than academic interest. Clearly, Congress had aggrandized its power. More than that, the legislative veto gave lobbyists and special interest groups a vitally important chance to influence policy after the administrative process had run its course. For example, rules for natural gas pricing could be canceled by the vote of only one house. A foreign trade regulation could be voided if both houses registered their disapproval.

The justices accepted the *Chadha* case at the beginning of the 1981 term. To Blackmun, the issue was straightforward: the legislative veto was unconstitutional, and the impact of such a ruling was not the Court's particular concern. But there was little straightforward in the way the Court handled the case. While mystified outsiders watched and waited, the Court would take more than twenty months before it stumbled its way to a decision.

After the oral argument, in February 1982, there was lively debate during the conference. Rehnquist said it was "too bad" and "a misfortune" that the case had reached the Court. A decision to strike down the legislative veto, he said, would "harm the practical workings of the government." Marshall took the opposite view, arguing that the challenge "should have been here earlier." In vetoing the attorney general's decision regarding Jagdish Chadha, Marshall said, Congress had, in effect, acted as a judge, but "nothing in the Constitution gives Congress the right to adjudicate." Burger said little, other than to emphasize how difficult and important he found the case. He did not cast a vote. Blackmun noted five votes to affirm the appeals court's finding of unconstitutionality: himself along with Marshall, Brennan, Powell, and Stevens. The conference ended with the opinion unassigned.

Signs of trouble emerged the next day, February 25. Powell sent a memo to Burger, with copies to the rest of the justices. "I share the concern expressed by you and others about having to decide the one-house veto issue," he said. "The Executive and Legislative branches have lived with it for decades—even though uncomfortably at times. If there were a principled way to avoid the issue, I would welcome it. In any event, it seems to me that the issue is of sufficient national importance to merit further discussion."

Brennan replied immediately. It was essential to decide the case as quickly as possible and "settle the persisting controversy between the Executive and the Congress concerning the lawfulness of these one-house veto provisions," he said. But Powell was not so easily put at ease. On March 9 he circulated another memo: "In thinking further about this worrisome case, I am now inclined to think a reargument is desirable." He suggested that the Court could combine a reargument in *Chadha* with the argument in a case another appeals court had just decided, invalidating the one-house veto for gas pricing regulations. "On an issue such as this where the fundamental structure of our government is implicated, it may be desirable to have more time for consideration, and also to have the benefit of arguments in both of these cases," Powell said.

Blackmun's clerk Harold Hongju Koh urged him to resist Powell's effort. Koh gave Blackmun a five-page memo arguing why the case should go forward toward a decision. Blackmun edited the law clerk's memo, turning it into a letter to the chief justice. In his own words he emphasized what was clearly, for him, the heart of the matter. Jagdish Chadha had remained in immigration limbo for nine years, Blackmun said. "We are here to decide cases, and he and the Government deserve an answer to the issues that are raised."

Burger asked for a special conference on Saturday, March 13, to take up Powell's reargument proposal. A decision to reargue a case requires a formal motion supported by the votes of five justices, a rule designed to prevent a minority from controlling the calendar and delaying a decision. Brennan replied to Burger's invitation with a memo opposing the special conference. He noted that no appeal had even been filed in the recently decided legislative veto case that Powell wanted to hear. Further discussion "seems to me a waste of time," he said; the Court should simply decide the case it had already heard. Stevens agreed. The case would not get any easier a second time, he observed. Rehnquist, O'Connor, and White expressed support for reargument, but White said he was busy on Saturday. Burger canceled his call for a special conference.

On Monday, the chief justice circulated a memo: "As I indicated at our original conference on this case, I think it is one of the most difficult we have had in a long time, and this is why I felt that a further conference would be useful. Neither of the dispositions, which seemed quite clear to five or six members of the Court, seemed that clear to me." Adding that "I find it difficult to understand why there is any time pressure in this matter," he said he was voting to schedule the case for reargument the next term. But no formal vote had taken place. The case remained unassigned.

In effect, Burger froze. His response differed from his behavior of earlier years when, as in the *Bakke* case, he tried to influence the course of events by circulating a preemptive opinion. What he now displayed was not heavy-handed leadership—it was the absence of leadership, a vacuum that had swallowed one of the most important cases of the decade. More than two months later, as the term was about to end, Burger circulated the schedule for announcing the term's final opinions. On June 25, Blackmun sent Burger a memo calling attention to the omission from his list of any reference to *Chadha*. There had been no formal vote to reargue the case, Blackmun pointed out. If a reargument order was to be issued, he said, "I wish to be shown on the public record that I dissent."

Burger replied later that day: "There were five votes at conference to put this case over; whether to call this a 'formal' or 'final' vote I am uncertain. It seems clear that everyone has assumed the case is to go over. You may recall I suggested a special conference to be held to discuss the matter and there were no 'takers.'"

Nothing of what was taking place inside the Court was known to the outside world. As far as anyone knew, July 2, 1982, the final day of the term, would be the day for announcing *Chadha,* along with any other remaining decisions. But there was, of course, no *Chadha* decision to announce. Later that day, the Court issued the term's final list of orders, noting that *Chadha* was "restored to the calendar for reargument" and that "Justice Brennan and Justice Blackmun dissent."

The second argument took place in December 1982; this time, the vote after conference was decisive: it was 7 to 2 to affirm that the legislative veto was unconstitutional, with White and Rehnquist dissenting. While expressing "regret that we must decide this issue after 50 years," Powell joined the majority. Burger assigned the opinion to himself. But that was scarcely the end of the Court's internal struggle.

Burger's first draft, circulated nearly four months later, referred to the history of the case. "The parties are properly before us and the difficult and sensitive issues have been fully briefed and twice argued in this Court," Burger wrote. To Blackmun, "difficult and sensitive" was out of place. Perhaps he remembered Burger's advice long ago, during that stressful first term, when Blackmun had called *Palmer v. Thompson,* the Jackson, Mississippi, swimming pool case, "excruciatingly difficult" and Burger had advised him never to concede that a case was close or difficult. Certainly, he now regarded Burger's description as a self-justifying rationalization for the Court's failure to decide *Chadha* the previous term. He asked Burger to remove "difficult and sensitive" from Part H of his draft opinion.

Burger refused. To a formal memo responding to a variety of suggestions on his draft, he added a postscript: "I do not contemplate changing sub-part H as Harry suggests. That is purely a matter of style and for better or worse—probably the latter!—I prefer my own style."

Blackmun, now even more offended, replied: "The handwritten postscript to your letter of May 27, I assume, was meant to be a 'brush-off,' and I must accept it as such. For me, Part H is *not* a matter of style. Had it been, I would not have objected to it. You say there that the issues are 'difficult and sensitive.' To say that they are difficult is substance, not style. The issues may well be sensitive, but for me they are not difficult." That, Blackmun concluded, was why he had opposed the reargument. He enclosed a concurring opinion that he

Re: No. 80-1832 - INS v. Chadha
    No. 80-2170 - U.S. House of Representatives v. INS
    No. 80-2171 - U.S. Senate v. INS

Dear Chief:

    The handwritten postscript to your letter of May 27, I
assume, was meant to be a "brush off," and I must accept it as
such. For me, Part H is not a matter of style. Had it been, I
would not have objected to it. You say there that the issues
are "difficult and sensitive." To say that they are difficult
is substance, not style. The issues may well be sensitive, but
for me they are not difficult. That is one of the reasons I
opposed the motion that the cases go over for reargument.

    I also assured Hugo that I would do my best not to have the
Court agonize in its opinions. I concede I did not take his
advice in Roe v. Wade, 410 U.S. 113, 116 (1973).

    I therefore am circulating the enclosed concurrence in
part.

                    Sincerely,

                    H.a.B

The struggle between Blackmun and Burger over the legislative veto case reaches a climax.

proposed to circulate, calling public attention to the internal dispute. "The issues decided today were ably briefed and argued before this Court in February 1982," the draft concurrence said. "Ordering reargument needlessly prolonged uncertainty in the halls of Congress about the constitutionality of many federal statutes that, had Congress deemed it desirable, could have been amended in response to the Court's judgment."

Burger replied the next day: "I am still puzzled as to what creates a problem and so far as I am concerned the reference to 'twice argued' is a simple historic fact that will make clear to a reader in, let us say, 1993, that there was no 'rush to judgment' on an important case." But he backed off, offering a compromise. He would replace "sensitive and difficult" with "important," and say only that "the important issues have been fully briefed and twice argued."

Blackmun was satisfied. On June 13, he dropped his concurring opinion and joined Burger's majority, now circulating in its sixth draft. His was the final "join." When the opinion was issued, on June 23, 1983, Burger used his bench announcement to get in the last word.

Describing the decision for the courtroom audience, he said: "We can all agree on one thing, that this is a very difficult and important case."

As Burger became more irascible, even erratic, he alienated even those justices who—like Rehnquist, years before, in his "Dover Beach" letter—were most ideologically compatible. Early in the 1984 term, the Court took up a case from Oklahoma that raised the issue of whether an indigent defendant whose sanity was in serious question must be provided with the psychiatric assistance necessary to prepare an effective insanity defense. The vote was 8 to 1 in favor of the defendant's claim, with only Rehnquist dissenting. But there was a puzzling aspect to the decision as it was eventually issued, on February 26, 1985. While concurring in the judgment, Burger refused to sign Thurgood Marshall's opinion for the Court.

Although *Ake v. Oklahoma* was a capital appeal—the defendant, Glen Burton Ake, had been sentenced to death for a double murder—Marshall viewed the decision as establishing the general principle that an indigent defendant who needed a psychiatric expert was entitled, as a matter of constitutional due process, to be provided with one. When Marshall circulated his opinion, Burger asked him to limit it to capital cases. Marshall declined, responding, "I have carefully considered your memorandum and cannot see my way clear to making the change you suggest." He canvassed the six other members of his majority. All said they would go along with whatever approach he chose. "Either way is all right with me," White told him. Blackmun said: "I shall leave this entirely to your good judgment."

The result was that Marshall wrote for seven justices, and Burger wrote two paragraphs for himself alone. "Nothing in the Court's opinion reaches noncapital cases," he declared, although, of course, with seven votes, it did.

Capital cases were very much on the justices' minds—and especially on Blackmun's mind—in the late 1970s and early 1980s. After the Court's reauthorization of capital punishment in *Gregg v. Georgia* and the other 1976 rulings, the death penalty pipeline filled steadily, but years passed before Blackmun had once again to confront his personal dilemma: how to reconcile his personal opposition to the death penalty with his belief that the Constitution neither prohibited it nor gave him a mandate as a judge to enact his view into law. For six years after the Court upheld the new state death penalty laws, there were never more than two executions a year. The Court permanently eliminated an entire category of death sentences when it ruled, by 7 to 2 in *Coker v. Georgia* (1977), that the death penalty for rape, which Blackmun had long found particularly troublesome, was unconstitutional. Burger and Rehnquist dissented, with Burger filing an opinion that quoted pointedly from Blackmun's paean to judicial restraint in his *Furman v. Georgia* dissent five years earlier. There, Blackmun had objected that the justices who voted in the majority to strike down the death penalty were acting on the basis of their personal views rather than the Constitution's command. "We should not allow our personal preferences as to the wisdom of legislative and congressional action, or our distaste for such action, to guide our judicial decision in cases such as these," he had declared. Now Burger, making the same point in his dissenting opinion in *Coker,* quoted Blackmun's words, identified him as the author, and included a commentary of his own: "Some sound observations, made only a few years ago, deserve repetition."

The landscape began to shift in the early 1980s. Thirty-seven states had reinstituted the death penalty, and by 1983 there were more than twelve hundred inmates on death row. There were five executions that year and twenty-one the next, with appeals reaching the Supreme Court in growing numbers. Most unsettling were the emergency requests for stays of execution that required last-minute action, outside the Court's normal procedures. The 1983 term alone saw eighty-six of these urgent requests. Some were filed by defense lawyers seeking one last chance for clients who had exhausted their previous appeals. But for others, the responsibility lay with impatient state courts that set execution dates for inmates who had not had the chance to file even an initial appeal with the Supreme Court.

As the Supreme Court "circuit justice" for his old jurisdiction, the Eighth Circuit, Blackmun was in the line of fire. Each of the nine justices had one or two circuit assignments that carried responsibility for administrative matters, including requests for stays of execution, arising in the state and federal courts within the circuit's boundaries. The Missouri Supreme Court was one of the most aggressive in setting an execution date within a few days of upholding a conviction, regardless of the fact that the rules of the U.S. Supreme Court provided ninety days, following a final judgment, for the filing of a petition for certiorari. The Missouri inmates' fervent requests for stays of execution came directly to Blackmun.

So the old dilemma was back. Years earlier, as *Furman* and the other death penalty cases were heading for the Court, Blackmun had sat at his typewriter and copied a passage from *Haley v. Ohio,* a 1948 opinion by his former law professor Justice Felix Frankfurter. Frankfurter had provided the deciding vote to overturn a fifteen-year-old boy's death sentence, on the ground that an all-night, secret interrogation had induced an involuntary confession. The justice stressed that he was ruling narrowly, based on the disturbing facts of the case, and was not condemning the death penalty as such. "I disbelieve in capital punishment," Frankfurter wrote. "But as a judge I could not impose the views of the very few States who through bitter experience have abolished capital punishment upon all the other States, by finding that 'due process' proscribes it." Blackmun placed a title over the paragraph that he copied, calling it "Re: Capital Punishment." Below the quotation he added his initials—not a claim of authorship but a personal endorsement of the view the passage expressed. Blackmun, who admired his former professor and had even corresponded with him after law school, took comfort from the knowledge that as a Supreme Court justice, Frankfurter had confronted the same contradiction between belief and duty and had found a way to resolve it. Perhaps the passage suggested for Blackmun a way out: stick closely to the facts, and try to make sure that justice is done in each case.

He granted a stay of execution to a Missouri inmate in 1983, intending it as a message of disapproval of the Missouri Supreme Court's precipitous scheduling of the execution date. But the Missouri court did not heed the message and continued its practice of setting immediate execution dates. On January 3, 1984, Blackmun granted stays to four

Re: Capital Punishment

"A lifetime's preoccupation with criminal justice, as prosecutor, defender of civil liberties, and scientific student, naturally leaves one with views. Thus, I disbelieve in capital punishment. But as a judge I could not impose the views of the very few States who through bitter experience have abolished capital punishment upon all the other States, by finding that 'due process' proscribes it. Again, I do not believe that even capital offenses by boys of fifteen should be dealt with according to the conventional criminal procedure. It would, however, be bald judicial usurpation to hold that States violate the Constitution in subjecting minors like Haley to such a procedure. If a State, consistently with the Fourteenth Amendment, may try a boy of fifteen charged with murder by the ordinary criminal procedure, I cannot say that such a youth is never capable of that free choice of action whith, in the eyes of the law, makes a confession 'voluntary.' Again, it would hardly be a justifiable exercise of judicial power to dispose of this case by finding in the Due Process Clause Constitutional outlawry of the admissibility of all private statements made by an accused to a police officer, however much legislation to that effect might seem to me wise." Mr. Justice Frankfurter, concurring in Haley v. Ohio, 332 U.S. 596, 602-603 (1948).

H.A.B.
4/16/71

Blackmun endorses the approach his old law professor, Felix Frankfurter, took toward the death penalty.

more Missouri inmates, who were all scheduled to die on January 6. None had yet filed a Supreme Court appeal. The opinion Blackmun issued in his capacity as circuit justice was explicit. "Every defendant in a state court of this Nation who has a right of direct review from a sentence of death, no matter how heinous his offense may appear to be, is entitled to have that review before paying the ultimate penalty," Blackmun wrote in *McDonald v. Missouri,* an opinion covering the four cases. "The right of review otherwise is rendered utterly meaningless." He pledged that he would continue to grant a stay for any Missouri inmate who had not yet had a chance to seek an appeal to the Supreme Court. "The stay, of course, ought to be granted by the state tribunal in the first instance, but, if it fails to fulfill its responsibility, I shall fulfill mine."

In response, the Missouri court modified its practice, but only slightly. It would no longer schedule an execution while the Supreme Court's ninety-day clock was running. But as soon as the inmate filed a petition, the Missouri court would set an execution date, without giving the justices a chance to act on the appeal. "In some respects, this is worse than their prior policy," Blackmun said in a memorandum he circulated to the other justices in late 1984, describing his "tug-of-war" with the Missouri court. "They just wish to pass the buck to us. In any event, I shall continue to stay these direct-review cases as long as they follow this new policy."

There was general agreement within the Court that this step was the proper course when all that was at issue was "direct review," a first appeal from the final judgment of a state's highest court. But there was deep disagreement over how to respond once a death-row inmate had exhausted his direct appeal and was now seeking "collateral review" through a challenge, in federal court, to the constitutionality of his conviction or sentence. Such a challenge was not a criminal appeal in the technical sense, because it took the form of a petition for a writ of habeas corpus, seeking an order from a federal court to the state authorities to provide an inmate with a new trial or sentencing hearing, or release him.

Habeas corpus was the legal system's safety valve, a way for the federal courts to monitor the quality of criminal justice being administered by the states. State prosecutors and courts regarded habeas corpus as intrusive, and many of the Supreme Court justices were becoming concerned about its growing role in death penalty litigation. In 1983, the Court ruled in *Barefoot v. Estelle* (with Blackmun, Brennan, and Marshall dissenting) that the federal appeals courts were not obliged to grant stays of execution for inmates who were seeking to appeal a federal district court's denial of habeas corpus. "It must be remembered that direct appeal is the primary avenue for review of a conviction or sentence, and death penalty cases are no exception," Byron White wrote for the majority, adding that "federal courts are not forums in which to relitigate state trials."

As circuit justice for the Eleventh Circuit, covering Florida, Georgia, and Alabama, Lewis Powell was on the front lines, just as Blackmun was. Florida had one of the country's most populous death rows, and in 1979 had carried out the first post-*Furman* execution of an inmate, John Spenkelink, who had resisted the death penalty. (Utah executed Gary Gilmore at his request in 1977.) Powell was increasingly vexed about stay requests from inmates whose lawyers had gone into federal court at the last minute with habeas corpus petitions. Suspecting that these petitions were "premeditated as a strategy," he proposed, in June 1985, a change in the Court's rules so that "where resort to federal habeas is deferred until a stay of execution is necessary to assure the requisite consideration by the district court, the court of appeals, and this Court, the burden of proof would be on the defendant to establish by affidavits reasons that satisfactorily explain the delay." Lawyers might be required, under oath, "to give a satisfactory reason for the delay," he suggested.

The term ended without action on Powell's proposals, but, before long, the Court was embroiled in a full-blown institutional crisis over how to handle the last-minute stays. As the justices were preparing to enjoy the Labor Day weekend, with a month to go before the start of the 1985 term, a stay application arrived from Willie J. Darden, a Florida death-row inmate whose name they knew quite well. Darden was scheduled to die in the electric chair at 7 A.M. on Wednesday, September 4. He had been convicted in 1974 for killing a Lakeland furniture-store owner during a robbery that netted $15, demanding oral sex from the victim's wife as her husband lay dying, and then shooting and wounding a sixteen-year-old neighbor who entered the store while the crime was in progress. The widow and the neighbor identified Darden, who had been on furlough from prison at the time of the crime, in court during his trial. The lower federal courts had turned down his petition for habeas corpus. His lawyer was asking for a stay of execution to enable him to appeal that denial to the Supreme Court.

The justices knew Darden's case because it had come before the Court on direct review in November 1976, only four months after the Court had upheld Florida's new death penalty law. At that time, Darden, who was black, had claimed that the prosecutor's inflammatory closing argument deprived him of a fair trial. The prosecutor had called Darden an "animal" who "shouldn't be out of his cell unless he has a leash on him." Oral argument was held in March 1977, and, at the conference, the justices were in basic agreement that the prosecutor's comments were unfortunate but not unconstitutional. Burger called the prosecutor a "clown" but said that, because of the evidence of Darden's guilt, any error was probably harmless. Blackmun agreed with that appraisal. In his preargument memo to himself, he had noted that there was "no question some ethical proprieties [were] violated" but that the prosecutor's "highly improper" comments were "not of reversal magnitude in light of all the evidence."

On April 19, 1977, the Court dismissed Darden's appeal without deciding the case. Although the justices did not explain their action, the Court typically uses such a disposition, known as a DIG, for "dismissed as improvidently granted," when a case turns out either not to present the question that the petition for certiorari had appeared to raise, or to contain a previously unrecognized obstacle to reaching that question. In Darden's case, the Court evidently had some doubt about whether his appeal in the Florida courts had encompassed the federal constitutional argument he sought to make to the Supreme Court.

Now Darden and his constitutional arguments were back. Several of the Court's death penalty decisions since his appeal would lend greater weight to some of his arguments. In addition, he was renewing an earlier claim of innocence. He could not have been the killer, he argued, because he crashed his car into a telephone pole miles from the scene while the crime was supposedly still in progress. The white victims who identified him had, classically, not been able to tell one black man from another, he said. As the circuit justice, Powell recommended denial of the stay application, asserting that the arguments had been fully considered and properly rejected.

But Blackmun's law clerk Pamela S. Karlan recommended granting the stay. In a sixteen-page memo, which she described as an "incredibly truncated discussion" of the complicated history of Darden's case, Karlan told Blackmun: "The fact that this case has bobbed around is not at all due to abuse of the writ or improper litigation by Darden. It is due instead to the incredibly cavalier treatment accorded Darden originally by the Florida Supreme Court which totally abdicated its supervisory responsibilities."

On Tuesday, September 3, 1985, Blackmun, Stevens, Brennan, and Marshall voted to grant the stay. The four votes would have been enough to grant a petition for certiorari, but that was not what Darden needed a day before his scheduled execution. A stay of execution—like a stay of any lower-court judgment—required a majority, five votes. At 6:05 that evening, the Court informed Darden's lawyer that there would be no stay of execution. Burger issued a concurring opinion, noting that the case had been before the Court previously and that "the issues raised in this application have been thoroughly considered and resolved by federal and state courts." Blackmun prepared a dissent. He emphasized that this was Darden's first federal habeas corpus petition and argued that the fact that the Court had examined the case once before, on direct review, was irrelevant. "Since 1976, this Court has come to a clearer understanding that the death penalty, although it may be imposed constitutionally, is so profoundly different from all other penalties that extraordinary safeguards must attend its imposition."

Darden's lawyer, recognizing that he had the support of four justices, sent a letter requesting that the Court treat the stay application as a petition for certiorari. The four who had voted for a stay now voted to grant the case. That meant that the Court would, sometime later that fall, be hearing an appeal from a dead man.

At one minute to midnight on September 3, Powell yielded and provided a fifth vote to grant the stay. His resentment was obvious in the memorandum he circulated. "I find no merit whatsoever in any of the claims advanced in the petition," Powell said, but "in view of the fact that this is a capital case with petitioner's life at stake, I feel obligated in this case, where the Justices are scattered geographically and unable to meet for a conference, to join in granting the application for a stay." Byron White noted his dissent. Burger added a dissenting opinion to the order by which the Court had granted the case. "Upon review of the petition and the history of this case, I conclude that no issues are presented that merit plenary review by this Court," Burger wrote. "Because we abuse our discretion when we accept meritless petitions presenting claims that we rejected only hours ago, I dissent."

The next day Powell sent a letter to the other justices: "The experience of last evening disturbs me—perhaps all of us," because it "illustrates how easily the system is manipulated in capital cases." Referring to the practice by which a minority of the Court can grant a case, he said: "If the Rule of Four can be so easily exploited, I am inclined to think we should reconsider that Rule and possibly—as many have suggested in recent years—adopt a Rule of Five." Powell then repeated his earlier assertion that there was no merit to Darden's appeal. "No one suggests that he is innocent—a fact that all too often under our law is irrelevant." Habeas corpus was becoming such an obstacle to the states' ability to administer their death penalty laws, Powell said, that the states should repeal those laws "unless the habeas corpus statute is substantially changed." He concluded: "I have no doubt as to the constitutionality of capital punishment, but I have grave doubts as to whether it now serves the purposes of deterrence and retribution, the principle purposes we identified in *Gregg*."

Blackmun, reading this last sentence, corrected the spelling of "principal" and added a comment: "So do others of us!" He placed question marks throughout Powell's letter, including the assertion that "no one suggests that he is innocent." He was not yet ready to respond publicly. But Stevens responded the next day, September 5. Explaining his actions, he said he had voted to grant the stay "based solely on my view that since the applicant was seeking an opportunity to have the Court grant certiorari to review denial of relief on his first federal habeas corpus petition, we should give the applicant the same time to present his case as would be available to any other litigant." Once the stay was denied, he said, he had at first considered that it would be "procedurally improper" to treat the stay application as a petition for certiorari, as the lawyer had requested. But he had concluded that "counsel really had no other choice" and that "it would be inappropriate to allow the execution to go forward without further study."

Brennan responded to Powell the next day. With sixty executions already scheduled to take place during the Court's coming term, he said, "I fully agree with Lewis that we should reconsider our procedures for dealing with capital cases." But that was the extent of his agreement. "My own view is that the Rule of Four is vital to the sound and just administration of the business of this Court," Brennan observed. Blackmun wrote "yes" in the margin of his copy of Brennan's letter. And he wrote "agree" in the margin next to Brennan's next sentence: "I must say that I am somewhat at a loss to comprehend how the Rule of Four was 'exploited' in Darden's case. As I understand what happened Tuesday, four of us believed that the petition raised certworthy issues and accordingly voted to grant. With respect, I do not foresee any danger that counsel will be able to 'exploit' our procedures. The votes of four Justices are required to grant cert. It is not possible for counsel to manipulate this rule."

Brennan had more to say: "What does concern me greatly is the prospect of what was narrowly avoided Tuesday evening, namely, the Court granting cert in a capital case while refusing to stay the execution, with the result that the petitioner dies even while his case is being docketed and scheduled for argument. I think we all agree that this would be intolerable, not only from the perspective of public reaction, but, more fundamentally, in terms of the unspeakable irony it would present." Brennan's proposal was, in fact, the opposite of Powell's: "that in capital cases we adopt a Rule of Four to stay executions," at least for an inmate's first federal habeas corpus petition. "The Court need not fear that such a Rule of Four would inexorably lead to the granting of a stay," Brennan continued. "However, where four Justices do require time to decide the merits of a petition, and where, as a consequence, the possibility that cert will be granted remains, it is clear to me that the state's interest in immediate execution must yield to the possibility of an erroneous execution." He concluded: "The point here is that if we continue to allow state-set execution dates to rush us to judgment, we run the risk of providing capital petitioners with less, rather than equal, justice." Blackmun annotated this last sentence with a vigorously underlined "yes."

The next response was from Rehnquist, who had been solidly

among the group opposed to granting the stay. He called Powell's proposal an "unwelcome departure from the tradition which allows four out of nine members of the Court to bring a case here for review." On the other hand, Brennan's proposal "would in capital cases turn the Court over to a minority of four." Rehnquist counseled taking no action. Perhaps the Darden case would prove to be unusual, he said. "I am as unhappy as anyone with the feeling that the capital defense lawyers are subtly switching the cart and the horse, so that instead of the grant of stay being ancillary to the granting of a petition for certiorari, the granting of certiorari becomes a means to obtain a stay. But I would prefer to wait and see what happens before moving on the basis of my present impressions."

Burger responded on September 10. The justices should discuss the entire issue at the new term's opening conference, he said. Although Burger agreed with Brennan that "we have 'exposed the Court to the criticism that its own decisions are arbitrary' by the events of last week," he was "not sure that he and I agree on what it is that merits criticism. Although criticism *per se* does not concern me, our sudden 'about face' performed late Tuesday evening surely raises valid questions in some minds." Noting that "thirteen years have elapsed since Darden was charged with murder," Burger went on to say that "any suggestion that our disposition of these cases is a 'rush to judgment' is unmitigated nonsense." Blackmun wrote in the margin: "here again!" It was a point that Burger had made before.

Burger continued: "At some point, the State's interest in carrying out a lawfully imposed judgment must certainly outweigh a petitioner's interest in a stay to allow prosecution of one more 'last appeal.' We must decide where we will draw the line in granting stays in these cases." A habeas corpus petition, even an initial one, did not merit an automatic stay, Burger said, because any inmate with such a petition had, by definition, already had a chance to bring a Supreme Court appeal. However, he concluded, he would advise adopting neither Powell's proposal for a Rule of Five for certiorari in capital cases nor Brennan's proposal for a Rule of Four in stays of execution. "If it is to be the case that four can grant a stay, does this mean that four should also be able to vacate a stay?" Burger asked, adding: "Remember Elizabeth Barrett Browning's lines: things 'so wrought may be unwrought so.'" In the margin, Blackmun wrote, witheringly: "our poet?"

Through these days Blackmun had been working on his own response, which he circulated on September 10. "The idea that a Rule of Five should be adopted in capital cases strikes me as especially pernicious, since it suggests that the Eighth Amendment concerns implicated by the death penalty are less compelling than the other issues we face," Blackmun wrote. He reminded his colleagues of his interaction with the Missouri Supreme Court. "I would not allow that court to rush us to judgment," he said. "I have had no trouble with the Supreme Court of Missouri since then. If we make clear to the States that this Court will insist upon having sufficient time adequately to review first federal habeas petitions, we shall eliminate the current incentive States possess to set execution dates that force hasty review of often problematic cases."

Blackmun observed that he found Darden's case troublesome, and "his claim of innocence is at least colorable." He pronounced himself "convinced" that the record of Darden's trial demonstrated "error." He explained that he had voted to grant certiorari in order to determine whether the error was of constitutional dimension. Addressing Burger and Powell directly, Blackmun said: "Two of you, of course, already have judged the case on the merits when you announced that there is no merit whatsoever in the case. I may reach that conclusion ultimately, but I certainly am not prepared to reach that conclusion on the papers presented to us initially."

In the first draft of his letter, Blackmun had concluded by saying that "the Court as an institution would surely look a little strange" if it granted certiorari while denying a stay. Karlan, his law clerk, told him the sentence was "far too tame, given what we're really talking about here." She suggested stronger language: the Court would appear "intellectually and morally bankrupt." Blackmun adopted her proposal, adding an elaboration of his own: "I think allowing an execution under such circumstances would do far more to discredit this Court than any delay in allowing a proper execution could ever entail."

The justices made no change in the Court's rules when they met in

October to discuss the competing proposals, and Darden's case was scheduled for argument in January 1986. At the conference after the argument, the justices all agreed that the prosecutor's behavior had been deplorable. In Burger's view, the remarks were a "gross violation" of the Code of Professional Responsibility; nonetheless, they did not make the trial unconstitutional. Rehnquist said the closing argument was "bizarre but did not overwhelm the jury." The vote was 4 to 4. Burger, Powell, White, and Rehnquist voted to affirm the denial of habeas corpus. Blackmun, Brennan, Marshall, and Stevens voted to reverse, with Stevens commenting that it was "tragic to say this is acceptable lawyer conduct." O'Connor, the junior justice, did not cast a vote at the conference, telling the others that she was still studying the case. The next week she informed Burger that she was voting to affirm. Burger assigned the majority opinion to Powell.

Preparation of the opinions in *Darden v. Wainwright,* during the spring of 1986, produced one last bitter exchange between Blackmun and Burger. Blackmun circulated a dissenting opinion that referred to "this Court's impatience with the progress of Darden's constitutional challenges to his conviction and death sentence." As evidence, he cited Burger's opinion, the previous September, dissenting from the last-minute grant of certiorari. Blackmun's opinion prompted Burger to circulate one concurring in Powell's majority opinion and reprising the certiorari dissent by reprinting it in full. "As my dissent makes clear," Burger's concurrence said, "I voted to deny the petition in this extraordinary case because the meritless claims raised did not require plenary review. Full briefing and oral argument have not changed my views. The dissent's suggestion that this Court is motivated by impatience with Darden's constitutional claims is refuted by the record; the 13 years of judicial proceedings in this case manifest substantial care and patience." He concluded: "At some point there must be finality."

Blackmun responded that if Burger published his proposed opinion, he would add a footnote to his own, criticizing Burger directly. "A public dissent from a grant of certiorari is extremely rare," Blackmun's footnote read. "Indeed, I know of no other recent case in which a Justice has dissented on the ground that the claims raised by the petitioner—which at least four Justices must have found worthy of full consideration—were meritless." By reprinting the dissent, he continued, "the Chief Justice suggests that he irrevocably had committed himself to rejecting those claims before he had received the benefit of the full briefing, oral argument, access to the record, and discussion of the issues by other Members of the Court that followed our grant of certiorari." Blackmun sent the proposed footnote to Burger on June 16: "Frankly, I would prefer not to indulge in this exchange of views. If, by chance, you should withdraw your writing, the footnote, too, will be withdrawn."

The next day Burger announced his retirement as chief justice. He would leave the Court to head a commission overseeing the observance of the bicentennial of the Constitution. There is no record that the two old friends exchanged any personal notes about this momentous transition. Instead, on the following day, their sniping at each other over the *Darden* opinions resumed uninterrupted. Burger sent Blackmun a letter refusing his colleague's request to drop the concurring opinion. "I too prefer not to indulge in the exchange of views that the Darden case has prompted," Burger said, but "so long as the incorrect statement remains in your opinion I am bound to set the record straight. Actually there is no point to any of this exchange." When the Court issued the decision, on June 23, Burger's concurring opinion was there; so was Blackmun's reference to the Court's "impatience" and, as footnote 9, his criticism of Burger. Addressing the merits of Darden's appeal, Blackmun said that the majority opinion "reveals a Court willing to tolerate not only imperfection but a level of fairness and reliability so low it should make conscientious prosecutors cringe."

The *Darden* case left Blackmun shaken, and he continued to dwell on it. At the Eighth Circuit's annual conference the following month, he told the appeals court and district court judges that "if ever a man received an unfair trial, Darden did." Blackmun called the 1985 term "the most difficult of the 16" that he had yet served on the Court. His dissenting opinion prompted several critical letters from members of the public, to whom he did not respond. "You evidently have been in the 'ivory tower' too long," a man wrote from Plano, Texas, telling Blackmun that he had almost been killed in a mugging. "Get back in the real world, you'll be shocked to find there are many two legged 'animals' out on the streets—thanks to many judges who think as you."

The Court's decision did not result in Darden's immediate execution. He filed two more federal habeas corpus petitions and brought a final stay application to the Supreme Court in March 1988 after the governor of Florida signed a seventh death warrant. By then, Darden was fifty-four years old and was the longest-serving death-row inmate in the country. His case had become the focus of an international campaign, with Pope John Paul II and Andrei Sakharov, the noted Russian dissident, among those who raised their voices on his behalf. The Court denied his application on March 7, 1988, with Blackmun, Brennan, and Marshall dissenting. Recalling his dissenting opinion two years earlier, Blackmun wrote: "I was not persuaded then, and I am not persuaded now, that petitioner Willie Jasper Darden received a fair trial in the Florida courts. A person should not be condemned to die and be executed under any system of justice in this country without a fair trial." On March 14, the ABC News program *Nightline* broadcast an interview in which Darden said: "I'm going to holler, I'm going to holler loud, and I'm not going to stop hollering, and I'll be hollering, 'Innocent, innocent, innocent' if they put me in the chair." He was executed the next day.

Blackmun's discomfort with the death penalty grew with each passing term. At the start of the 1986 term, the Court heard arguments in *McCleskey v. Kemp*, a challenge to Georgia's administration of capital punishment that was based on a statistical study showing sharp racial disparities; those who killed whites, as had the defendant in the case, Warren McCleskey, were 4.3 times more likely to receive a death sentence than those whose victims were black. Writing for a 5-to-4 majority in the decision that was issued in April 1987, Powell said the statistics did not show sufficient evidence of intentional discrimination. Blackmun wrote, in dissent, that "the Court's rejection of McCleskey's equal protection claims is a far cry from the 'sensitive inquiry' mandated by the Constitution." He had changed his mind since his first encounter, on the Eighth Circuit, with a statistical challenge to the death penalty. Back in 1968, Blackmun had rejected an appeal based on a study that demonstrated racial disparities in the way Arkansas imposed the death penalty for rape. A black man convicted of raping a white woman had a 50 percent chance of receiving a death sentence, compared to a 14 percent chance if the rape victim was black. "We are not yet ready to condemn and upset the result reached in every case of a Negro rape defendant in the state of Arkansas on the basis of broad theories of social and statistical injustice," Blackmun had written in his majority opinion in the case, *Maxwell v. Bishop.* Now, nearly twenty years later, he concluded that these studies had merit.

In 1993 the Court ruled, in *Herrera v. Collins,* that a state death-row inmate presenting belated evidence of innocence is not ordinarily entitled to a writ of habeas corpus. Leonel Herrera, who had been on death row in Texas since 1982 for killing two police officers, tried to reopen his case by offering evidence that his brother, who had since died, had been the killer. Herrera turned to federal court because Texas law provided only sixty days after conviction for filing a motion for a new trial based on recently discovered evidence. He argued that his claim of "actual innocence" made his case different from the ordinary complaint of errors at trial. Rehnquist, who had succeeded Burger as chief justice, wrote for the Court that even if a "truly persuasive demonstration of actual innocence," presented long after the fact, might theoretically entitle a defendant to habeas corpus, Herrera's evidence fell far short of that "extraordinarily high" threshold.

Blackmun announced his dissent from the bench. Added to his legal analysis was a bitter final paragraph. "I have voiced disappointment over this Court's obvious eagerness to do away with any restriction on the States' power to execute whomever and however they please," he said. "I have also expressed doubts about whether, in the absence of such restrictions, capital punishment remains constitutional at all. Of one thing, however, I am certain. Just as an execution without adequate safeguards is unacceptable, so too is an execution when the condemned prisoner can prove that he is innocent. The execution of a person who can show that he is innocent comes perilously close to simple murder."

In his *Herrera* dissent, Blackmun had come close to disavowing capital punishment entirely. But still he did not cross the line, as his longtime colleagues William Brennan and Thurgood Marshall had done. Their blanket opposition to capital punishment, expressed in every death penalty case in which they voted, was based on their view that "the death penalty is in all circumstances cruel and unusual punishment forbidden by the Eighth and Fourteenth Amendments."

But during the summer after the *Herrera* decision, one of Blackmun's law clerks, Andrew H. Schapiro, came to him with a proposal. "You have on occasion this Term expressed frustration with the Court's capital jurisprudence, and have suggested more generally that the death penalty itself may be invalid," Schapiro wrote. "I want to outline briefly in this memo why I believe the time has come to abandon the effort to craft a constitutional death penalty." His eight-page memo traced the tortured effort, in the Court's post-*Furman* death penalty decisions, to ensure that juries consider each defendant's case on an individual basis without, at the same time, reintroducing the arbitrariness that had led to *Furman* in the first place. Some members of the Court evidently believed those conflicting goals could be reconciled, Schapiro said, but he doubted that Blackmun was among them. "I can only guess what twenty years of experience has shown you in that regard, but even a single Term's set of executions has left me extremely dubious of that proposition," he wrote. "Twenty years of applying the Eighth Amendment to the death penalty has demonstrated that the rationalizing enterprise has failed. Efforts to fine-tune the machinery of death cannot succeed, because a process sufficiently accurate with respect to individual circumstances requires so much discretion as to be unacceptably arbitrary, and a process that can avoid being unacceptably arbitrary can never be accurate enough with respect to individual circumstances."

Schapiro told Blackmun that "of the justices on this Court, you are uniquely situated to assess the system's performance. You have spent thirty years on the federal bench." True, he said, Blackmun had refused, by his votes in *Furman* and *Gregg,* to invalidate the death penalty. "As particular aspects of the system were challenged, however, you expressed a firm desire to ensure its fairness and a deep concern about the ever-accelerating rush to execution." According to Schapiro, "it would be entirely consistent with your history on this issue to conclude that the death penalty finally has proven itself constitutionally unworkable." Reverting to his role as law clerk rather than counselor, Schapiro provided a list of recent "worthwhile articles" and ended with: "I hope you find this of use."

Blackmun was ready. Frankfurter's credo, to which he had clung since his first term on the Court, no longer sustained him, and the promise of fairness to which he had subscribed in *Gregg v. Georgia* had proven empty. He had never forgotten his experience in the case of *Pope v. United States,* from his Eighth Circuit days, when he had meant to speak his mind but had held back in the face of criticism. Now, approaching his eighty-fifth birthday, it was time. He told his law clerks to go ahead and draft an opinion by which he would renounce the death penalty.

Andrew Schapiro's clerkship year was expiring, so the task of completing what he had begun passed to the four clerks who were arriving to start the 1993 term. The project, known in the Blackmun chambers as the "death penalty dissent," had two parts: to draft an opinion and then to select a case—a "vehicle," they called it—in which the opinion could be used to best effect. Blackmun wanted to get the opinion out by the end of 1993, but the task of finding the right case—an ordinary death penalty appeal that raised no exotic issues and that the Court would predictably deny—proved harder than expected. The opinion would then be filed as a dissent. The Blackmun chambers wanted to be ready when the moment arrived.

The clerks collaborated, with Michelle L. Alexander doing most of the drafting. By late October, she had a draft to show Blackmun. "This is a very personal dissent, and I have struggled to adopt your 'voice' to the best of my ability," she wrote. "I have tried to put myself achieved in the administration of the death penalty, see

McCleskey v. Kemp, 481 U. S. 279, 313 ~~n.37~~) n.37 (1987), the Court

has chosen to deregulate the entire enterprise, replacing ~~(in any area)~~

substantive constitutional requirements with mere aesthetics, and

abdicating its statutorily and constitutionally imposed duty to

provide meaningful judicial oversight to the administration of

death by ~~the States.~~ *considerable governmental authority,*

From this day forward, I w~~i~~ll *shall* no longer tinker with the

machinery of death. For more than twenty *20* years I have struggled, — *(endeavored — indeed, have)*

Blackmun edits a law clerk's draft of his "death penalty dissent."

in your shoes and write a dissent that would reflect the wisdom you have gained, and the frustration you have endured, as a result of twenty years of enforcing the death penalty on this Court." Aside from some minor editing, Blackmun accepted nearly everything. Alexander had written: "From this day forward, I will no longer tinker with the machinery of death." Blackmun changed "forward" to "on," but Alexander persuaded him to change it back. Blackmun changed "will" to "shall" and later reversed the word order for emphasis: "From this day forward, I no longer shall tinker with the machinery of death." It became one of the best-known lines ever to be attached to his name.

The opinion Blackmun and his clerks worked on was generic: "In the early hours of the morning, ___ will be executed by the State of ___. Intravenous tubes attached to his arms will carry the instrument of death. . . ." Meanwhile, the clerks kept track of the death penalty cases reaching the docket. A petition for certiorari arrived from Bruce E. Callins, a Texan who had killed a bar patron during a robbery. The very ordinariness of the case commended it.

On February 22, 1994, the Court denied review in *Callins v. Collins,* over Blackmun's twenty-two-page solitary dissent. Callins was scheduled to be executed by the state of Texas at one o'clock the next morning, Blackmun's opinion began. "Intravenous tubes attached to his arms will carry the instrument of death, a toxic fluid designed specifically for the purpose of killing human beings. The witnesses, standing a few feet away, will behold Callins, no longer a defendant, an appellant, or a petitioner, but a man, strapped to a gurney, and seconds away from extinction."

The opinion continued: "Twenty years have passed since this Court declared that the death penalty must be imposed fairly, and with reasonable consistency, or not at all, see *Furman v. Georgia,* and, despite the effort of the States and courts to devise legal formulas and procedural rules to meet this daunting challenge, the death penalty remains fraught with arbitrariness, discrimination, caprice, and mistake." Blackmun's position was subtly different from that of Marshall and Brennan. For him, capital punishment remained conceptually acceptable, at the level of theory; he had decided that in practice, it could not be made to operate in a constitutionally acceptable way. "Rather than continue to coddle the Court's delusion that the desired level of fairness has been achieved and the need for regulation eviscerated, I feel morally and intellectually obligated simply to concede that the death penalty experiment has failed."

After the opinion was released, Justice Brennan, frail and four years into retirement, telephoned and left word for Blackmun: thank you for "the present."

The Court clerk's office asked Blackmun how he wished to phrase the standard dissent that he would now be attaching to every death penalty decision. His law clerk suggested something very close to the wording that had been used by Brennan and Marshall: "Adhering to my view that the death penalty in all cases is violative of the Eighth Amendment." But that wording did not convey the nuance Blackmun wanted. "Adhering to my view that the death penalty cannot be imposed fairly within the constraints of the Constitution" is what he told the clerk's office to use.

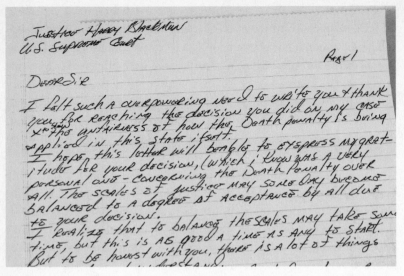

Bruce E. Callins writes from the Texas death row to thank Blackmun for his effort.

Six months later, Blackmun received a letter from Bruce Callins's lawyer, Brent E. Newton of the Texas Resource Center, in Houston. Callins had won a temporary reprieve in state court and was still fighting his execution. The lawyer enclosed a letter from the inmate, written in ballpoint pen on lined paper torn from a pad.

Dear Sir:
I felt such a overpowering need to write you & thank you for reaching the decision you did on my case & to show the unfairness of how the death penalty is being applied in this state itself. I hope this letter will be able to express my gratitude for your decision (which I know was a very personal one—covering the death penalty over all. The scales of justice may someday become balanced to a degree of acceptance by all due to your decision.

The inmate told Blackmun that "I hope that you are at peace within yourself for doing as you did."

Blackmun thanked the lawyer for writing; he did not reply to Callins. In June 1997, Callins's sister, Nadeline Robinson, wrote from Dallas to tell Blackmun that her brother had been executed on May 21. "He had mentioned your name to me a number of times with great respect for you as an individual."

8

SAVING *ROE*

AMONG THE REALITIES of Harry Blackmun's life on the Court were the periodic death threats from antiabortion militants. Late at night on February 28, 1985, a bullet shattered the window of his apartment in Rosslyn, Virginia, just across the Potomac River from the Georgetown neighborhood of the capital. At first, the natural assumption was that the shooting was an act of antiabortion terrorism. Although the police quickly concluded that the shot was a random one, fired from a distance and not aimed at Blackmun, the incident led to a significant change in the justice's daily routine. The Supreme Court police deemed it no longer prudent for him to drive himself to work. No longer would he be parking his Volkswagen Beetle among the larger cars in the Supreme Court garage. While it was convenient to be driven the few miles back and forth in a Court car, it was also a daily reminder to Blackmun of the impact that *Roe v. Wade* had had on his life.

Not that he needed to be reminded: during the mid-1980s, *Roe* remained at the center of the political and judicial landscape. New abortion cases, each one a potential test of the Court's continued loyalty to *Roe,* were making their way through the judicial pipeline, and the six justices who had joined Blackmun's opinion in 1973 were aging, retiring, or drifting away. First to go had been William O. Douglas, in 1975, but Blackmun held out hope for his replacement, John Paul Stevens, who had joined Blackmun in dissent in the Hyde Amendment case in

Blackmun kept this newspaper cartoon on the wall of his chambers, a reminder of the 1985 shooting incident.

1980 and might well vote against any attempt to overturn *Roe.* Potter Stewart's retirement in 1981 had brought Sandra Day O'Connor to the Court, and her vote in *Akron v. Akron Center for Reproductive Health* (1983) did not augur well for Blackmun or for *Roe.* As the 1985 term got under way, another blow came, this one from Warren Burger.

A new abortion case had come before the Court, *Thornburgh v. American College of Obstetricians and Gynecologists,* a challenge to Pennsylvania's Abortion Control Act of 1982. The law differed in minor respects from the Akron, Ohio, ordinance the Court had struck down, but the *Thornburgh* case was essentially a repeat of the first, with two exceptions: the Reagan administration asked the Court directly to over-rule *Roe,* and Burger, after years of coyness and hand-wringing, finally abandoned the decision. Blackmun wrote a note for his files: "We reaffirm the general principles of *Roe v. Wade,* a 7 to 2 decision of the Court from which the Chief Justice—for reasons of his own—has now defected." Predictable as it was, Blackmun still found the defection hard to accept. When he received a draft of Byron White's dissenting opinion, he wrote in the margin: "Well, he says about what there is to say. He does not like *Roe*. SOC & WHR [O'Connor and Rehnquist] can join this. But how can the CJ, who joined *Roe*?"

Burger did not, in fact, sign White's dissent, but filed one of his own. He said it was "astounding" that the Court was invalidating Pennsylvania's informed consent provision that required clinics to provide descriptions of fetal development at two-week intervals and to inform women of the "detrimental physical and psychological effects" of abortion. "Can it possibly be that the Court is saying that the Constitution *forbids* the communication of such critical information to a woman?" Burger asked. "We have already passed the point at which abortion is available merely on demand. If the statute at issue here is to be invalidated, the 'demand' will not even have to be the result of an informed choice." If the Court meant what it said, Burger concluded, "I agree that we should reexamine *Roe*."

O'Connor also filed her own dissent. "Suffice it to say that I dispute not only the wisdom but also the legitimacy of the Court's attempt to discredit and pre-empt state abortion regulation regardless of the interests it serves and the impact it has," she wrote. Next to this passage in her draft opinion, Blackmun placed an exclamation point and the comment: "She is just against abortion."

Blackmun wrote the opinion for the shrinking majority, now barely holding on at 5 to 4. His original draft contained explicit criticism of the solicitor general's brief that urged the reversal of *Roe*. Noting that Pennsylvania was arguing more narrowly that its regulations were consistent with *Roe*, Blackmun wrote: "For the Solicitor General to ask us to discard a line of major constitutional rulings in a case where no party has made a similar request is, to say the least, unusual. We decline his invitation." Stevens and Powell urged Blackmun to omit the direct criticism. The opinion should simply speak for itself, Powell said: "My judgment is that even those who will applaud your decision will find the reaffirmation of *Roe v. Wade* that is implicit throughout your opinion and explicit on page 10 to be sufficient."

Blackmun accepted the advice. When the *Thornburgh* decision was issued, on June 11, 1986, the last paragraph of the majority opinion rephrased the rationale for *Roe* in language that was more directly centered on the woman than any of the Court's previous formulations. "Our cases long have recognized that the Constitution embodies a promise that a certain private sphere of individual liberty will be kept largely beyond the reach of government," the paragraph began. "That promise extends to women as well as to men. Few decisions are more personal and intimate, more properly private, or more basic to individual dignity and autonomy, than a woman's decision—with the guidance of her physician and within the limits specified in *Roe*—whether to end her pregnancy. A woman's right to make that choice freely is fundamental. Any other result, in our view, would protect inadequately a central part of the sphere of liberty that our law guarantees equally to all."

Burger's defection was but a harbinger of even more profound change that would come to the Court in the next few years and put *Roe* more deeply in doubt. Burger announced his retirement six days after the *Thornburgh* decision (and in the midst of the wrangling over the *Darden* death penalty case). President Reagan named Rehnquist to succeed Burger as chief justice and chose Antonin Scalia, a respected and sharp-tongued conservative from the District of Columbia Circuit, to fill the vacancy created by Rehnquist's elevation. Given Burger's defection in *Thornburgh* from the *Roe* majority, the new appointment was likely to be a substitution of one anti-*Roe* vote for another, leaving Blackmun's majority narrow but still firm.

By this point, the friendship between Burger and Blackmun had vanished. The letters and cards had petered out. "WEB announces retirement," Blackmun recorded laconically in his "chronology" for June 17, 1986. In place of the nonexistent correspondence, Blackmun now filed away unflattering articles about Burger. In 1989, he declined an invitation from the William Mitchell College of Law, Burger's alma mater, to join the retired chief justice in St. Paul for a ceremony breaking ground for the Warren E. Burger Law Library. In 1993, the former best man congratulated Warren and Vera Burger on their sixtieth wedding anniversary, recalling their departure on their honeymoon. "I well remember when the little car took off down the road on a fairly bright November day bound for Washington, D.C.," he wrote. "Look at all that you have accomplished since then." It took more than a month for Burger to respond. He had been in the hospital, he said. "Tempus doth fugit and we may as well get used to it. Best wishes for the season." The letter was signed by his secretary.

The relationship between Harry Blackmun and Warren Burger was complex, multilayered, encrusted with a lifetime of shared experiences and mutual expectations. And its dissolution was equally complex: not one or several events, not clashes over particular cases, but an accretion of disappointments, like water dripping on stone and, over the years, wearing it away. The expectations on both sides may well have been unrealistic. Having spent the crucial decades of their adult lives a thousand miles apart, each carried an image of the other that no longer reflected reality. Blackmun may have believed, based on how warmly his advice was solicited and received during Burger's solitary first year on the Court, that he would be his old friend's confidant and helpmate there. But he arrived at the Court as the junior justice, struggling through a difficult adjustment, while Burger had already found his equilibrium and was moving ahead on his own agenda.

Burger had clearly believed that Blackmun would enlist in his causes, but his agenda was not Blackmun's. It did not take long for that fact to become clear. According to data compiled by Joseph F. Kobylka, a political scientist at Southern Methodist University, Blackmun voted with Burger in 87.5 percent of the closely divided cases during his first five terms (1970 to 1975) and with Brennan, the Court's leading liberal, in only 13 percent. By the next five-year period, 1975 to 1980, Blackmun was joining Brennan in 54.5 percent of the divided cases and Burger in 45.5 percent. During the final five years that he and Burger served together, he joined Brennan in 70.6 percent of the close cases and Burger in only 32.4 percent.

Yet ideological divergence alone is an unsatisfactory explanation for the rupture of a lifelong friendship. For instance, Blackmun maintained a warm relationship with William Rehnquist while agreeing with him on very few of the issues that mattered most to both of them. Neither took their disagreements personally. But Blackmun perceived that Burger did. "I do not know what he expected, but surely he could not have anticipated that I would be an ideological clone," Blackmun wrote in a brief reminiscence of Burger for the *William Mitchell Law Review* in 1996. "He knew me better than that. But when disagreement came, his disappointment was evident and not concealed."

For his part, Blackmun, always thin-skinned, was hypersensitive to slights from Burger, perhaps perceiving slights when, in the rough-and-tumble of daily combat, nothing particularly personal was intended. The difficult 1977 term offered one striking example. As a result of his prostate surgery, Blackmun had missed the December argument session, and consequently received no assignments from that two-week period. In April he sent a private letter to Burger listing the number of majority opinion assignments that each member of the Court had received during the term so far. Burger and Stevens had the most, fourteen each. Blackmun had the fewest, with ten. Brennan, who had also missed an argument session, had more opinions than he did. The low number, he told Burger, "makes me feel somewhat humiliated not only personally, but publicly." In June of that term, with the *Bakke* decision still pending, Burger sent his customary note on the anniversary of Blackmun's arrival at the Court. This year, the tone was different. "Cheer up—there can't be any more as tough as this one!" Burger said.

Instances of perceived slights also appeared in Blackmun's "chronology." "CJ for the first time very cool," Blackmun recorded at the beginning of the 1980 term. "CJ picks on me at conference," he wrote on February 15, 1985. Since each year's chronology included, at most, a few dozen entries, many of them dealing with family and public events rather than with the Court, Blackmun's inclusion of these remarks indicated how easily hurt he was by any indication from Burger of a lack of regard. He was acutely sensitive to the "Minnesota Twin" label that the press had been quick to pin on him when he joined the Court. Years later, he would reflect on the moniker and say he had expected it, "particularly as it was widely assumed that I would vote constantly with the new Chief Justice. I warned the Chief of this, but he seemed disinterested. The appellation, of course, died of its own weight, as the Chief's vote and mine came to diverge. It never had validity anyway." Or perhaps, for a brief time that Blackmun cared not to remember, it did. If *Roe v. Wade* had been his baptism, the break with Burger was his coming of age. Now, with the chief in retirement, Blackmun was truly on his own.

A year after Burger's departure, another significant retirement occurred—that of Lewis Powell, whose moderate demeanor and institutional skills had helped build coalitions on the Court and who had been a solid vote for *Roe* and its progeny for fourteen years. For this seat, Reagan nominated Judge Robert H. Bork of the District of Columbia Circuit. He was a powerful advocate for the view that any deviation by the Supreme Court from the text of the Constitution or the intent of its framers was illegitimate. Testifying before a Senate Judiciary subcommittee in 1981, Bork had denounced *Roe v. Wade* as "an unconstitutional decision, a serious and wholly unjustifiable usurpation of state legislative authority," a perspective that, he claimed, was shared by "almost all constitutional scholars." Bork also rejected *Griswold v. Connecticut,* the 1965 birth control decision that had established the framework for the constitutional right to privacy. Time appeared to be running out for *Roe v. Wade.*

The debate over Bork's nomination consumed Washington during the summer and well into the fall of 1987. Finally, on October 23, the Senate defeated the nomination by a vote of 58 to 42, the widest margin of defeat for any Supreme Court nominee in history. In no small measure, the Bork battle had been a referendum on modern constitutional law. Once the anti-Bork forces persuaded the public that confirmation would mean "turning back the clock" on civil rights and abortion rights, the nomination had become a lost cause.

But there was still a vacancy to fill. Reagan's next nominee, Judge Douglas H. Ginsburg of the D.C. Circuit, quickly withdrew his name after allegations surfaced that he had smoked marijuana during his days as a professor at Harvard Law School. The third choice, Anthony M. Kennedy, presented a profile much different from Bork's. A soft-spoken Californian, he had compiled a moderately conservative

> Dear Tony:
>
> You have my sincere congratulations on your nomination as an Associate Justice of the Supreme Court of the United States. You should, I feel, have comparatively little difficulty on the road to confirmation. I look forward to your being here. Your chambers will be next to mine. Please do not hesitate to let my secretaries or me know if we ever can be of assistance to you.
>
> The transition will be a major one, but Dottie and I survived. You will, too.
>
> I told Richard that I am a founding member of a very exclusive organization called "the good old #3 club." You now qualify for this unusual but worthy distinction. It happened to me in 1970, and it has served to keep me a little humble whenever Dottie suggests that I might be getting too "judgie." The other characters around here do not qualify.
>
> Good luck in the days ahead. You will enjoy being here and will make a worthwhile contribution to what is a common calling for us.
>
> Sincerely,

Blackmun welcomes Anthony M. Kennedy into the "good old #3 club."

record during thirteen years on the Ninth Circuit Court of Appeals. Although he did not take a position on *Roe* during his confirmation hearing, Kennedy endorsed *Griswold* as well as the right to privacy, which he described as "a zone of liberty, a zone of protection, a line that's drawn where the individual can tell the Government, 'Beyond this line you may not go.'" Some liberal scholars who had opposed Bork endorsed the new nominee. On February 3, 1988, the Senate confirmed Kennedy by a vote of 97 to 0.

Even before Kennedy's confirmation, Blackmun had welcomed him as another "old number three." On November 12, 1987, the day after Kennedy's nomination, Blackmun had written to the man who, he evidently assumed, would be his new colleague. "I am a founding member of a very exclusive organization called 'the good old #3 club,'" he told Kennedy, whom he had not met. "You now qualify for this unusual but worthy distinction. It happened to me in 1970, and it has served to keep me a little humble whenever Dottie suggests that I might be getting too 'judgie.' The other characters around here do not qualify."

Within a year, abortion was back before the Court. Blackmun's old court, the Eighth Circuit, had invalidated a Missouri abortion law that declared, in its preamble, that "the life of each human being begins at conception." Among other provisions, the Missouri law barred abortions in public facilities, prohibited public employees from performing them, and required extensive prenatal testing for viability if a doctor believed a pregnancy was at least twenty weeks along. Missouri's Supreme Court appeal was backed by the Reagan administration, which urged the Court to use the case, *Webster v. Reproductive Health Services,* as a vehicle for overturning *Roe.*

"Missouri is Missouri and will push and push," Blackmun wrote in notes to himself before the argument, which was scheduled for April 26, 1989. He was offended by the brief the new Bush Administration had filed, citing his 1985 opinion in the federalism case, *Garcia v. San Antonio Metropolitan Transit Authority,* as proof that "in similar circumstances, the Court has 'not hesitated' to overrule a prior interpretation of the Constitution." Blackmun wrote to himself, "This is a personal attack on me."

Blackmun expected the worst. In his "chronology" for the term, he referred to O'Connor, Scalia, and Kennedy as "the Reagan crowd cabal." Adding Rehnquist and White to the list, he wrote: "The 5 coalesce." As he made notes on the Missouri case before the argument, he sketched out the dissenting opinion he fully expected to be writing soon: "16 years . . . An entire generation of women. To overthrow would create the chaos created by Prohibition. It will turn thousands of American women into criminals & their MD's too. Or court will return us to the back alley, and a number of these women, an unconscionable number, will die. And it is not on any collision course with itself. 23½ weeks is it." By that last comment he rejected O'Connor's prediction, in her *Akron v. Akron Center for Reproductive Health, Inc.* dissent, that medical advances would inevitably push the date of fetal viability back toward conception. In the margin of his notes, Blackmun jotted one more: "hold for writing, not in conference." He would wait to see what happened, and he would keep his counsel.

"All very tense in the courtroom," Blackmun wrote in the notes he took during the oral argument. The justices' conference, two days later, ended in some ambiguity. It was not certain, after all, that the Court would use the *Webster* case to overturn *Roe*. According to Rehnquist, the media had blown the case "out of proportion." *Roe* did not have to be overturned in order to reinstate the Missouri law, he said, and he did not propose to do so. O'Connor agreed. She would "adhere to what I have written," she said, but would go no further in this case.

White and Scalia made clear that they would be happy to see *Roe* overturned, but—given the absence of a readily apparent majority for that result—neither committed himself to pushing for it. White said he would "join four"—provide a fifth vote—to "overrule *Roe* or modify." Otherwise, he would join Rehnquist in simply upholding the challenged provisions of the Missouri law. Scalia agreed. "Perhaps we need not reach the issue here." Nonetheless, "I may have to confront *Roe*. I just disagree with it." The decision did not get better as time went on, he said, adding that he "would set it aside when we can."

The newest justice gave the fullest account of his views. As an adjunct professor at the McGeorge School of Law in Sacramento, Anthony Kennedy had taught *Roe* for fifteen years; as a matter of "pure stare decisis," he said, he would leave it alone. But the decision "continues to do damage to the Court and judicial review and conception of judges' proper role." The Court should "return this debate to the democratic process," where the rights of women would be protected. "Reach the merits and alter the method and structure of *Roe*," he recommended. From the discussion, Blackmun counted five votes to uphold the Missouri law. As to the question of *Roe*'s fate, he drew no conclusion.

The draft majority opinion that Rehnquist circulated on May 25 left no doubt as to where he stood. While the opinion noted that the case "affords us no occasion to revisit the holding of *Roe*," Rehnquist proceeded to do precisely that: "We do not see why the State's interest in protecting potential human life should come into existence only at the point of viability." Throughout pregnancy, a regulation that "reasonably furthers the state's interest in protecting potential human life" should be upheld.

Stevens, J. ±

O'Connor, J. —

Scalia, J. —

Kennedy, J. —

Blackmun's notes during the conference after the argument in the *Webster* abortion case, April 1989

Stevens, who had observed during the conference that the *Webster* case provided no occasion to revisit *Roe* and that the "administration did us a disservice by raising the issue," reacted vigorously. "If a simple showing that a state regulation 'reasonably furthers the state interest in protecting potential human life' is enough to justify an abortion regulation, the woman's interest in making the abortion decision apparently is given no weight at all," Stevens wrote to Rehnquist, with copies to the others. "A tax on abortions, a requirement that the pregnant woman must be able to stand on her head for fifteen minutes before she can have an abortion, or a criminal prohibition would each satisfy your test." He concluded: "As you know, I am not in favor of overruling *Roe v. Wade,* but if the deed is to be done I would rather see the Court give the case a decent burial instead of tossing it out the window of a fast-moving caboose."

Blackmun, who placed check marks in the margins throughout Stevens's letter, did not engage Rehnquist in debate. Instead, he turned to work on his dissent. It followed the outline he had made six weeks earlier. "Today, a majority of this Court disserves the people of this Nation, and especially the millions of women who have lived and come of age in the 16 years since the decision in *Roe v. Wade,*" the draft began. He had revised a more vitriolic opening proposed by his law clerk Edward P. Lazarus, who had begun his version with these words: "Today, a bare majority of this Court perpetrates a fraud."

Although Rehnquist had assumed that he was writing for a majority in *Webster v. Reproductive Health Services,* he had failed to persuade Sandra Day O'Connor that the moment had come to revisit *Roe.* On June 23, nearly a month after the chief justice circulated his opinion, O'Connor distributed her own. While she agreed that the Missouri provisions were constitutional, such a conclusion, she believed, was consistent with the Court's precedents, including *Roe* itself. "Where there is no need to decide a constitutional question, it is a venerable principle of this Court's adjudicatory processes not to do so," O'Connor wrote. "When the constitutional invalidity of a State's abortion statute actually turns on the constitutional validity of *Roe v. Wade,* there will be time enough to reexamine *Roe.* And to do so carefully."

Scalia was furious. Three days later, he circulated a separate opinion of his own. He agreed with Blackmun that the Rehnquist opinion would effectively overrule *Roe,* but he wanted the Court to do so explicitly. O'Connor's view that the rule of judicial restraint should stay the Court's hand "cannot be taken seriously," Scalia wrote, venting his anger at the fact that unexpectedly, almost inexplicably, *Roe v. Wade* had survived.

Blackmun amended his dissenting opinion to reflect Rehnquist's failure to hold a majority. "Today, *Roe v. Wade,* and the fundamental constitutional right of women to decide whether to terminate a pregnancy, survive but are not secure," he wrote.

Initially, his final paragraph had begun: "With *Roe*'s passing, a political revolution in the law takes hold." To replace it, Lazarus proposed a substitute: "Today, the law of abortion stands perfectly still. Today, the women of this Nation retain the liberty to control their destinies. Oh, but an icy wind blows." Once again, Blackmun took up his editing pencil as he worked out the final sentences of the dissent, which he announced from the bench on the term's final day, July 3, 1989. "For today, at least, the law of abortion stands undisturbed. For today, the women of this Nation still retain the liberty to control their destinies. But the signs are evident and very ominous, and a chill wind blows."

The term was over, but there was no letup in the flow of abortion cases. The issue for the next term to consider was parental involvement in a teenager's decision to have an abortion, a question with which the Court had grappled since shortly after deciding *Roe.* Earlier decisions had established that if a state required parental consent, it had to offer a "judicial bypass," the opportunity for a minor to go before a judge and demonstrate either that she was mature enough to make the decision on her own or that an abortion was in her best interest. The new cases posed the question of the necessity and adequacy of bypass procedures for statutes that did not give parents a veto power but that did require doctors to notify one or both parents before performing an abortion.

At issue in one of the cases, *Ohio v. Akron Center for Reproductive Health,* was a state law requiring notice to one parent, with a bypass

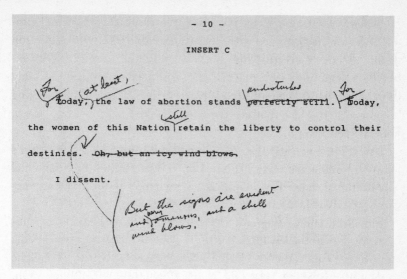

- 10 -

INSERT C

For (at least,)
~~Today,~~ the law of abortion stands *undisturbed* ~~perfectly still~~. *For* ~~Today,~~

(still)
the women of this Nation retain the liberty to control their

destinies. ~~Oh, but an icy wind blows.~~

I dissent.

But the signs are evident and very ominous, and a chill wind blows.

Blackmun edits his dissent in *Webster v. Reproductive Health Services.*

procedure that the federal appeals court in Cincinnati had found constitutionally inadequate. The Supreme Court reversed the lower court's ruling, by a vote of 6 to 3, with Blackmun, Brennan, and Marshall dissenting. Kennedy, assigned the majority opinion, included in his draft a final paragraph that stepped back from the legal analysis to offer some reflections in an unusually personal tone. "A free and enlightened society may decide that each of its members should attain a clearer, more tolerant understanding of the profound philosophic choices confronted by a woman who is considering whether to seek an abortion," Kennedy wrote. "Her decision will embrace her own destiny and personal dignity, and the origins of the other human life that lie within the embryo. The State is entitled to assume that, for most of its people, the beginnings of that understanding will be within the family, society's most intimate association. . . . It would deny all dignity to the family to say that the State cannot take this reasonable step in regulating its health professions to ensure that, in most cases, a young woman will receive guidance and understanding from a parent."

Blackmun found Kennedy's language "paternalistic." He circulated a dissent, calling the paragraph "hyperbole that can have but one purpose: to further incite an American press, public, and pulpit already inflamed by the pronouncement made by a plurality of this Court last Term in *Webster v. Reproductive Health Services*." On June 21, 1990, he received a handwritten letter from Kennedy.

Dear Harry,

After much hesitation, I decided it best for our collegial relation and, I hope, mutual respect to tell you that I harbor deep resentment at your paragraph on page 17 in *Ohio v. Akron Center*. You say my hyperbole is to incite an inflamed public. To write with that purpose would be a violation of my judicial duty.

I am still struggling with the whole abortion issue and thought it proper to convey this in what I wrote. . . . I do not question the depth of your compassion and understanding, but neither do I yield to the charge that my own is somehow a mask for some improper purpose.

In any event, though it is late in the term, I thought you would want to hear this; and perhaps it will prompt you to reconsider what is a most unfair attribution of motives not consonant with the conscientious discharge of my office.

Yours, Tony

Blackmun replied the next day. "In the thought that it will help to assuage your feelings," he said, he would remove the word "purpose" and substitute "result." He concluded: "This should help, but, of course, I do not know whether it will."

In the end, two members of Kennedy's majority, O'Connor and Stevens, also objected to his paragraph of personal reflections and declined to sign it. While the core of Kennedy's opinion commanded six votes, he had only four for the final section.

At the same time, the Court was considering *Hodgson v. Minnesota*, a case challenging a Minnesota law that required notice to both parents and contained a judicial bypass provision designed to take effect only if a court found one to be necessary. The law was being challenged by

Dr. Jane Hodgson, the Minneapolis gynecologist and Mayo Clinic alumna who had defied Minnesota's abortion law twenty years earlier when she performed an abortion on a patient who had contracted German measles. The Eighth Circuit ruled that the statute would be unconstitutional without a judicial bypass but that the bypass provision saved it.

Only half the children in Minnesota lived with both biological parents, but the law made no allowance for that fact, requiring notice to noncustodial parents and even to those who had never lived with the girl. At the justices' conference after the argument, O'Connor expressed discomfort with the law's sweep. She said the rigid two-parent requirement "entails risk" to the pregnant teenager and failed to meet even a "rationality standard," the lowest standard of judicial review. Kennedy agreed that "two-parent notice does increase the risk" but noted that the law provided exemptions for minors who faced danger or abuse in the home: "The law stands ready to protect the child." He also pointed out that the bypass procedure, which was in effect as the result of the lower court's ruling, seemed to be working as designed, with judges granting all but a handful of requests to authorize abortions without parental notice.

With O'Connor in the middle, there were five votes for each of two holdings: first, that the two-parent notice requirement, alone, was unconstitutional; second, that the law was valid with the judicial bypass. O'Connor joined Stevens, Brennan, Marshall, and Blackmun for the first, and Rehnquist, Scalia, White, and Kennedy for the second. It was a muddled outcome, but one thing was clear: for the first time in nearly nine years on the Court, O'Connor had found an abortion regulation that she could not accept. But Blackmun had little time to savor the possible implications of that development. Less than a month later, on July 20, 1990, the eighty-four-year-old William Brennan announced his retirement, effective immediately. He had suffered a small stroke while on vacation during the Court's summer recess. One of the most stalwart of *Roe*'s remaining defenders was gone.

Three days later, President George H. W. Bush named David H. Souter, a fifty-year-old New Hampshire Republican and protégé of

Senator Warren Rudman, to succeed Brennan. In seven years on the New Hampshire Supreme Court, Souter had encountered no abortion cases, and relatively few constitutional cases of any kind. Only two months earlier, he had been confirmed to the First Circuit Court of Appeals, in Boston, but he had barely moved into his chambers there and had not yet participated in any cases. He was, in other words, still an unknown. Liberals were wary but somewhat reassured by his testimony at his confirmation hearing, during which he avoided any comment on *Roe* but expressed support for *Griswold* and described the doctrine of stare decisis as "a bedrock necessity if we are going to have in our judicial systems anything that can be called the rule of law." Souter was no Brennan, clearly, but neither was he at war with the trajectory of modern constitutional law. He was no Bork, either. On October 2, 1990, as the new term was getting under way, the Senate confirmed Souter's nomination by a vote of 90 to 9.

An abortion-related case was already on the docket for the 1990 term. On October 30, the Court heard argument in *Rust v. Sullivan,* a challenge to a regulation that prohibited employees of family-planning clinics receiving federal money from counseling their patients on abortion. The ban extended even to answering a patient's direct questions. The plaintiffs—Planned Parenthood and the city and state of New York—argued that the regulation had not been authorized by Congress and that it violated the free speech rights of the clinic employees.

The discussion at conference was something of a surprise. Souter joined Rehnquist, White, Scalia, and Kennedy to uphold the regulation. O'Connor dissented, on the grounds that the underlying statute, a public health law that provided family-planning grants, "cannot be reasonably interpreted" to authorize the restriction. Blackmun, Marshall, and Stevens believed that the regulation was unconstitutional, although Stevens, like O'Connor, did not think it was necessary to reach the constitutional issue. Blackmun began working on a dissent.

The outcome of the case remained in doubt for some months. Although Rehnquist began circulating a draft of his majority opinion in December, Souter did not formally join it until May. He asked Rehnquist to add a paragraph making clear that in other contexts, such as a university that receives federal grants, acceptance of government money does not carry with it acceptance of government control over the recipients' speech. The chief justice complied.

Blackmun's dissent was bitter. "While technically leaving intact the fundamental right protected by *Roe v. Wade,* the Court, through a relentlessly formalistic catechism, once again has rendered the right's substance nugatory," he said in a final paragraph. Citing the *Webster* decision from two terms earlier, he continued: "This is a course nearly as noxious as overruling *Roe* directly, for if a right is found to be unenforceable, even against flagrant attempts by government to circumvent it, then it ceases to be a right at all. This, I fear, may be the effect of today's decision."

Stevens tried to warn Blackmun that his tone could alienate rather than attract wavering colleagues. "I think it may be poor strategy to assume that either Sandra and David—and certainly not both—are prepared to overrule *Roe v. Wade,*" Stevens wrote in a private note to Blackmun. "Moreover, I really think that the opinion does not do quite that much damage because, at least for the woman who can afford medical treatment, the right remains intact." Blackmun decided against softening his final paragraph. Marshall joined his dissent, but Stevens omitted the final paragraph from his "join." *Rust v. Sullivan* was issued May 23, 1991. A month later came another blow to Blackmun, as Thurgood Marshall announced his retirement. Of the original *Roe* majority, only Blackmun remained. He could count on Stevens, but it was not clear who could save the right to abortion now.

To replace Marshall, President George H. W. Bush nominated Clarence Thomas, a judge on the District of Columbia Circuit who had served in the Reagan administration as chairman of the Equal Employment Opportunity Commission and was one of the country's most prominent black conservatives. At his contentious confirmation hearing, Thomas testified that he had never expressed a view on *Roe v. Wade,* even in private, and that he had no personal opinion of the ruling. "The Clarence Thomas hearings!" was all Blackmun wrote in his "chronology of significant events." During the hearing, attention shifted abruptly from Thomas's judicial philosophy to his personal behavior after Anita Hill, a lawyer who had worked for him at the employment commission, accused him of sexual harassment. He vigorously denied the charge and was finally confirmed, on October 15, 1991, by a vote of 52 to 48, the closest margin in the twentieth century for a successful Supreme Court nominee. Three weeks later, another abortion case arrived at the Court, *Planned Parenthood v. Casey*. With the new makeup of the Court, *Roe* had never looked so imperiled.

At issue was Pennsylvania's Abortion Control Act, a law similar to many the Court had reviewed in the past. The Third Circuit Court of Appeals, in Philadelphia, had struck down a provision requiring a husband to be notified before a married woman could obtain an abortion. But the court had upheld provisions that the Supreme Court had found unacceptable in the past: a twenty-four-hour waiting period and an informed consent provision. In upholding these provisions, the appeals court had declared that abortion regulations were no longer to be subjected to "strict scrutiny" because, it explained, there were no longer five votes on the Supreme Court for the highest standard of review. Rather, the appeals court said, Justice O'Connor's "undue burden" test was all that could command five votes and was consequently "the law of the land." In her first vote in an abortion case, her dissenting opinion in the first *Akron* case in 1983 (*Akron v. Akron Center for Reproductive Health*), O'Connor had proposed that even in early pregnancy, any regulation that did not "unduly burden the right to seek an abortion" should be upheld as long as the state could show a "rational basis" for it. This standard, which O'Connor reiterated in subsequent cases, had marked a retreat from the Court's insistence in *Roe v. Wade* that regulations other than those intended to protect a pregnant woman's health were unconstitutional before fetal viability, the point at which the state's interest in the fetus became "compelling." While the Third Circuit's ruling in the new case was thus a challenge to the Supreme Court to affirm *Roe* or dilute it in favor of O'Connor's lesser standard, it was far from clear that the Court, if it took the case, would stop there.

The appeals court had issued its decision on October 21, 1991; therefore, the abortion-rights groups had until late January to file their petition for certiorari. On that schedule, the Supreme Court would likely hear the case, if it chose to hear it at all, in October 1992 at the earliest, and would decide it the following spring. But the abortion-rights groups had a different strategy. If *Roe v. Wade* was to be over-ruled, as seemed highly likely, it might as well happen sooner—while President Bush was in the middle of a reelection campaign—rather than later. Let the 1992 presidential election be a referendum on the right to abortion. With that scenario in mind, the plaintiffs spent barely two weeks drafting their petition and filed it on November 7, in time for the Court to add the case to its calendar for decision during the current term. Whether the justices chose to do so would, of course, be up to them.

The petition for certiorari went to the Court's first conference after the Christmas recess, on January 10, 1992. White, Stevens, and Scalia provided three definite votes to grant. Blackmun "passed," without speaking or casting a vote. His conference notes do not provide a rea-son, but he may have been deeply conflicted over whether *Roe*'s inter-ests would be better served by granting the case or by denying it, by joining the issue then or by deferring the ultimate confrontation to some indefinite future. Souter voted tentatively to grant, but asked that the case be carried over until the next week. That set off alarm bells in the Blackmun chambers, where the law clerks, if not the justice himself, were persuaded that the election-year strategy of the abortion-rights groups was correct and that *Roe* should meet its fate as quickly as possi-ble. Perhaps Souter—a Bush appointee, after all—was stalling in an ef-fort to delay the grant long enough to put the argument over until next October and push the eventual decision off until after Election Day.

Blackmun's clerk Stephanie A. Dangel investigated and reported back that this was not the new justice's goal. "Unlike the Chief and SOC," Souter was "not concerned about the election," she said. His clerk Peter Rubin had told her that while Souter did "hope that he would have the summer to think about this question," he had re-quested the delay so that he might rephrase the question presented in the petition "in such a way as to *avoid* overruling *Roe*." The Planned Parenthood petition, in challenging the Third Circuit's analysis, had posed a provocative question designed to force the Court to confront the ultimate issue: "Has the Supreme Court overruled *Roe v. Wade*, holding that a woman's right to choose abortion is a fundamental right protected by the United States Constitution?" Souter was evidently looking for a way to avoid pushing the Court to the limit.

The day before the second conference, Blackmun's clerks urged him to do what he could to make sure the case was not delayed further. "We feel strongly that the case should be heard this spring," they said. Before the January 10 conference, one of the clerks, Molly S. McUsic, had given him a more extensive memo on the timing issue. "If you believe that there are enough votes on the Court now to overturn *Roe*, it would be better to do it this year before the election and give women the opportunity to vote their outrage," she advised. Blackmun was now persuaded; he would vote to grant. In the event of further delay, the clerks drafted an unusual "dissent from the relisting" for Blackmun to submit. "I feel that this Court stands less tall when it defers decision for political reasons," the draft said. The dissent did not prove necessary.

On January 17, the Court voted in conference to grant both the Planned Parenthood petition and the cross-petition of Governor Robert P. Casey of Pennsylvania, who was appealing the invalidation of the husbands' notification provision. The Casey petition asked the Court explicitly to overturn *Roe*. There were seven votes to grant the petitions—all except Rehnquist and O'Connor. All nine justices agreed with the substitute questions, as proposed by Souter and edited by Stevens. They were studiedly neutral: Did the court of appeals err when it upheld the waiting period, informed consent, and several other provisions of the Pennsylvania law? Did it err when it struck down the spousal notice provision?

The Court issued its order granting the case on January 21, 1992, the eve of *Roe*'s nineteenth anniversary. Tens of thousands of antiabortion demonstrators were gathering in Washington for what had become an annual march, and 350 people were arrested for trying to block the entrances to two local abortion clinics. The contrast between the quiet at the Court and the violence in the streets of

Washington—the latter a vivid reminder of the ferocious emotions still surrounding the issue after all these years—was striking.

Planned Parenthood v. Casey was argued on April 22. As in the *Webster* case, three years earlier, it was not clear from the discussion at the postargument conference whether *Roe v. Wade* itself was on the table. To uphold the waiting period and informed consent provisions, Rehnquist said, the Court would have to overrule the *Akron v. Akron Center for Reproductive Health* and *Thornburgh* decisions that had struck down nearly identical requirements. In Blackmun's view, a majority was prepared to do at least that much. Rehnquist also indicated his support for the spousal notice provision: "The father has sufficient interest, so the state can require that he be notified." Stevens called the provision "outrageous," and O'Connor and Souter also appeared to oppose it. While there was uncertainty as to the details, Blackmun knew he would be writing a dissent. "I, of course, shall be writing in these cases," he said in a memo that he sent to colleagues several days later.

On May 27, Rehnquist circulated a twenty-seven-page draft majority opinion. "Wow! Pretty extreme!" Blackmun wrote in the margin of the first page. All the Pennsylvania law's provisions were upheld. Further, Rehnquist said the Court had been wrong to find "any all-encompassing right of privacy" in the Constitution: "The Court was mistaken in *Roe* when it classified a woman's decision to terminate her pregnancy as a 'fundamental right' that could be abridged only in a manner which withstood 'strict scrutiny.'" As in his *Webster* opinion, he maintained that "States may regulate abortion procedures in ways rationally related to a legitimate state interest." If Rehnquist actually spoke for a majority, *Roe* would effectively be overruled. Blackmun continued working on his dissent.

Then, suddenly, everything changed. Two days later, a handwritten note arrived from Anthony Kennedy.

Dear Harry,

I need to see you as soon as you have a few free moments. I want to tell you about some developments in Planned Parenthood

v. Casey, and at least part of what I say should come as welcome news.

If today is not convenient, I will be here tomorrow. Please give me a call when you are free.

Yours, Tony

When the two met the following day, Kennedy revealed that he, O'Connor, and Souter had been meeting privately and were jointly drafting an opinion that, far from overruling *Roe,* would save it—not in its details, but in its essence. The *Akron v. Akron Center for Reproductive Health* and *Thornburgh* decisions would be overruled; the waiting period and informed consent provisions of the Pennsylvania law would be held constitutional. The spousal notice provision would fall. The opinion would adopt O'Connor's "undue burden" test, substituting it for *Roe*'s trimester approach. But the constitutional right to abortion was preserved.

"Roe sound," Blackmun wrote on a small piece of pink Supreme Court memo paper after his meeting with Kennedy ended. The choice of this slightly old-fashioned word was significant. To a lawyer, "sound" conveys not just survival but correctness and legitimacy. *Roe* had survived its test in the *Webster* case, only because of O'Connor's unwillingness to confront the issue at that time. But now five justices would reaffirm—would affirmatively declare—the constitutional basis of a right to abortion. On the pink paper, Blackmun drew a schematic lineup of the Court. As he had done for years, he referred to each justice by a single initial, but since there were now three justices whose last names began with "S," he had worked out his own code. Reflecting Kennedy's news, he placed the justices into three groups: "CJ-W-T-N" (Rehnquist, White, Thomas, and Scalia—"Nino") were in one camp; "O-K-D" (O'Connor, Kennedy, and Souter—"David") in another; "X-S" (himself and Stevens) in the third. *Roe* was sound, by a vote of 5 to 4.

O'Connor, Kennedy, and Souter circulated their sixty-one-page draft on June 3. Immediately, Stevens said he would join "substantial parts of it," and after a week, Blackmun told the three justices the same

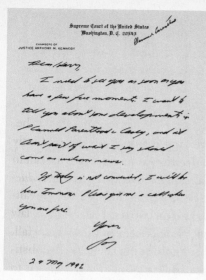

Anthony Kennedy alerts Blackmun to an unexpected development in *Planned Parenthood v. Casey.*

Blackmun's note summarizes Kennedy's news and diagrams the Court's new abortion lineup. "The 3"—Kennedy, O'Connor, and Souter—now propose to declare "*Roe* sound, though not the trimester system."

thing. Stevens began negotiating over the specifics, on his behalf and Blackmun's. If the three would move their criticism of the trimester framework from the beginning of their opinion to the end, Stevens said, he and Blackmun would be able to join the first three sections and thus express unified support for the basic principle. The three agreed. The first section now contained a strong, unambiguous statement: "After considering the fundamental constitutional questions resolved by *Roe*, principles of institutional integrity, and the rule of *stare decisis*, we are led to conclude this: the essential holding of *Roe v. Wade* should be retained and once again reaffirmed." When Blackmun came to this passage, he made a big check with the comment "this OK."

Blackmun still needed to speak for himself. The lower courts would have to apply the new opinion, and Stephanie A. Dangel, Blackmun's clerk, said it was important for him to convey the message that even though he did not favor the "undue burden" test, it was a standard with teeth that the lower courts could properly invoke to strike down future abortion restrictions. "I think the tone in this section cannot be harsh—it must be the more consoling tone of an older, wiser uncle, whose views on abortion have evolved as he has faced the issue over and over again," Dangel said.

Now, she continued, Blackmun faced the choice of whether to make a direct link between the upcoming election and the future of abortion. It is "the one substantive decision you will have to make," she said. She had drafted such a final paragraph and urged him to use it, although Stevens was advising otherwise. "You are the person American women look to in order to find out what is really happening in this case," Dangel told Blackmun. "I can't help but fear that without that last paragraph women are going to think they can rest easy, because *Roe* has been reaffirmed once and for all."

Blackmun was persuaded. He thanked Stevens for his advice but he would keep the final section, as drafted. The two sides of the Court were "worlds apart," Blackmun wrote, "and yet in another sense, the distance between the two approaches is short—the distance is but a single vote.

"I am 83 years old. I cannot remain on this Court forever, and when I do step down, the confirmation process for my successor may well focus on the issue before us today. That, I regret, may be exactly where the choice between the two worlds will be made."

It was June 29, 1992, nineteen years after *Roe,* three years after Blackmun had warned, in his *Webster* dissent, that "a chill wind blows." For now, at least, the air was calm. He, and *Roe,* had come to a safe place. There might well be battles ahead, but they would be fought by others. Blackmun knew his own journey was nearing its end. Marking Election Day in his "chronology," he wrote: "Now what for HAB?"

9

IMPROBABLE ICON

HARRY BLACKMUN'S LAW clerk was right: by 1992, he had indeed become "the person American women look to" as a barometer for the status of abortion rights. His identification with *Roe v. Wade* had long since bestowed on him the mantle of champion not only of abortion rights but of women's rights in general. On Harry Blackmun's improbable journey, becoming a feminist icon was perhaps the most improbable destination of all. To those who lionized him late in his career, his presence in the place of honor on their podiums and at their testimonial dinners may have seemed inevitable, but it was not. The long shadow of *Roe v. Wade* obscured the ambiguities, the halting and tentative footprints that marked Blackmun's path toward a full embrace of women's rights. Even the reality of *Roe* itself, the extent to which its author's focus was on doctors rather than on women, was largely lost to myth and the mists of memory. Blackmun's summary paragraph, the sentences that expressed his own view of what he intended *Roe v. Wade* to accomplish, did not appear in the tribute programs.

> The decision vindicates the right of the physician to administer medical treatment according to his professional judgment up to the points where important state interests provide compelling justifications for intervention. Up to those points, the abortion decision in all its aspects is inherently, and primarily,

a medical decision, and basic responsibility for it must rest
with the physician.

These were not the words that speakers read when they introduced
the aging justice to standing ovations.

The fact is that Blackmun worked hard to understand the issues
that the feminist movement began bringing to the Court in the early
1970s—harder, in a way, than he worked on the abortion and death
penalty cases. Those cases presented issues that Blackmun understood on an instinctive level: the utility of safe and legal abortion, the
societal degradation of capital punishment. His challenge was to find
a stance and a voice with which to address the issues as a judge. The
sex discrimination cases were different. They questioned policies that
often appeared sensible and reasonable. Far from being matters of life
and death, the specific complaints the plaintiffs in these cases brought
to the Court often seemed petty, almost self-indulgent, and Blackmun
could easily have turned away. He did not always give the answers that
the women's-rights advocates wanted to hear. But his attention was
unwavering.

It was not that Blackmun was hostile to women's rights. He
scarcely could have been, with one of his daughters having earned a
law degree and another a doctorate in psychology. While the family
lived in Rochester, Dottie Blackmun was a partner in a business called
Designing Women, which designed and made women's clothes to order. At a time when many men of his generation disregarded women's
professional accomplishments, Blackmun appreciated them. By the
time he retired, he had hired more female law clerks than the other sitting justices combined, and during his last ten years on the Court, a
majority of his clerks were women.

On the other hand, he was not particularly engaged by the women's
movement, which was becoming increasingly visible in the early 1970s
and was making the courts a focus of its efforts to eliminate barriers to
women's full participation in society. The Supreme Court was the target
of a carefully constructed campaign designed to create a body of law that
would make official discrimination on the basis of sex as unacceptable as

discrimination on the basis of race. The litigation effort made Blackmun wary and a little grumpy; the cases struck him as contrived, the arguments overbearing. In one of the earliest cases, *Reed v. Reed*, the Court was asked to invalidate an Idaho law that gave automatic preference to men over women in being selected as administrators of estates. Ruth Bader Ginsburg, then a law professor and an attorney for the American Civil Liberties Union, worked on the brief for the appellant, Sally Reed, although she did not argue the case. The Supreme Court appeal had a purpose beyond resolving the sad family dispute that it presented, a battle between the estranged parents of an adopted son who died by suicide and left no will. The goal of the appeal was to persuade the justices to apply the Fourteenth Amendment's guarantee of equal protection to sex discrimination and to declare for the first time that, as with race, official policies that discriminated on the basis of sex were presumptively unconstitutional.

Blackmun's initial response was one of skepticism. "The case, of course, is a test case and much ado about nothing," he wrote in his memo to himself before the argument in October 1971. "Apparently the estate in question amounts to less than $1,000. Why, then, should there be this great battle over the appointment of an administrator for this small estate, and why should four courts struggle with the underlying issue when so little is involved?"

He was also impatient with the brief that Ginsburg had filed, calling it "mildly offensive and arrogant" and "a very lengthy brief filled with emotion and historical context about the inferior status of women." At sixty-eight pages, the brief was indeed longer than most, although not drastically so, providing dramatically worded background information for what Blackmun saw as "a very simple little case." The Idaho probate code commanded the "subordination of women," the brief said. "American women have been stigmatized historically as an inferior class and are today subject to pervasive discrimination. . . . A person born female continues to be branded inferior for this congenital and unalterable condition of birth."

But even as he criticized the ACLU brief, Blackmun was attentive to it; almost despite himself, his response to the case was shaped by

No. 70-4 - Reed v. Reed, Administrator

Well, here we are with a very simple little case raising the issue of statutory discrimination between the sexes. An Idaho statute repealed as of July 1, 1971 provides for preferences in the appointment of the administrator of a decedent's estate. One category includes the father or mother. The decedent here is an adopted child, and both parents survive. Another statute provides that, of several persons equally entitled to administer, the male must be preferred to the female, and relative of the whole to those of the half blood. The Idaho probate court appointed the father under this statute. The mother appealed to the district court, and that tribunal held the statute unconstitutional as violative, among other things, of the Fourteenth Amendment. The father then appealed to the Idaho Supreme Court, and they unanimously reversed.

This is all there is to the case. The ACLU, on behalf of the appellant mother here, has filed a very lengthy brief filled with emotion and historical context about the inferior status of women. Its first point is that the statute creates a

Blackmun's negative response to Ruth Bader Ginsburg's brief in an early sex discrimination case, *Reed v. Reed*

the appellant's presentation. His preargument memo makes that clear. Barely four pages long, internally inconsistent in places, the memo is the record of an interior monologue that shows a judge wrestling with his instincts and biases in order to get to the heart of a challenging legal problem. "All in all, I am inclined to feel that sex can be considered a suspect classification just as race," he wrote.

This does not mean that every statute which makes a distinction based on sex is automatically invalid. It merely sets as the starting point the proposition that such a distinction is suspect and strong justification is needed to uphold it. There can be no question that women have been held down in the past in almost every area.

The Fourteenth Amendment approach is a fascinating one. After all, this statute stands or falls on the Fourteenth Amendment. Clearly, however, it was not intended to meet any sex differentiation when it was adopted a hundred years ago. One certainly cannot argue that had this case arisen in 1890, the Court would have held that the Fourteenth Amendment has no possible application to it. The logic of this may be a little difficult to refute. On the other hand, my own feeling is that these constitutional provisions must have some flexibility and expansiveness in them as, in theory, we ourselves progress and expand in our concepts of equality.

In the end, Blackmun persuaded himself that the Idaho law was unconstitutional. "We certainly could write a fairly brief and simple opinion accomplishing that very result. I would hope that we do not get into a long and emotional discussion about women's rights. I think we can avoid a good bit of the historical material that fills the appellant's brief at such great length."

The Court's unanimous decision in *Reed v. Reed,* in a six-page opinion written by Burger and issued barely a month after the argument, reflected little of the deeper debate. Idaho's preference for men over women to administer estates was arbitrary and unreasonable, the Court held. Because the law did not bear a "rational relationship to a state objective," it failed to meet even the most forgiving standard of judicial review and thus made it unnecessary for the justices to decide what standard should be applied in a closer case.

The Court was only one front in the struggle for women's rights. The following year, 1972, Congress passed the Equal Rights Amendment to the Constitution and sent it to the states for ratification. If three-quarters of the states ratified it, the amendment would accomplish what the ACLU brief had asked the Court to do in *Reed v. Reed:* make discrimination against women subject to strict judicial scrutiny, the most rigorous standard of review. Soon, the highly charged politics of the amendment and the uncertainty within the Court about how far and how fast to move the law converged in a new case. *Frontiero v. Richardson* began as a suit by a female Air Force officer for the right to claim her husband as a dependent for the purpose of obtaining housing and medical benefits, although the husband was not financially dependent on her. Under the laws governing military benefits, a male service member could automatically claim his wife as a dependent, regardless of their relative circumstances, while a woman could claim her husband only if she contributed more than half of his support.

"This must be stricken down," Blackmun wrote in his notes before the argument on January 17, 1973. "The question is by what route and how far." That, indeed, was the question: whether to make sex, like race, a "suspect classification," an outcome that would accomplish the goals of the Equal Rights Amendment by judicial decree and make its ratification unnecessary. The battle inside the Court went back and forth for weeks. All the justices except Rehnquist agreed that the distinction between male and female service members was unsustainable. Brennan wanted to use the case to establish strict scrutiny, arguing that *Reed v. Reed* had already done so, implicitly, in its rejection of administrative convenience as a sufficient justification for the state's policy. If the Court had truly applied the lowest standard of review in *Reed,* Brennan said, it would have accepted the state's justification as at least rational; therefore, no matter what the Court said, it rejected, in that case, the low-level, rational-basis test. Burger, who had written the *Reed* opinion, vigorously disagreed. "Some may construe *Reed* as supporting the 'suspect' view but I do not," he wrote to Brennan. "The author of *Reed* never remotely contemplated such a broad concept but then a lot of people sire off-spring unintended!"

In *Frontiero v. Richardson,* Ruth Bader Ginsburg filed a seventy-page brief for the ACLU, urging the Court to adopt strict scrutiny. Blackmun's law clerk James W. Ziglar found the brief persuasive and urged the justice to "go the whole route and find that sex is a 'suspect classification.'" But Blackmun resisted. There was no need to reach the question, he said, because rational basis was sufficient to strike down a distinction that lacked even a reasonable justification. "This case has afforded me a good bit of difficulty," he told Brennan on March 5, 1973. "After some struggle, I have now concluded that it is not advisable, and certainly not necessary, for us to reach out in this case to hold that sex, like race and national origin and alienage, is a suspect classification. It seems to me that *Reed v. Reed* is ample precedent here and is all we need and that we should not, by this case, enter the arena of the proposed Equal Rights Amendment."

Brennan, who was monitoring the amendment's sagging fortunes, argued that the time for the Court to act was now. The Equal Rights Amendment had already been rejected by eleven state legislatures, he pointed out, and two more would be sufficient to kill the measure. Douglas, White, and Marshall agreed, but Brennan could not find a fifth vote for strict scrutiny in the *Frontiero* case. Blackmun joined Powell, Burger, and Stewart in concurring only in the judgment that military benefits had to be equal. Rehnquist, alone, dissented, with a one-sentence statement expressing his agreement with the lower court's judgment that the distinction between military men and women was administratively and economically rational. So while the Court voted 8 to 1 that the distinction in benefits was unconstitutional, the *Frontiero* decision, issued on May 14, 1973, did not establish a new standard of review for sex discrimination.

The cases came quickly, but they did not get any easier for the nine men of the Supreme Court, who were being asked to see impermissible discrimination in government policies that had long been accepted as sensible and inoffensive. Mandatory pregnancy leaves for public school teachers, for example, were extremely common; teachers were typically required to take unpaid leave, without a guarantee of reemployment, by the fifth month of pregnancy, when their condition was likely to become apparent to their students. Suddenly, these policies were being challenged in lawsuits around the country. Two cases reached the Court early in the 1973 term, one from Cleveland and one from Chesterfield County, Virginia.

The mandatory leave policies struck most of the justices as unfair, but it was not obvious what exactly, as a constitutional matter, was wrong with them. In his preargument memo in *Cleveland Board of Education v. LaFleur,* Blackmun explored a variety of theories. Did the case even present an issue of sex discrimination? he wondered:

It is easy to say initially that any regulation which relates to pregnancy is automatically and per se sex discriminatory. I am not at all certain that this is necessarily so. Actually, what the regulation does is to draw distinctions between classes of women, that is, those who are pregnant and those who are not pregnant, rather than between male and female. It is somewhat similar to an Army regulation requiring that enlisted men be shaved and not wear beards or mustaches. Such a regulation discriminates between one class of men and another class of men, and not as between men and women.

On the other hand, it is only women who become pregnant. Thus, it is easy to say that a regulation directed to pregnancy is discriminatory as against women.

But having raised this possibility, Blackmun rejected it:

This approach, although initially attractive, is logically unsound. I think I personally prefer to classify in still another way. My initial preference is between those who are disqualified to teach for reasons of pregnancy and those who are disqualified for other medically indicated reasons. If one is to draw this type of classification, then a proper required leave must be determined on an ad hoc basis, that is, in the light of the facts of each case. We certainly determine leave for any temporary disability on this approach. Is pregnancy really different? It is different, of course, in that pregnancy is to be classified as voluntary rather than involuntary, whereas another health disability is probably to be classed as involuntary rather than as voluntary. Even so, elective surgery has its voluntary aspects. One thinks immediately of prostatectomy, cosmetic surgery, hemorrhoidectomy, tonsils and adenoids, teeth extractions and the like, all of which are often done at a time convenient to the patient rather than a matter of immediate compulsion.

If this classification approach is sound, then I think it follows that a mandatory leave policy for pregnancy, particularly when it is inflexible as is the Cleveland system, is violative of equal protection.

Blackmun ultimately joined the majority opinion, by Potter Stewart, that invalidated the leave policy, not on equal protection grounds but as a violation of due process. A single decision, issued January 21, 1974, resolved the Cleveland case as well as *Cohen v. Chesterfield County School Board*. The excessive and arbitrary mandatory leave, Stewart wrote, placed a "heavy burden" on the exercise of a woman's constitutionally protected liberty to decide to have a child. The word *discrimination* did not appear in the Court's opinion. A Court that had confidently announced the right to abortion only a year earlier now appeared almost tongue-tied in the presence of pregnant schoolteachers.

During the same 1973 term, the Court heard another of Ruth Ginsburg's cases. *Kahn v. Shevin* was her second Supreme Court argument, following the *Frontiero* case. Representing a male plaintiff this time, Ginsburg challenged a Florida law that gave an annual, automatic $500 property tax exemption to widows but not to widowers. The Florida Supreme Court had upheld the law, finding that it bore a "fair and substantial relation" to the goal of reducing "the disparity between the economic capabilities of a man and a woman." To a majority of the Court, including Blackmun, that reasoning seemed to produce a sensible outcome. The justice graded Ginsburg's argument as a B—better than the C+ he awarded her in *Frontiero* and higher than the C he gave her opponent in the Florida case, an assistant state attorney general. "Too smart" was Blackmun's comment on Ginsburg's argument. Brennan, Marshall, and White voted to apply strict scrutiny and overturn the Florida law, but Blackmun agreed with Douglas that the law was "reasonably designed to further the state policy of cushioning the financial impact of spousal loss upon the sex for which that loss imposes a disproportionately heavy burden," as Douglas wrote in an almost cursory four-page opinion.

But Blackmun objected to a footnote in Douglas's draft. "Gender has never been rejected as an impermissible classification in all instances," the footnote said. "When we had before us *Roe v. Wade*, the Court proceeded to treat the abortion problem on the basis that it pertained to the prerogative of the mother in which the putative father had no concern."

Blackmun told Douglas that he was "somewhat disturbed" by the reference to *Roe*. Directing Douglas to footnote 67 in *Roe,* which said that the Court was deferring consideration of "the father's rights, if any exist in the constitutional context," until the issue was specifically raised in a future case, Blackmun found his colleague's comment "not consistent" with the Court's decision to avoid the subject. In response, Douglas called Blackmun's point "very well taken" and removed the footnote. Blackmun then signed the opinion upholding the Florida law.

That it took fourteen months after *Roe v. Wade* for any mention of abortion to seep into the Court's evolving conversation about sex discrimination showed how unrelated the two subjects appeared to the justices. Eventually, reproductive rights would be seen by many as an indispensable component of women's rights, but it was a connection that Blackmun, for one, had not yet made. Even two years later, when the question of whether a state could give a man veto power over his wife's decision to have an abortion finally reached the Court, in *Planned Parenthood of Missouri v. Danforth,* Blackmun's tone, in his majority opinion finding a husband's veto unconstitutional, was detached. In preparing for the oral argument in *Danforth,* he read a brief that framed the issue in overtly feminist terms; in his preargument memo, he dismissed the presentation. "This brief, of course, presents the extreme on the female side," he said. The Court's abortion cases and sex discrimination cases would continue to run on parallel tracks for years, with no connection established between them.

Ruth Ginsburg's next argument came during the 1975 term, in *Weinberger v. Wiesenfeld,* a challenge to a provision of the Social Security Act making still another distinction between men and women in calculating government benefits. If a male wage earner died, both his widow and their minor children would receive benefits. But if the wage earner was a woman, benefits would go only to her children and not to her husband. The difference was based on the government's assumption that a father was more likely to be a family's primary breadwinner and would not need the support of his wife's Social Security benefits. Ginsburg's client was a man, Stephen C. Wiesenfeld, a self-employed consultant whose wife, a schoolteacher, provided most of the couple's income. She died in childbirth, and he applied for and received Social Security survivors' benefits for their son but was told that, as a man, he was not eligible for benefits himself.

The case initially struck Blackmun as little different from *Kahn v. Shevin*, in which the Court, just a year earlier, had rejected Ginsburg's argument on behalf of a male client and upheld Florida's preferential tax exemption. "Widows with children are more likely to need social security benefits than widowers with children," Blackmun wrote in his preargument memo. If the federal law was to be changed, he continued, the Court should leave the responsibility to Congress: "That is where it belongs really if changing times are equalizing incomes as between men and women. . . . So long as the objective of the differential is to alleviate need, I suspect that we shall have to hold that the differential is not unconstitutional."

Blackmun's law clerk Richard Blumenthal agreed. "No doubt, the statute's provision rests on a stereotype—a stereotype that has greatly diminished validity," Blumenthal wrote in his analysis of the case. "But the basis for the differential treatment appears to be a ground of difference—income disparities—that has a fair and substantial relation to the statute's objective. . . . Women are more likely to be needy, even in this increasingly liberated age. The statute would seem to be constitutional."

But as he listened to the oral argument, Blackmun began to change his mind. He gave Ginsburg a B and wrote, in his notes, that "it is a good clean case, factually. The dif. [his abbreviation, most likely for *differential*] does seem rather useless." At the postargument conference he voted, initially, to uphold the law; eventually, however, he joined Brennan's majority opinion that found the sex-based distinction "entirely irrational."

Although Blackmun had not taken a leading role in any of the sex discrimination cases, he got the opportunity, in another 1975 case, to add his voice to the growing body of law. *Stanton v. Stanton,* argued as the Court was considering *Wiesenfeld,* was a modest case, a child-support dispute from Utah, where, by law, girls attained the age of majority at eighteen and boys at twenty-one. When a divorced father stopped paying child support for his daughter when she turned eighteen, the mother went to court to ask for support until both the daughter and the son reached twenty-one. The divorce court's decision that the father's obligation to the daughter ended at age eighteen but continued until the son turned twenty-one was then upheld by the Utah Supreme Court, which found a "reasonable basis" for the differential: girls matured earlier and married younger; boys had a greater need for education. That these were "old notions" did not make the law unconstitutional, the Utah court said.

After reading the briefs, Blackmun decided that "we have some kind of violation of equal protection here," as he wrote in his preargument notes. "One is hard put to find any reason for the justification of the age differential." As a result, he said, there would be no need to apply any standard more searching than rational basis. The decision "should be in the context of child support without wandering all over the lot with respect to different ages for males and females in other contexts."

Blackmun was assigned the majority opinion. He concluded that "under any test—compelling state interest, or rational basis, or something in between," the Utah law violated the constitutional guarantee of equal protection. *Stanton v. Stanton* did not make new law, but it did something else that, for the moment, was almost as important: it placed the Court on record as declaring that society's stereotypes were not, by any standard, a legitimate basis for official policies that treated men and women differently. "A child, male or female, is still a child," Blackmun wrote. "No longer is the female destined solely for the home and the rearing of the family, and only the male for the marketplace and the world of ideas. Women's activities and responsibilities are increasing and expanding. Co-education is a fact, not a rarity. The presence of women in business, in the professions, in government and, indeed, in all walks of life where education is a desirable, if not always a necessary, antecedent is apparent and a proper subject of judicial notice. If a specified age of minority is required for the boy in order to assure him parental support while he attains his education and training, so, too, is it for the girl."

The next term, in *Craig v. Boren,* the Court formally adopted an intermediate level of scrutiny in sex discrimination cases, neither as forgiving as rational-basis review nor as searching as strict scrutiny. The 7-to-2 decision, issued on December 20, 1976, invalidated an Oklahoma law that allowed the sale of 3.2 percent beer to women beginning at age eighteen but required men to be twenty-one. Blackmun joined Brennan's majority opinion, holding that "classifications by gender must serve important governmental objectives and must be substantially related to achievement of those objectives." But finally resolving the question of which standard to use in sex discrimination cases did not make the cases any easier.

Ginsburg next came before the Court in the 1976 term, in *Califano v. Goldfarb,* another Social Security benefits case. It was Ginsburg's fifth oral argument before the Court, and she was a familiar figure. "In red & red ribbon today," Blackmun wrote in his argument notes. Once again, Ginsburg's client was a man, Leon Goldfarb—a retired federal employee whose wife had died after having paid Social Security taxes for twenty-five years as a secretary in the New York City public school system. Goldfarb was denied widower's benefits because his wife had not provided half of his support. Widows were automatically eligible for benefits, without the need to show dependency.

The Court was growing weary. "Here we go again," Blackmun wrote in his memo. At the conference after the argument, Potter Stewart said he was "getting disturbed by these Social Security Act cases. The whole body of law is filled with arbitrary line drawing. Many tear jerkers, as this case is not." John Paul Stevens also expressed great difficulty in deciding how to vote. Blackmun had no difficulty in upholding the law. While the case had obvious similarities to *Wiesenfeld,* it was not controlled by that precedent, Blackmun wrote in his memo to himself, because the welfare of a child was not in the mix, as it had been in the earlier case. "My basic philosophy in this general area is to leave this kind of thing to Congress. I dislike to dignify every classification with constitutional rigidity. If the classification is wrong, the Congress should rectify it. I think there is some rationality in requiring the surviving husband to prove dependency and in foregoing that for the surviving wife; comparatively few people are going to be involved anyway." Nonetheless, the Court voted, 5 to 4, to overturn the statute. Blackmun joined Rehnquist, Burger, and Stewart in dissent.

In 1979 the Court considered the validity of a Massachusetts law that bestowed on veterans an absolute, lifetime preference in state employment. Under the law, any veteran who qualified for a state civil service job was hired in preference to any nonveteran. There was no dispute that the law placed women at a severe disadvantage. A federal district court, finding that the law favored a class from which women had traditionally been excluded, declared it unconstitutional. "The preference here *is* extreme and annoying," Blackmun wrote to himself, preparing for the argument in *Personnel Administrator of Massachusetts v. Feeney*. On the other hand, the law was "neutral on its face." And, the state argued, it served two valid purposes: to promote enlistment and to help veterans readjust. Blackmun searched for a way to rationalize upholding the law. "Women's role in the military is increasing, so the difference will lessen," he wrote. On a law clerk's memo on the case, he penciled a question: "Do we dare to disturb the veterans' preference?" He voted with six others to uphold the law; only Marshall and Brennan dissented.

All seven justices in the majority then received a letter from Kathryn Christenson, a woman in St. Peter, Minnesota. "Women, since the time of Eve, have been told to bear children instead of arms," Christenson wrote. "Now, finally, many enlightened societies are realizing that waging war and raising families aren't the only appropriate work for adult men and women, respectively. However, you have decreed that men may continue to be rewarded for having played the role in which society has long cast them, while women are, in effect, penalized, particularly when compared with the opposite sex." Blackmun did not respond. Two years later, in *Rostker v. Goldberg*, he voted, with the 6-to-3 majority, to uphold the military's male-only draft registration.

When Sandra Day O'Connor took her seat on the Supreme Court in 1981, it was far from clear what difference the Court's first woman might make on the issue of sex discrimination. O'Connor did not present herself as a feminist, and Blackmun did not expect her to be one. The first test came in her first term, when the Court accepted *Mississippi University for Women v. Hogan,* a challenge to the constitutionality of a state-supported single-sex college. Joe Hogan, a male student who was denied admission to the university's nursing school, sued and won a ruling from the federal appeals court in New Orleans that the state had not proved that the exclusion of men from the nursing program was "substantially related to an important governmental objective." The university appealed.

Blackmun's law clerk Kit Kinports urged him to vote to affirm the decision and admit men to the nursing program. "The opinion need not be a sweeping one," she wrote reassuringly, noting that there would be "very little practical impact" because there were only two other single-sex state universities in the country, Texas Women's University and the all-male Virginia Military Institute. The university's defense was "based on outdated, stereotypical attitudes about women that the Court has repeatedly refused to accept," she added.

Blackmun was unpersuaded. He would vote to reverse "despite my clerks," he wrote in his preargument memo. "True, the statute is a stereotype and the case is sticky," he said, but "I am not qualified to say single sex situation cannot be educationally sound, though it is controversial."

During the oral argument, on March 22, 1982, Blackmun jotted down his prediction that O'Connor would join him in a vote to reverse. He was wrong. At the conference, O'Connor announced that she agreed with Brennan that the admissions policy was unconstitutional. The Court was closely divided, with Brennan, O'Connor, White, Marshall, and Stevens voting to affirm and Burger, Powell, and Rehnquist agreeing with Blackmun to reverse. *Mississippi University for Women v. Hogan* engaged the Court on an emotional level that had been missing from the cases parsing the finer points of Social Security law. "We all belong to all-male organizations," Burger observed. Powell, who had graduated from Washington and Lee University when it was all-male, said that "all Powells have gone to single-sex schools."

They were "perfectly legitimate," he said, noting that the plaintiff in this case could enroll in any of the Mississippi system's other nursing programs. He was not, therefore, the victim of sex discrimination.

The Court's 5-to-4 division held. Assigned by Brennan to write the majority opinion, O'Connor circulated a draft that emphasized the university's anachronistic mission. The exclusion of men from admission to the nursing school "tends to perpetuate the stereotyped view of nursing as an exclusively woman's job," she said, and "makes the assumption that nursing is a field for women a self-fulfilling prophecy." Quoting from its 1884 charter, O'Connor noted that the university's stated purpose was to train "the girls of the state" in such subjects as needlework, bookkeeping, stenography, telegraphy, and typewriting, "to fit them for the practical affairs of life."

"A bit of a low blow," Blackmun wrote in the margin of O'Connor's draft. Although Kinports, his law clerk, urged him to join O'Connor's "persuasive, analytical, and exceedingly narrow opinion," Blackmun held firm. In his dissenting opinion, he conceded that "the University long ago should have replaced its original statement of purpose and brought its corporate papers into the 20th century." Nonetheless, "I have come to suspect that it is easy to go too far with rigid rules in this area of claimed sex discrimination, and to lose—indeed destroy—values that mean much to some people by forbidding the State to offer them a choice while not depriving others of an alternative choice." He warned against "needless conformity" in the name of equality.

Blackmun's attention soon returned to abortion, especially after O'Connor's vote in the first *Akron* case, in 1983, served notice that *Roe v. Wade* would need the most tenacious goal-line defense he could give it. And it was in the course of protecting *Roe* that he began to see himself as protecting the rights of women.

Blackmun wrote at the end of his majority opinion in the *Thornburgh* case, in 1986, that "few decisions are more personal and intimate, more properly private, or more basic to individual dignity and autonomy" than a woman's decision to terminate her pregnancy. The almost clinical tone of *Roe* was replaced by something close to passion. The rights of women, rather than those of doctors, were moving toward the center of Blackmun's focus. The abortion-funding cases the next year, 1987, moved him further down the road toward seeing abortion rights as women's rights. These were cases, after all, that concerned not doctors, not husbands, but women, alone and in great need.

Two years later, in his dissenting opinion in *Webster v. Reproductive Heath Services* (1989), equality as well as liberty entered Blackmun's discourse on abortion for the first time. In an early draft of his dissent, prepared when he believed that Rehnquist had five votes for effectively overturning *Roe*, Blackmun had written: "I rue this day. I rue the violence that has been done to the liberty and equality of women." Later, when O'Connor's refusal to join the Rehnquist opinion preserved *Roe* for another day, Blackmun changed his opinion to read, in its final, published version: "I fear for the future. I fear for the liberty and equality of the millions of women who have lived and come of age in the 16 years since *Roe* was decided."

In 1991, Blackmun wrote an opinion for the Court holding that employers could not exclude women of childbearing age from jobs where exposure to toxins might harm fetuses. These so-called fetal protection policies had generated considerable concern among women's groups, who saw the measures not only as paternalistic but also as an excuse for companies to avoid meeting the obligation to ensure safety for all their workers. "Decisions about the welfare of future children must be left to the parents who conceive, bear, support, and raise them rather than to the employers who hire those parents," Blackmun wrote in *Automobile Workers v. Johnson Controls*. Soon after, he received a letter from Fay Clayton, a Chicago lawyer who was active in abortion-rights litigation. Blackmun's opinion was "very reassuring," Clayton said. "It was not too long ago that women were kept out of the legal profession for *their* own good." She cited a notorious case from 1873, *Bradwell v. Illinois,* in which the Court had upheld the refusal of the Illinois bar to admit Myra Bradwell, one of the first female lawyers in the country, on the ground that "the natural and proper timidity and delicacy which belongs to the female sex" made women unsuited for a lawyer's life. Clayton's letter to Blackmun continued: "More than a century later, Johnson tried to keep women out of some professions for the good of theoretical others who may not have even been conceived. Thank you for telling them that it is not a decision for the *employer* to make."

The justice replied a week later, in a letter that showed his pleasure at being ascribed a role in the forward trajectory of women's rights: "I think the result was a correct one and that the decision will show the way in certain future cases. It took a bit of doing, but all these seem to require effort. It should put *Bradwell v. Illinois* to proper rest."

For Blackmun, the abortion and sex discrimination cases, having run on parallel tracks for nearly twenty years, were about to converge. The result would be a unified jurisprudence of women's rights in which reproductive freedom was established as an essential aspect of women's equality. In *Planned Parenthood v. Casey,* the 1992 decision that unexpectedly saved *Roe v. Wade,* Blackmun's separate opinion contained this paragraph:

> A State's restrictions on a woman's right to terminate her pregnancy also implicate constitutional guarantees of gender equality. State restrictions on abortion compel women to continue pregnancies they otherwise might terminate. By restricting the right to terminate pregnancies, the State conscripts women's bodies into its service, forcing women to continue their pregnancies, suffer the pains of childbirth, and in most instances, provide years of maternal care. The State does not compensate women for their services; instead, it assumes that they owe this duty as a matter of course. This assumption—that women can simply be forced to accept the "natural" status and incidents of motherhood—appears to rest upon a conception of women's role that has triggered the protection of the Equal Protection Clause.

And then Blackmun did something remarkable. He cited *Mississippi University for Women v. Hogan,* the decision on single-sex state colleges that had provoked his heartfelt dissent ten years before. The convergence was complete.

A year later, in June 1993, President Bill Clinton named Ruth Bader Ginsburg to the Supreme Court to succeed Byron White, who retired after thirty-one years. Her advocate's voice, so familiar during the 1970s, had been missing from the Court since 1980, when President Jimmy Carter had named her to the D.C. Circuit. With White never having reconciled himself to *Roe,* his replacement by one of the country's leading women's-rights lawyers should have cheered Blackmun greatly. Yet he was wary. In her scholarly way, Ginsburg had been a critic of *Roe*—not for its outcome, which she fully supported, but for its reasoning. *Roe* was unnecessarily weakened, she wrote in a 1985 law review article, "by the opinion's concentration on a medically approved autonomy idea, to the exclusion of a constitutionally based sex-equality perspective." She repeated this analysis early in 1993 in a lecture at New York University Law School. After her nomination to the Supreme Court, the *Washington Post* printed excerpts from the lecture. Blackmun read the *Post* article and recorded his responses: "She picks at Roe. Better to have been decided on equal protection. With all respect, could not have been done. . . . A professor's appraisal 20 years after. One has to be in the heat of the battle to appreciate this. She will be in it now. Can she stand up to AS?" It was well known that Ginsburg and Antonin Scalia were friends from their years together on the D.C. Circuit.

Ginsburg's first term demonstrated that she was not about to temper her views to please her friend Nino. The Court had accepted *J.E.B. v. Alabama,* a case on whether the Constitution permitted removing potential jurors from a trial on the basis of their sex. Seven years earlier, in *Batson v. Kentucky,* the Court had barred the use of peremptory challenges to remove jurors based on race, and the question in *J.E.B.* was whether the same prohibition applied to sex. *J.E.B.* began as a contested paternity and child support case. An Alabama prosecutor had used peremptory challenges to remove all the men from the jury—a common practice in such cases, based on the belief that women would favor the prosecution while male jurors would be

The Court during the 1993 term, Blackmun's last. Standing, left to right: Clarence Thomas, Anthony M. Kennedy, David H. Souter, Ruth Bader Ginsburg. Seated, left to right: Sandra Day O'Connor, Harry A. Blackmun, Chief Justice William H. Rehnquist, John Paul Stevens, Antonin Scalia.

sympathetic to a man who was denying paternity. The defendant argued unsuccessfully in the Alabama courts that in constructing an all-female jury, the state had violated his right to equal protection.

To Blackmun, the male defendant clearly had the winning argument. "Inevitable," he called the outcome in his memo before the case was argued in November 1993. The conference discussion after the argument was lively, with Scalia particularly energized. To bar the use of sex in jury selection, he said, would be the "most radical decision in 30 years" and a "terrible thing." But the vote was 6 to 3 to overturn the Alabama decision and extend the race-discrimination precedent to sex. Scalia, Rehnquist, and Thomas dissented.

With Byron White's retirement, Blackmun had become the senior associate justice, with the power to assign opinions when he was in the majority and the chief justice was in dissent. He assigned this case to himself. "We hold that gender, like race, is an unconstitutional proxy for juror competence and impartiality," he wrote. His opinion traced the history of the court system's discrimination against women, citing four of Ruth Ginsburg's cases. His draft included a footnote that treated as still an open question whether claims of sex discrimination should be subject to strict judicial scrutiny; it was not necessary to decide the issue in this case, he said, because sex-based jury challenges failed even mid-level scrutiny. "I am pleased to join your opinion and particularly appreciate footnote 6," Ginsburg told him.

In an angry dissent, Scalia accused the majority of adopting a "unisex creed," of obscuring its reasoning behind "anti-male-chauvinist oratory" in order to "pay conspicuous obeisance to the equality of the sexes." Sandra O'Connor, while joining Blackmun's opinion, wrote a separate concurring opinion to express her view that the decision should be binding only on prosecutors, who were "state actors," but not on defendants or civil litigants.

Ruth Ginsburg said nothing. She had no need to. Harry Blackmun had, finally and improbably, spoken for her.

IN THE CENTER

IF, AS HARRY BLACKMUN liked to say, there was another world "out there," beyond the justices' everyday experiences, few people came to exemplify that world as starkly as Joshua DeShaney, whose case came before the Supreme Court in the fall of 1987. Joshua was a four-year-old boy from Winnebago County, Wisconsin, whose father obtained custody after a divorce. When Joshua was admitted to a local hospital with multiple bruises, the staff suspected child abuse and notified the county Department of Social Services. But the department, deeming the evidence insufficient, returned the boy to his father's custody after the father promised to enroll Joshua in preschool and get counseling for himself. Although the promises were not kept and suspicious head injuries kept occurring, the county social worker who made monthly visits did not intervene. After a year, a beating left Joshua comatose, permanently brain damaged, and profoundly retarded. The father, Randy DeShaney, was convicted of child abuse. Joshua's mother sued the county for depriving Joshua of his liberty without due process of law, by failing to protect him against a known or foreseeable risk of violence. The lower federal courts rejected the suit on the ground that the government is not obliged to protect its citizens from private violence.

The case was disturbing, both as a personal tragedy and as a proposition of constitutional law. There was no clear precedent. The mother's lawsuit had an obvious appeal: Shouldn't someone be held accountable for what looked like gross negligence? But it also had its problems. Could the Court draw a line that would bring Joshua within the Constitution's protection without, at the same time, obliging the government to protect people against all manner of foreseeable danger at the hands of others? Blackmun's law clerk Danny Ertel urged him to vote to deny the petition for certiorari in *DeShaney v. Winnebago County Department of Social Services* and to wait for the issue to be presented in a context where the government's obligation would be less open to dispute, such as a prison in which the government has taken an inmate into its custody and then fails to protect him.

When the justices first considered the petition, at the start of the 1987 term, the Court voted to deny it. But Byron White circulated a dissent from the denial. White, who believed more strongly than any other justice that the Court should act promptly to resolve conflicting rulings among the federal appeals courts, identified a conflict with another case, in which a different appeals court had held that once a state learns that a child is at risk, a "special relationship" obliges the state to remove the child from a dangerous home environment. Brennan and Marshall joined White's dissent. Blackmun then decided to "join three," a fairly common practice in which a justice who is on the fence about a case offers to provide the necessary fourth vote for a grant of certiorari. Blackmun gave his vote. The case was set for argument in November 1988.

In his preargument memo, Blackmun said he would vote to permit the lawsuit, but on "very narrow" grounds that would confine the decision to the child abuse context. "This is a dangerous area and must be carefully delineated," he wrote. "When a state places a child in a situation of danger, if it learns at some time of the danger it has caused and is causing, it is constitutionally obliged to remove the child from that situation of danger."

After the argument the vote was 6 to 3 to affirm the lower court's dismissal of the mother's case against Winnebago County, with White joining the five justices who had opposed granting certiorari. Rehnquist assigned himself the majority opinion, and Brennan said that he would file a dissent for himself, Marshall, and Blackmun, who was not committed to writing on his own. But the draft dissent that Brennan circulated in January 1989 went beyond Blackmun's comfort level, suggesting, for example, that the failure by a police officer to intervene and rescue a victim of a rape or other crime would violate the victim's constitutional rights. Blackmun authorized his law clerk Edward B. Foley to draft a narrower dissent.

The draft majority opinion that Rehnquist circulated also struck Blackmun as unnecessarily broad, and particularly heartless as well. "Our cases have recognized that the Due Process Clauses generally confer no affirmative right to governmental aid, even where such aid may be necessary to secure life, liberty, or property interests of which the government itself may not deprive the individual," the chief justice wrote, citing *Harris v. McRae,* the Hyde Amendment abortion-funding decision, in support of this proposition. At the urging of John Paul Stevens, Rehnquist had toned down some provocative passages. He had initially written that while the people of Wisconsin could choose to create a system in which state officials bore responsibility for failing to act in similar situations, "they should not have it thrust upon them by this Court's distortion of the Due Process Clause of the Fourteenth Amendment." Yielding to Stevens, Rehnquist changed "distortion" to "expansion."

While his law clerk was working on a draft for his dissenting opinion, Blackmun took up a legal pad and began writing a dissent in his own voice. "Poor Joshua!" he began:

Victim of repeated attacks by an irresponsible, bullying, obviously cowardly, and intemperate father, and neglected by respondents who placed him in a dangerous predicament and who knew or learned what was going on and yet did essentially nothing except, as the Court revealingly observes, "dutifully recorded these incidents in their files." It is a sad commentary upon American life, and constitutional principles—so full of late of patriotic fervor and proud proclamations about "liberty and justice for all," that this child, Joshua DeShaney, now is

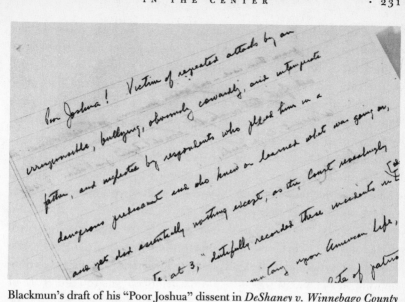

Blackmun's draft of his "Poor Joshua" dissent in *DeShaney v. Winnebago County Department of Social Services*

assigned to live out the entire remainder of his life profoundly retarded. Joshua and his mother, as petitioners here, deserve—but now are denied by this Court—the opportunity to have the facts of their case considered in the light of the constitutional protection that Section 1983 is meant to provide.

His reference was to the federal civil rights law that provides a means for suing state officials for constitutional violations.

Eventually Brennan dropped, from his powerful dissent, the expansive language that had troubled Blackmun. "My disagreement with the Court arises from its failure to see that inaction can be every bit as abusive of power as action, that oppression can result when a State undertakes a vital duty and then ignores it," Brennan wrote. Blackmun joined Brennan's opinion. And with only minor editing, he filed his heartfelt dissent on behalf of "Poor Joshua" as well.

Of the hundreds of opinions Harry Blackmun would write during his years on the Court, "Poor Joshua" would become one of the best

232 ·   BECOMING JUSTICE BLACKMUN

known and, as a matter of judicial style, one of the most controversial. It was unusual, "the unmediated expression of self," in the words of Judge Richard A. Posner, who had written the appeals court decision in the *DeShaney* case. The opinion has been the subject of dozens of commentaries in the legal literature. In 2002, one academic observer, Laura Krugman Ray, wrote that along with the deeply personal tone of Blackmun's separate opinions in two abortion cases—*Webster v. Reproductive Health Services* and *Planned Parenthood v. Casey*—his opinion in *DeShaney* offered "the remarkable spectacle of a justice speaking directly and emotionally to the reader without any pretense of dispassionate neutrality."

In response to his opinion in the *DeShaney* case, Blackmun received a dozen appreciative letters from members of the public. To one writer, who said he was surprised to find himself praising a Nixon appointee, Blackmun replied: "Do not condemn me too much about the Nixon appointment—after all, I was his third choice." Later, Blackmun would explain his choice of words in his dissent by saying that the majority had lost sight of the individual behind the case: "Sometimes we overlook the individual's concern, the fact that these are live human beings that are so deeply and terribly affected by our decisions."

Blackmun had now passed his eightieth birthday, and in the early fall of 1990, soon after William Brennan's retirement, he began drafting a farewell letter to his colleagues. Perhaps he was just trying the idea on for size; he put the letter aside. In November he had lunch with his old friend Erwin N. Griswold, the former solicitor general and dean of Harvard Law School. Blackmun admired Griswold, four years his senior, and trusted his judgment. "ENG tells me to retire," he noted in his "chronology." But it was too soon: *Roe v. Wade* was not safe. The following summer, Thurgood Marshall, Blackmun's age-mate at eighty-three, retired after twenty-four years on the Court, leaving Blackmun the oldest sitting justice by nine years. He was now second to Byron White in seniority as an associate justice. That meant a move closer to the center of the bench, to the immediate left of the chief justice's middle seat. "Here I am in the center!" he noted as the

Court began the 1991 term. Then he added: "Shadows lengthen." But it was still too soon.

Two events in 1992 changed the calculation. The first was the preservation of *Roe* in *Planned Parenthood v. Casey*, with the emergence of Sandra Day O'Connor, Anthony Kennedy, and David Souter as *Roe*'s committed defenders. The second was the election of Bill Clinton as president. In late December, Harry and Dottie Blackmun joined the president-elect and some 1,400 other guests at Renaissance Weekend, on Hilton Head Island, South Carolina. The last night of the four-day event turned into a celebration of Clinton's election. After the inauguration, Blackmun wrote to congratulate the new president. Recalling the festivities of the weekend's final evening, he said: "I write merely to say that you have many friends 'out there' who, as was said that night, are supportive and behind you as you go through these difficult initial weeks. I seem to sense this as I travel about the country. There is an attitude of fresh air and anticipation, coupled with an understanding that all cannot be accomplished immediately and perhaps some things cannot be accomplished at all."

During the early months of 1993, Blackmun and Byron White kept up a private joke about which of the two would retire first. White, named to the Court at age forty-four by his friend John F. Kennedy, was the only remaining justice to have been appointed by a Democratic president. "We'd pass each other in the hall and he'd ask, 'Have you retired yet?' I'd say, 'Nope, have you?'" Blackmun later told the Associated Press. Although White was considerably more conservative than the new president and was relatively young at seventy-five, the stars were properly aligned for him. On March 19, 1993, White announced that he would leave the Court at the end of the term.

Later that afternoon, Blackmun received a letter from Anthony Kennedy. "Dear Harry," Kennedy began.

My own devotion to the Court and its constitutional place have been shaped in most profound ways by your splendid juristic dedication, and you still inspire me to try to do better in my own work.

It would be a great loss to this institution if Byron's successor were to be deprived of that same instruction. You and Dottie have much to weigh, and I must not intrude, but I considered that the warm relation between us might justify this brief letter. If you were to stay here a while longer, it would influence the Court for years to come.

You ought not feel the necessity to respond.

With admiration and respect, I remain,

Yours, Tony

Blackmun replied immediately. He was touched and deeply grateful, he said:

This institution we are privileged to be part of is precious, despite the pain it causes each of us now and then. I do not want it damaged by acting or failing to act. Departure of a member always is an emotional moment. I shall not act at a time of emotion, but I shall think carefully about what I shall do. Your note was a comfort and affords me much strength.

With thanks from my heart, Harry.

He would wait.

The years since Warren Burger's retirement, in 1986, had brought not only four new justices to the Court—Kennedy, along with Antonin Scalia, David Souter, and Clarence Thomas—but a new atmosphere. Burger's departure removed a constant irritant from the Court's group dynamic. Rehnquist ran the Court efficiently: conferences were much shorter and more sharply focused, and opinion assignments were unambiguous. Rearguments, almost an annual ritual under Burger, became rare. Some of the old rules were relaxed. Blackmun had complained to Burger in 1978 that the rule against taking notes by those in the courtroom audience seemed to make little sense. At the very least, Blackmun urged, members of the Supreme Court bar—lawyers entitled to practice before the Court, who received preferred seats when they attended an argument—should be able to take notes. Years went by without a response from Burger. In 1988, under Rehnquist, the Court lifted the ban on note taking by bar members.

The other justices respected Rehnquist even when they disagreed with him, as Blackmun increasingly did. In fact, Blackmun's voting record had become ever more liberal. According to data compiled by Joseph F. Kobylka (see chapter 8), from the 1981 term through the 1985 term, Blackmun voted with William Brennan 77.6 percent of the time and with Thurgood Marshall 76.1 percent. From 1986 to 1990, his rate of agreement with the two most liberal justices was 97.1 percent and 95.8 percent. After Brennan and Marshall retired, Harry Blackmun was, by wide consensus, the most liberal member of the Supreme Court.

Although the new chief justice had a firm hand, his touch could also be light. He liked politics and gambling, preferably in combination. On the bench on January 20, 1987, Blackmun passed Rehnquist a note. "Mr. CJ—Two years from today (noon) we shall have a new President. Who will it be?" Rehnquist replied that if a Republican was to be inaugurated, it would be George H. W. Bush or Kansas senator Robert Dole. "If a Dem," the chief justice went on, "maybe someone who is now regarded as a total dark horse." As it turned out, the Democratic nominee for 1988 was Michael Dukakis, governor of Massachusetts—if not a total dark horse, then close.

Blackmun also took part in Rehnquist's Election Day betting pools. "Sandra proved to be positively prescient," Rehnquist wrote in a memo he circulated immediately after the 1992 presidential race, in which he had invited his colleagues to make state-by-state forecasts. O'Connor, who alone had predicted Bill Clinton's victories in Georgia and Nevada, was owed $18.30, and Rehnquist ordered the other players, all but Blackmun, to pay her. Blackmun was also a statistical winner, but his lucky guesses had been shared rather than solitary. He was owed $1.70.

In one of the notes they passed back and forth on the bench, Rehnquist offered a personal revelation, although what prompted it remains unclear. "I was once William D. (Donald) until I changed my

A feathered visitor to chambers, 1987

middle name while in high school to H (Hubbs—my grandmother's maiden name)," the man known to the world as William H. Rehnquist disclosed to Blackmun in January 1993.

Under the new regime, everyone seemed more relaxed. In the spring of 1987, a Court employee stopped by Blackmun's chambers to show off a pet bird, a blue-and-yellow macaw. The law clerks were afraid to touch the bird, but Blackmun allowed it to perch on his shoulder, and posed for a photograph.

For Blackmun, the arrival of David Souter, who succeeded William Brennan in 1990, was one of the most positive developments of this period. He sensed a kindred spirit in the younger man, who, like him, was a graduate of both Harvard College and Harvard Law School; was given to long, solitary hours at his desk; and had been wrenched out of familiar surroundings (in Souter's case, New Hampshire) and was struggling through a difficult first term. Occasionally the Blackmuns invited Souter for supper at their apartment; Blackmun tried and failed to persuade Souter to join him in spending part of the summer at the Aspen Institute, in Colorado, where for twenty years he led a two-week seminar on justice and society. Souter said he needed to spend quiet time in New Hampshire. "It has taken far longer to relax than I'd expected," Souter wrote to Blackmun during the summer recess after his first term on the Court. "In part, I suppose, that is because I've been doing some work, but I think it is also partly due to the necessity of facing another unexpected fact, that being home is different from what it used to be. Life has changed, and it does not just switch itself back onto the old track for three summer months."

Their communications were not all so somber. A few months after *Planned Parenthood v. Casey,* Souter sent Blackmun a copy of a postcard with a photograph of two men in a lake, one in hip boots casting a fishing line, the other one fishing from an inflatable rowboat. ROW VS. WADE: THE GREAT WESTERN FISHING CONTROVERSY was the caption printed on the card. It was for his collection, Souter told Blackmun. The two also engaged in a long-running private joke about the New Hampshire roots that Blackmun claimed to have. In March 1992, Blackmun sent Souter a tongue-in-cheek letter about an unnamed ancestor who, Blackmun said he had been told as a child, was executed in the state by hanging. Promising to "make a discreet inquiry," Souter observed that it was "hard to believe that anyone would have wanted to hang a Blackmun (although that may not be Dottie's view)."

In May, Souter reported on the fruits of his investigation. With the research assistance of the state attorney general, he said, he had learned that New Hampshire had, in fact, executed not one but six Blackmuns. "How amazing it seems to me that none of this ever came up while your nomination to the Court was pending in 1970," Souter added. He enclosed a list of the executed Blackmuns: Esmerelda, Jebediah "The Butcher," Obediah, Lydia, Zachariah, and Everett "Hatchetman" Blackmun—"an embarrassment of riches." Blackmun, deadpan, sent a letter thanking Attorney General John Arnold for his "research and scholarship." More than a year later, Souter wrote to

Blackmun: "The sight of the N.H. State Prison the other day reminded me of you and your family."

Harry Blackmun and Antonin Scalia had little in common
philosophically—Scalia was the Court's most conservative justice—but
they shared a love of language and an insistence on linguistic precision. Blackmun reflexively corrected the spelling and grammar on
any document that fell into his hands. Scalia invited Blackmun to join
the Chancellor's English Society, of which Scalia was the founder
and sole member. They were allies in an effort to stamp out the word
"viable" except in abortion cases; it was, perhaps, the only abortion-
related subject on which the two could have agreed. Fighting the over-
use of this adjective had been Blackmun's solitary battle, and he
warned Scalia that it appeared to be a losing one. But Scalia reassured
him: "You have not 'lost the battle' on that one; those with taste never
use it, except in its literal medical context. I would sooner be caught
watching a rock video than referring to a 'viable option.' "

Few justices have had as acrimonious an arrival at the Supreme
Court as Clarence Thomas, who clearly would not have been Blackmun's choice to succeed Thurgood Marshall. But Blackmun quickly
reached out to his newest colleague, as he had to the others, inviting
Thomas to breakfast a week after he joined the Court, in October
1991. Thomas was grateful. "That was very generous of you," he said
in a handwritten note. "I look forward to sitting down and chatting
with you." Six weeks later, the Blackmuns received a handwritten letter from Thomas's wife, Virginia, thanking them for welcoming her
and her husband "with so much dignity and warmth."

The bond Blackmun established with Thomas in those early
months endured on a personal level even as it became unmistakably
clear that the two occupied opposite ends of the Court's ideological
spectrum. Following Blackmun's death penalty dissent in *Callins v.
Collins*, Thomas Sowell, a conservative commentator who was one of
Clarence Thomas's most vocal supporters, denounced Blackmun in
his syndicated column as a "vain and shallow old man whom the media have puffed up for their own ideological reasons . . . a tawdry
symbol of what has gone so wrong in American law over the past few

Row vs. Wade: the Great Western Fishing Controversy

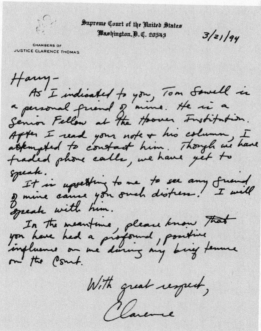

Top: David Souter sent Blackmun a copy of this postcard. **Bottom**: Clarence Thomas expresses his dismay that his friend Thomas Sowell has castigated Blackmun in a newspaper column.

decades." After receiving the column in the mail from a man in St. Louis who said he agreed with it, Blackmun showed it to Thomas, who responded with a handwritten note. Sowell was, indeed, a personal friend, he told Blackmun. "It is upsetting to me to see any friend of mine cause you such distress. I will speak with him. In the meantime, please know you have had a profound, positive influence on me during my brief tenure on the Court. With great respect, Clarence."

In the fall of 1993, Blackmun resumed drafting a retirement letter. Byron White had left, and the confirmation of Ruth Bader Ginsburg to succeed him had gone smoothly. Despite her qualms about *Roe v. Wade* as an opinion, it was clear that the substitution of Ginsburg for White gave the Court an additional vote, a sixth, in support of the right to abortion. *Roe* was safe, and a sympathetic president was in the White House. Blackmun talked privately with President Clinton at the next Renaissance Weekend, in December 1993, and told him that he was seriously considering retiring when the Court's term ended in June. The president and his aides kept Blackmun's secret while quietly beginning the search for a successor. On the bench on March 29, 1994, Blackmun passed Rehnquist a note on a small pink sheet torn from a Supreme Court memo pad. "May I have 5–10 minutes with you sometime this week? After the conference on Wednesday?" Rehnquist, no doubt guessing the reason for the unusual request, scrawled and underlined a large "Yes!" and handed the page back.

Throughout official Washington, word was now starting to leak. "Rumors rumors," Blackmun wrote in his "chronology" for April 4, 1994. Two days later, he stood with President Clinton in the White House for the announcement. "It's not easy to step aside, but I know what the numbers are, and it's time," he said. He was eighty-five years old, the fourth oldest person ever to serve on the Court. In praising the retiring justice, Clinton invoked "poor Joshua" by name. "Those of us who have studied the law can at times be lost in its abstractions," the president said. "The habits, the procedures, the language of the law can separate lawyers from the people who look to the bar for justice. Justice Blackmun's identification was firmly and decisively with

With President Bill Clinton in the White House for the retirement announcement, April 6, 1994

the ordinary people of this country, with their concerns, and his humanity was often given voice not only in majority opinions but in his dissents." Clinton added: "Justice has not only been his title; it has been his guiding light."

Blackmun's letter to the president read:

It has been a distinct privilege to have served on the Federal Bench since November 4, 1959, a period of over 34 years, and on this Court since June 9, 1970, a period embracing 24 Terms. It has been an extraordinary experience, one that comes to very few lawyers. Being a Justice places one in a position of controversy—as Justice Holmes described it, "in the fray"—but the Federal Judiciary is in the business of resolving controversy, developing the law, and seeking and determining "justice." One does the very best he can with such talent as he possesses. Through you, as Chief Executive, I express my gratitude to the Nation.

At the news conference that followed the brief White House ceremony, reporters asked Blackmun for his reflections on *Roe v. Wade*. Describing the decision as one that "hit me early in my tenure," he said, "I think it was right in 1973, and I think it was right today. It's a step that had to be taken as we go down the road toward the full emancipation of women."

Along with the praise, the nostalgic reflections, and the invitations that poured into Blackmun's chambers came a steady flow of letters from abortion opponents. "Dear 'Justice' Blackmun," one began. "I am thankful you are leaving office. I wish to tell you what an evil man you are to legalize abortion. I hope it is all of your heirs that get aborted." Another concluded: "Now if your Mom only had an abortion. . . ." Blackmun did not answer these letters, but he read them, even putting a question mark in the margin of a paragraph: "Well the good news this day is that you're out as a Judge. That means my tax money doesn't go to an old fool." The letter writer clearly was not aware that retired federal judges receive their full salary.

Blackmun's colleagues issued formal statements of congratulations and farewell; it was a practiced ritual. David Souter's public statement consisted of two words: "I dissent." He delivered a handwritten private letter on the afternoon of April 6.

Dear Harry,
In the public statement I was asked to make in the aftermath of your announcement, I feared I would say too much and, so, said only that I dissented. I persist in the dissent, majority view that it is. You may have been pigeonholed as a liberal, but you have been the center of the Court's integrity, and for four terms you have been to me the wisest and kindest elder brother that a junior justice could ever dream of having. I will never be able to give you thanks enough for your kindness in receiving me here, or for the friendship that your change of chambers address will not interrupt.

Respectfully and affectionately, David.

Clarence Thomas also sent a private letter. "I have truly enjoyed serving with you. Indeed, it has been an honor," he wrote. "There is much about the way you conduct yourself and go about the business of this Court that I intend to emulate as best I can. I deeply appreciate the wonderful example you have set for this junior colleague. In addition, Harry, I will be forever grateful for the courteous and dignified manner in which you treated me during my most difficult first Term. I wish you much happiness."

Scalia wrote a week later: "The announcement of your retirement came around when I was out of town. It was an unwelcome surprise. The Chancellor's English Society will have to be disbanded. You have done long and honorable service on the Court, and can retire with the good feeling of a race well run."

Even the crusty Byron White sounded almost sentimental in his handwritten note. "You have certainly left your very substantial and meaningful tracks all over the Federal law during your many years on the bench," he wrote. "Congratulations on a great career, and don't worry about retirement. I am finding very much to my liking." Another retired justice, Lewis Powell, wrote: "You will rank in history as one of the truly great Justices. I have been proud to have you as a friend."

If Warren Burger wrote, his letter did not find its way into Blackmun's "retirement" file. A month later, six months after the Burgers' sixtieth wedding anniversary, Vera Burger died. Blackmun did not attend her funeral. He told Burger, "with deep regret," that he had an "irrevocable commitment" to be in Boston that afternoon. His grandson, Nicholas Coniaris, was graduating from Concord Academy, a private secondary school in suburban Concord, and Blackmun was the graduation speaker, although he did not offer this further explanation to Burger. There was evidently no other personal correspondence about Vera's death between Burger and his best man. The Blackmuns made a gift to the Mayo Foundation in Vera's memory and received an engraved card: "The family of Elvera Stromberg Burger will hold in grateful remembrance your kind expression of sympathy." Barely a year later, on June 25, 1995, Warren Burger died, of

From Blackmun's "chronology of significant events," noting Warren Burger's death, June 25, 1995

congestive heart failure, at the age of eighty-seven. "WEB dies," Blackmun noted tersely in his "chronology."

Now it was Blackmun's turn to issue a formal statement. "Chief Justice Burger served extraordinarily well as the head of our national Judiciary for 17 years," Blackmun said in a statement, along with those of the other sitting and retired justices, issued by the Court's press office. "He was imaginative and innovative and did so much to improve the judicial process and to bring about the timely dispensation of justice. I personally knew him for 80 years, a friendship that indeed was lifelong. His leaving instills a sensation of loneliness, not only for me but for the Court." Blackmun sent a $50 check in Burger's memory to the Supreme Court Historical Society.

At the request of Burger's alma matter, the William Mitchell College of Law, Blackmun submitted an essay for publication in a tribute issue of the law review. It was more revealing than the formal Court statement—indeed, more revealing than most such posthumous tributes. Clearly, this was Blackmun speaking directly, not Blackmun editing a law clerk's draft. "Of course, Chief Justice Burger and I disagreed now and then as to the results to be reached in submitted cases," he wrote in a decided understatement. "When we did, the disagreement was basic and, on occasion, emphatic. He had little patience for disagreement. I do not know what he expected, but surely he could not have anticipated that I would be an ideological clone. He knew me better than that. But when disagreement came, his disappointment was evident and not concealed. The situation was not comfortable."

A note of nostalgia crept in at the end of the three-page essay. "So Warren Burger is gone now. He has put in his seventeen years of service and made his record. Evaluators will find it good, for he has contributed to the cause of justice in this country and to its dispensation. That is a large 'plus' that the rest of us will be hard put to match. Eighty years is not only a lifetime. It is a particularly long lifetime. I was privileged to have shared most of it with him."

On June 30, 1994, the last day of Harry Blackmun's final term on the bench, Chief Justice Rehnquist, on behalf of all the justices, formally wished his retiring colleague well. "Your colleagues are sad that you have chosen to retire from the Court," Rehnquist read from a letter written by Blackmun's eight colleagues. "You are undoubtedly best known for having authored the Court's opinion in *Roe v. Wade* in 1973, but that distinction should not obscure the many other important issues on which you have spoken for the Court. . . . We shall miss you."

Two of the six decisions announced that morning were Blackmun's—one in a labor case and another clarifying the jurisdiction of the federal district courts to grant stays of execution for death-row inmates who were still seeking lawyers to help prepare their habeas corpus petitions. The most widely noted majority opinion that morning was one by Rehnquist in *Madsen v. Women's Health Center, Inc.,* upholding most of a Florida court's injunction intended to keep disruptive protesters from blocking access to an abortion clinic. Scalia, speaking for Kennedy and Thomas as well as himself, read an angry dissent.

"Last day on bench for me," Blackmun noted in his "chronology." His retirement became official on August 3, the day his successor, Chief Judge Stephen G. Breyer of the First Circuit Court of

Blackmun in his chambers on his last day on the bench, June 30, 1994

Appeals, was sworn in. Blackmun noted the passage with one word: "Retired."

He kept busy in retirement. Freed from the constraints he had felt as a sitting justice, he accepted awards and tributes from abortion-rights and women's-rights organizations. "The truth is: You have saved more American women's lives than anyone in our nation's history," Gloria Steinem wrote in 1995, in presenting him with the Reproductive Freedom Award from the Voters for Choice Education Fund. When he was in Washington, he went to the Court four days a week and ate breakfast, as usual, in the cafeteria. David Souter regularly brought his yogurt into Blackmun's chambers in order to join him for lunch. Although Blackmun, of course, no longer participated in the Court's decisions, he paid close attention to them. At the end of the 1995 term, after Antonin Scalia had issued several impassioned dissents, Blackmun wrote to offer some cheer. "Dear Nino: I know that this has not been an easy year for you. But it is over with, and next October one will be rejuvenated and a new chapter will unfold. As a group or individually, we cannot get discouraged. May the summer be a good one for you."

Scalia replied: "How kind of you to write the nice note you did! You are right that I am more discouraged this year than I have been at the end of any of my previous nine terms up here. I am beginning to repeat myself and don't see much use in it any more. I hope I will feel better in the fall. A cheering note from an old colleague—one whom, God knows, I was not always on the same side with—sure does help."

Early in 1997, the director Steven Spielberg invited Blackmun to play the role of Justice Joseph Story in the movie *Amistad,* based on the true narrative of a slave ship mutiny that led to a Supreme Court decision, in 1841, freeing fifty-three African slaves. Blackmun's secretary, Wanda S. Martinson, encouraged him to accept. "It would be awfully fun!" she wrote. Blackmun sent a message to the chief justice's office, asking whether Rehnquist would have any objection. There was none. "The Chief seemed amused and said he was happy for you," Martinson told Blackmun after receiving a report from Rehnquist's administrative assistant. In March an entourage traveled to Newport, Rhode Island, for two days of filming. The former justice was paid the required minimum of $540 a day and had three lines to read, taken directly from the Court's decision and beginning with the declaration: "We are unanimous in our finding that the Africans are individuals with legal and moral rights with regard to their liberty." Blackmun's daughter Nancy and his grandson, Nicholas, were cast as extras in the film.

On his ninetieth birthday, November 12, 1998, Harry Blackmun was greeted in the Supreme Court cafeteria with balloons and cake. His daughters were there, along with Chief Justice Rehnquist and several other justices. Among those joining the festivities were ninety eighth-grade students from Anaheim, California, who happened to be visiting the Court and were urged by the cashier to serenade the justice with a rendition of "Happy Birthday."

There would be no more celebrations. In February, Blackmun fell at home and broke a hip. He underwent surgery at Arlington Hospital, in Virginia. On March 4, 1999, Wanda Martinson—effectively a member of the family after twenty-five years as Blackmun's secretary— sent an e-mail message to the 103 former law clerks: "We are very sorry to let you know that our Justice died early this morning." Some details followed, and then Martinson continued:

> HAB remained true to his character to the last: After his surgery he told all of us to "get back to work," and yesterday afternoon we read to him from the sports page—all the news on baseball spring training—and one of his favorite stories, Casey at the Bat.
>
> We ~~will~~ (shall) let you know about the funeral plans as soon as possible.

The last line was guaranteed to bring a smile to all who received the e-mail. No one who ever worked in the Blackmun chambers was spared the justice's editing.

An early spring storm brought ice and snow to Washington on the morning of his funeral, March 9, 1999. Before the public service, there was a private service at Arlington National Cemetery. The family rented a blue Volkswagen Beetle, which carried his ashes to the cemetery at the head of a procession of limousines. Police officers along the route, assuming the VW was an interloper, tried to wave it out of the procession. (Not all his ashes were buried at Arlington. A few days after the funeral, Wanda Martinson; Todd Gustin, Blackmun's longtime chambers messenger; and William McDaniel, a clerk from the 1978 term, returned to the Court on a special mission. On the southwest corner of the Court grounds, directly visible from the window of his chambers, where Blackmun often sat and ate his lunch, stands a perfectly proportioned Japanese cherry tree. Blackmun so enjoyed looking at it that he called it "my tree." It was not yet in bloom during that wintry week in March, but within weeks it would be a cloud of pink blossoms. Martinson, Gustin, and McDaniel carried with them a small portion of Blackmun's ashes, which they placed under his tree. Later, family members scattered small quantities at places that had particular meaning: the grounds of the Aspen Institute and the Mayo Clinic; the old family home in Rochester; and at Spider Lake in Wisconsin, where the family had spent summer vacations.)

At the memorial service on the afternoon of March 9, at the Metropolitan Memorial United Methodist Church, Garrison Keillor, a fellow Minnesotan who had bestowed on Blackmun the title of "the shy person's justice," led the congregation in singing the Whiffenpoof Song: "We are poor little lambs, who have gone astray"—a Yale song for a Harvard man. It was Blackmun's favorite piece of music, his daughter Nancy explained in her eulogy. When she and her sisters were young, he sang it every night in the shower. "For Sally and Susie and me, its beauty and sadness are inextricably tied up with the daddy who goes back as far as we do."

"Gentlemen songsters, off on a spree / Doomed from here to eternity." In the odd disjunction of the lyrics, there was, perhaps, something of Harry Blackmun's voice. "I have bounced around from despair to privilege and perhaps have benefited from both sides," Blackmun had written in 1995, gently correcting a speaker who, Blackmun thought, had suggested, in introducing him to an admiring audience, that he had been born to privilege.

Although Blackmun dictated shards of a memoir, he never settled on a narrative that explained or even described his life. Serving on the Court was a "fantastic experience" and a privilege, he said in a speech at the Aspen Institute, but "it has not been much fun." After twenty-four years, he continued, "I feel as though I have been a cork on a fast moving stream propelled by forces over which I had little control." In its melancholy tone, the self-assessment rang true. The public career that had made Blackmun a figure of history brought him little joy. He often said that his happiest time was the decade he spent with the doctors at the Mayo Clinic. For the forty years of his life that followed, Mayo remained for him a welcoming haven. The Supreme Court, on the other hand, was where he performed his duty.

The passivity in Blackmun's self-description was another matter. Was he really, merely, a cork carried along by fast-moving water? It is an image that belies the dogged determination that marked his response to every challenge, from the lonely years at Harvard to the tenacity of his defense of *Roe v. Wade*. His successor, Stephen Breyer, spoke, at the funeral, of his "enormous diligence." Breyer observed that "it is not often that a man or woman of sixty-one, in a cloistered office, manages through the years to find, not a narrowing, but a broadening of mind, of outlook, and of spirit. But that is what Harry Blackmun found."

But perhaps Blackmun meant something different by the image he invoked: not that he bobbed passively on the waves but, rather, that the waters carried him to places he had never expected to go. And once having arrived at the destination, he stepped onto dry land and performed in ways that neither he nor others would have predicted. It was not the fortuities themselves, but the responses they evoked from him, that shaped his life.

He almost acknowledged as much in December 1995, during the final recording session for his oral history, a joint project of the Supreme Court Historical Society and the Federal Judicial Center. His interviewer, Harold Hongju Koh, a former law clerk who was now a professor at Yale Law School, asked, "Do you think that writing *Roe v. Wade* was a piece of bad luck or good luck?" Blackmun replied that he had asked himself that question over the years and had finally concluded that he had been lucky to get the assignment. "I think one grows in controversy," he said. He noted that his friend Sol Linowitz, an eminent Washington lawyer who helped develop the Xerox Corporation while still in his thirties, "feels very strongly that one needs something like that in his career, particularly early in his career." Linowitz had told him that *Roe* was "the kind of case every justice should have once in his lifetime."

Blackmun often grumbled that he knew he would "carry *Roe* to my grave," despite having spoken for a 7-to-2 Court and notwithstanding his hundreds of opinions in other areas of law. His complaint was valid, and yet, in so many ways *Roe v. Wade* was not just another case. The world attached it to Blackmun in a manner that few Supreme Court decisions are ever linked to their authors. The popular attribution of *Roe* to Blackmun alone was a distortion of the Court's reality that baffled him at first, and he resisted the notion that he was *Roe*'s only creator. Eventually, though, he yielded; continued resistance would have been futile, in any event. In yielding, he locked *Roe* in a tight embrace and never let it go. Its defense carried him in new directions: to commercial speech in *Bigelow v. Virginia,* the abortion advertising case; to the other world "out there" of poverty and need in the abortion-funding cases; and, most significant, to his eventual commitment to the struggle for women's equality in the sex discrimination cases. Warren Burger could never have suspected that in turning to his reliable friend for one unwelcome assignment, he was launching Blackmun on a journey that would open him to new ideas and take him far from their common shore of shared assumptions. Burger sent Blackmun into dangerous waters without a life preserver, and then turned aside. But Blackmun kept swimming. In defending his legacy, he created his legacy. He became Justice Harry Blackmun.

A NOTE ON SOURCES

THIS BOOK IS based on the personal papers, correspondence, and case files in the Harry A. Blackmun Collection at the Library of Congress, as well as the transcript of the oral history Blackmun recorded with his former law clerk Harold Hongju Koh during the eighteen months following his retirement. The oral history, which includes thirty-eight hours of videos and a 510-page transcript, is available on the library's Web site, www.loc.gov/rr/mss/blackmun/. The same site contains a detailed index to the documents in the collection. Viewing the documents themselves, aside from a small sample posted on the Web site, entails a visit to the library's Manuscript Division reading room.

Because Harry Blackmun saved so much written material, telling his story required only minimal investigation of other sources. To provide context for the narrative, I drew on my years of observing and reporting on the Supreme Court, as well as on such reference works as Clare Cushman's *The Supreme Court Justices* (Congressional Quarterly, 1995). For my account of life on the United States Court of Appeals for the District of Columbia Circuit during Warren Burger's tenure there (1956–1969), I relied, in large part, on Jeffrey Brandon Morris's authoritative work *Calmly to Poise the Scales of Justice: A History of the Courts of the District of Columbia Circuit* (Carolina Academic Press, 2001). For the history of Court nomination strategy and confirmation battles, I consulted David Alistair Yalof's *Pursuit of Justices: Presidential Politics and the Selection of Supreme Court Nominees* (University of Chicago Press, 1999). Sally Blackmun provided an account of her unplanned pregnancy and its consequences in the introduction she wrote to *The War on Choice,* by Gloria Feldt (Bantam Books, 2004).

Readers interested in the history of the abortion-rights movement, including *Roe v. Wade* and its antecedents, will find no more authoritative work than David J. Garrow's monumental *Liberty and Sexuality: The Right to Privacy and the Making of* Roe v. Wade (University of California Press, 2nd ed., 1994). Another helpful, and more compact, account is Roe v. Wade: *The Abortion Rights Controversy in American History,* by N. E. H. Hull and Peter Charles Hoffer (University Press of Kansas, 2001).

For further reading on the Supreme Court itself, two biographies of justices who served with Harry Blackmun offer vivid depictions of life on the Court during his tenure: *Justice Lewis F. Powell, Jr.,* by John C. Jeffries, Jr. (Scribners, 1994) and *The Man Who Once Was Whizzer White,* by Dennis J. Hutchinson (Free Press, 1998). *The Brethren,* by Bob Woodward and Scott Armstrong (Simon and Schuster, 1979), covers the Burger Court's first seven terms (1969 through 1975). Its reliance on anonymous sources has made that best-selling book controversial, but, in many instances, Blackmun's case files attest to its accuracy.

A final comment on method: deciphering Harry Blackmun's notes became easier over time but remained a challenge. His handwriting was tiny, and he used an idiosyncratic, although consistent, system of abbreviations. To avoid continual distraction for the reader, I translated his abbreviations into full words when quoting from his notes: "not," for example, rather than "n[ot]." But there were some passages that simply remained indecipherable.

ACKNOWLEDGMENTS

I AM INDEBTED to Sally A. Blackmun, Esq., and to the committee that advised her on her father's papers, for giving me the two-month head start that launched my yearlong immersion in the Harry A. Blackmun Collection. The committee's members were three former law clerks, Dean Harold Hongju Koh of Yale Law School, Professor Pamela S. Karlan of Stanford Law School, and Richard A. Meserve, president of the Carnegie Institution, along with Wanda S. Martinson, the justice's secretary. Both Wanda and Francis J. Lorson, the retired chief deputy clerk of the Supreme Court who was my research assistant during the first phase of the project, placed their long memories at my disposal. Frank also made helpful suggestions on the manuscript.

The staff in the Manuscript Division reading room at the Library of Congress and Daun van Ee, the division's historical specialist, were not only professionally helpful but personally interested in the project. Their enthusiasm added to the pleasures of working in the collection. Professor Stephen Wermiel of the Washington College of Law at American University gave me valuable advice. Professor Joseph F. Kobylka of the Southern Methodist University political science department generously shared his insights gleaned from years of studying Harry Blackmun's judicial career.

I am grateful to those who read part or all of the manuscript and made helpful comments: Professor Laurence H. Tribe of Harvard Law School; Professor James J. Brudney of the Moritz College of Law at Ohio State University; Judge Myron H. Bright of the U.S. Court of Appeals for the Eighth Circuit; and Anthony Lewis, my longtime colleague at the *New York Times*. I thank Dorothy Toth Beasley, former chief judge of the Georgia Court of Appeals, for her unflagging enthusiasm.

Philip Taubman, the *Times* Washington bureau chief, indulged my efforts to juggle the demands of finishing the book and attending to my day job at the Court. Also at the newspaper, I'm thankful to Alex Ward, editorial director of book development; to Doug Mills and Yoni Brook for their expert photography of the documents; and to Michele McNally, director of photography, assisted by Rebecca Cooney, for research in the photo archives. At the Supreme Court, Catherine Fitts, the curator, and Steve Petteway, the Court's photographer, were most helpful in giving me access to the Court's collection of photographs.

I was skeptical when Paul Golob, editorial director of Times Books at Henry Holt and Company, first tried to persuade me that this project was feasible within reasonable limits of time and length. I thank him for persisting and for being the kind of editor that every writer needs but few are lucky enough to have. His assistant, Brianna Smith, attended to the many details of book production. My husband, Eugene R. Fidell, the first reader of every chapter, was my initial line of defense against sloppy writing and thinking.

Finally, I appreciate the moral support and enthusiasm of all three Blackmun daughters, Sally, Nancy, and Susie. None of them saw any portion of the manuscript before publication, and consequently bear no responsibility for any mistakes of fact or interpretation, which are completely my own.

ILLUSTRATION CREDITS

Unless otherwise noted, the documents that illustrate this book are from the Papers of Harry A. Blackmun in the Manuscript Division at the Library of Congress.

85 Collection of the Supreme Court of the United States

94 Doug Mills/*The New York Times*

100 Left: Photoduplication Service, Library of Congress; right: Doug Mills/*The New York Times*

105 Left and right: Yoni Brook/*The New York Times*

118 Yoni Brook/*The New York Times*

126 Yoni Brook/*The New York Times*

128 Yoni Brook/*The New York Times*

130 Yoni Brook/*The New York Times*

142 Yoni Brook/*The New York Times*

152 Doug Mills/*The New York Times*

159 Yoni Brook/*The New York Times*

163 Yoni Brook/*The New York Times*

178 Yoni Brook/*The New York Times*

180 Doug Mills/*The New York Times*

183 Collection of the Supreme Court of the United States

189 Yoni Brook/*The New York Times*

192 Doug Mills/*The New York Times*

195 Doug Mills/*The New York Times*

205 Left and right: Doug Mills/*The New York Times*

210 Yoni Brook/*The New York Times*

226 Collection of the Supreme Court of the United States

231 Doug Mills/*The New York Times*

236 Courtesy of Chai Feldblum

239 Top and bottom: Yoni Brook/*The New York Times*

241 Stephen Crowley/*The New York Times*

244 Doug Mills/*The New York Times*

246 Paul Hosefros/*The New York Times*

INDEX

ABOUT THE AUTHOR

LINDA GREENHOUSE has covered the Supreme Court for *The New York Times* since 1978 and won a Pulitzer Prize in 1998 for her coverage of the Court. She appears regularly on the PBS program *Washington Week* and lectures frequently on the Supreme Court at colleges and law schools. She graduated from Radcliffe College and holds a master of studies in law from Yale Law School.